Media Framing of the Muslim World

Conflicts, Crises and Contexts

Halim Rane
Griffith University, Australia

Jacqui Ewart
Griffith University, Australia

John Martinkus
University of Tasmania, Australia

First published 2014 by
PALGRAVE MACMILLAN

Palgrave Macmillan in the UK is an imprint of Macmillan Publishers Limited, registered in England, company number 785998, of Houndmills, Basingstoke, Hampshire RG21 6XS.

Palgrave Macmillan in the US is a division of St Martin's Press LLC, 175 Fifth Avenue, New York, NY 10010.

Palgrave Macmillan is the global academic imprint of the above companies and has companies and representatives throughout the world.

Palgrave® and Macmillan® are registered trademarks in the United States, the United Kingdom, Europe and other countries.

ISBN 978–1–137–33481–7 hardback
ISBN 978–1–137–33482–4 paperback

This book is printed on paper suitable for recycling and made from fully managed and sustained forest sources. Logging, pulping and manufacturing processes are expected to conform to the environmental regulations of the country of origin.

A catalogue record for this book is available from the British Library.

A catalog record for this book is available from the Library of Congress.

Transferred to Digital Printing in 2015

Media Framing of the Muslim World

Contents

Preface and Acknowledgments

Only a little over a decade into the 21st century and the prospects for global peace and security look quite grim from the perspective of Islam–West relations. We have already witnessed a plethora of terrorist attacks that have caused widespread fear and insecurity, and two long and bloody wars in Afghanistan and Iraq that have created significant instability and devastation in the Middle East and South Asian regions. We have also witnessed violent protests against offensive depictions of the Prophet Muhammad. By the close of the first decade of this century, the Arab Spring offered hope that the tide might be turning in the Muslim world as long-standing dictators were either overthrown or forced to make social and political reforms. Recent developments in both Egypt and Tunisia, however, indicate a reversal of the democratic gains of the Arab Spring, while there seems to be no end in sight to the civil war in Syria. Meanwhile, in Western countries, news stories about Muslims have focused on the threat of home-grown terrorism in addition to the infiltration of terrorist cells from abroad. Muslim culture and religious practice have also come under scrutiny, raising debates about national values, the failure of multiculturalism and the challenges to social cohesion posed by immigrants and asylum seekers. Such is the picture as viewed through the media lens.

The central premise of this book is that those for whom the media are a primary source of information are likely to have a perception of the Muslim world that, first, falls within frames of crises and conflicts, and, second, isolates them from the broader context of the histories, geographies, societies, cultures, people, issues and developments in the Muslim world. This book draws on its authors' expertise in Islamic and media studies and experience as journalists and foreign correspondents to examine the processes of news production and consumption and the impact of media content on society.

The topics addressed in this book include how news values and media frames contribute to Western audiences' perceptions and understandings of Islam and Muslims; the extent to which historic conceptions of orientalism remain salient and are manifested in Islamophobia; how reporting on terrorism and asylum seekers relates to public opinion and policy making; how the relationship between mass and social media

contributes to the changing socio-political landscape and our understanding of the Muslim world; and how journalism and audiences
have evolved in the decade since 9/11. Key concepts and approaches
including the fourth estate, news values, framing, agenda-setting and
orientalism inform our analysis of these issues. Throughout this book,
we also consider the role of Islamophobia and the clash of civilizations
in the future direction of Islam–West relations.

This is not the first book on the media coverage of the Muslim world.
Other prominent books include *Fueling Our Fears* by Nacos and Torres-
Reyna and *Framing Muslims* by Morey and Yaqin. This book is unique,
however, in the breadth and depth with which it engages with key
concepts, theories and issues in media studies as they pertain to Islam–
West relations. Additionally, it is written by three scholars with specific
expertise in Islamic studies, media studies and journalism.

The authors would like to thank our research assistant, Ms Elise
Stephenson, for her fine work on this project. We would also like to
thank our respective universities and research centers for their support
during the process of writing this book.

About the Authors

Dr Halim Rane is Associate Professor of Islam–West Relations at Griffith University. He researches and writes extensively on Islamic and Muslim issues including political Islam, the Israel–Palestine conflict, Islam in the West and the media coverage of Muslims. He is the author of *Reconstructing Jihad amid Competing International Norms*; *Islam and Contemporary Civilization: Evolving Ideas, Transforming Relations* and *Making Australian Foreign Policy on Israel-Palestine: Media Coverage, Public Opinion and Interest Groups* (co-authored with Eulalia Han). He is also a co-editor of *Islam and the Australian News Media*.

Dr Jacqui Ewart worked as a journalist and media manager for more than a decade and is currently Associate Professor of Journalism and Media Studies at Griffith University. Her research includes terrorism and the media, community media, talkback radio and cultural change in newsrooms. She is the author of the book *Haneef: A Question of Character*, which was long-listed for the John Button prize and the CAL Waverly prize. She is a co-editor of *Islam and the Australian Media* and an associate editor of *Media International Australia*.

John Martinkus has worked for almost two decades as a foreign correspondent and became Lecturer in Journalism, Media and Communications at the University of Tasmania in 2009. Since 1995 he has covered conflicts in East Timor, Indonesia, Iraq and Afghanistan, among other countries. He has written three books and works predominantly outside Australia in wire service, newspaper and magazine journalism. He has been nominated for three Walkley Awards for his coverage of East Timor, Iraq and Afghanistan, and in 2002 his book on East Timor, *A Dirty Little War*, was shortlisted for the NSW Premier's Literary Award. For the last four years he has been working for the SBS *Dateline* program, filming and reporting stories mostly in Iraq and Afghanistan.

Introduction

From the printing press to Twitter, media tools have enabled people to articulate their perceptions of the 'other' and potentially shape how 'we' relate to 'them'. For over a millennium, and certainly within recent decades, the major 'other' for the West has been Muslims. This book examines how the Western media frames the Muslim world and the implications of this for Islam–West relations, both intercommunity and international. It is concerned with how news values and media frames contribute to Western audiences' perceptions and understandings of Islam and Muslims; the extent to which historic conceptions of orientalism remain salient and are manifested in Islamophobia; how reporting on terrorism and asylum seekers relates to public opinion and policy making; how the relationship between mass and social media contributes to the changing socio-political landscape and our understanding of the Muslim world; and how journalism and audiences have evolved in the decade since 9/11. A synopsis of the book's chapters is provided at the end of this chapter.

It is essential to clarify from the outset some of the key terms used in this book, particularly 'Islam' and the 'Muslim world' on the one hand and the 'West' and 'Western world' on the other. We use these terms in reference to broad geographical locations that, in spite of their many commonalities, historical interactions and contemporary interconnectedness, have distinct characteristics that continue to be identified by both sides as markers of distinction. In respect to the term 'Islam', we are referring to both the monotheistic religion that emerged in 7th-century Arabia founded by the Prophet Muhammad (d. 632) and the civilization that developed in the lands under Muslim rule from the 8th century. As we note in Chapter 1, while the overwhelming majority of Muslims reside in what we refer to as the Muslim world, increasing

1

numbers of Muslims now live in what we term the Western world. By the term 'Muslim world', we are referring to the approximately 50 countries in which the majority of the population is Muslim, followers of Islam. These countries tend to be developing countries, concentrated in the Middle East and North Africa as well as Central, South and Southeast Asia. However, we reject the notion that religion is the key determinant of issues and events in the Muslim world. Rather, we contend that it is within human factors – society, economy, education, politics and history – that we are most likely to find the soundest explanations. By the terms 'West' and 'Western world', we are referring to the countries that comprise Western Europe and North America, as well as Australia, which are characterized by their developed economies, democratic political systems and an affiliation with Christianity as the dominant religious identity of the people. We use the term 'Islam–West relations' in reference to the state of the relationship between these two broad entities.

This introductory chapter focuses on the power and potential of the media. The news media, in particular, tell people *what* to think about by way of the issues and events they decide to cover. The way these issues and events are framed in terms of the images and information that are included or excluded influences *how* people think about these issues and events. The way people learn and retain information from the media varies widely, however. Prior knowledge, education, experiences and interest regarding the information received affect how the receiver retains and employs the information in shaping their opinions and attitudes. The power of the media stems from an ability to reach mass audiences and to become a primary source of information about people, places and events that the audience has not directly experienced. Such is the case in respect to the media's coverage of Muslims.

The central problem with the Western media's coverage of the Muslim world is not that the reporting is inaccurate per se. Indeed, individual and groups of Muslims are responsible for acts of violence and terrorism, human rights violations and the oppression of women. There are also groups of Muslims who oppose Western values, systems and institutions and are avowed enemies of the Western world. The problem is that the coverage of Islam and Muslims in the Western media tends to focus on the views and actions of these individuals and groups, and, in the absence of other, more representative stories and images that provide a more complete picture, audiences are left with a very narrow, skewed perspective. The stereotypical Muslim terrorist, misogynist and fanatic are not representative of the majority of Muslims. Indeed, 'Muslims themselves are a far more varied set of communities and individuals

than this picture allows' (Morey and Yaqin, 2011, p. 1). Edward Said put
it best in the introduction of his book *Covering Islam*, when he said:

> the term 'Islam' as it is used today seems to mean one simple thing
> but in fact is part fiction, part ideological label, part minimal desig-
> nation of a religion called Islam. In no real significant way is there a
> direct correspondence between the 'Islam' in common Western usage
> and the enormously varied life that goes on within the world of
> Islam, with its more than 800,000,000 people [now over 1.6 billion],
> its millions of square miles of territory principally in Africa and
> Asia, its dozens of societies, states, histories, geographies, and cul-
> tures. On the other hand, 'Islam' is peculiarly traumatic news today
> in the West.... During the past few years, especially since events in
> Iran caught European and American attention so strongly, the media
> have therefore covered Islam: they have portrayed it, characterized it,
> analyzed it, given instant courses on it, and consequently they have
> made it 'known'.
>
> (1997, pp. x–xi)

Here Said refers to a version of Islam that, in reality, corresponds to
the life, experiences and interpretations of only a very small minority of Muslims, but this version is the dominant media representation.
The Western media's reporting on Islam and Muslims, particularly since
the events of 9/11, has had a significant impact on political and public
discourse. As Morey and Yaqin explain,

> There is no conspiracy between politicians and the media to restrict
> the way Muslims are represented and treated ... it is, rather, the habit-
> ual workings of the mainstream press and news media that lead to a
> sometimes inadvertent complicity with power agendas. Since 9/11
> this has meant elevating the threat from Islamist terrorism to the
> number one priority impacting on both domestic and foreign policy.
> This political priority is duly reported, but some of its more para-
> noid implications and inferences, we have suggested, are taken up
> too in the way Muslim issues are identified and relayed to the broader
> public.
>
> (2011, p. 77)

The mass media are fundamental to how people in the Western world
think about the Muslim world. For many Westerners, what is 'known'
about Islam and Muslims is minimal, inaccurate and misrepresentative.
Central to understanding the media's coverage are three concepts that

relate to the selection, presentation and prevalence of news. In the field of media studies, these are respectively discussed as news values, framing and agenda-setting. Another key factor is a tendency of the Western media to approach Islam and the Muslim world from a point of difference and opposition, an approach known as orientalism.

News values

Often called newsworthiness, news values is a term used in reference to the criteria news organizations apply in selecting stories on which to report. Seminal studies include those of Galtung and Ruge (1965) and Gans (1980). Galtung and Ruge (1965) were specifically interested in how overseas events and issues become news for Western audiences. They identified that the likelihood of an event making the news is determined by criteria based on 12 factors: frequency, threshold, unambiguity, meaningfulness, consonance, unexpectedness, continuity, composition, as well as reference to elite nations, people, persons, and something negative. Considering these criteria, a terrorist attack in a Western country or against Western interests by a Muslim individual or militant group is newsworthy, as it is an event that has occurred at a particular point in time (frequency), it has a certain intensity and is likely to be gruesome and involve casualties (threshold), it can be easily interpreted as an attack by an enemy against 'us' (unambiguity), the attack was against 'us' or those who are culturally similar to 'us' (meaningfulness), the attack may be a precursor to subsequent or counter-attacks (consonance), the attack was unanticipated (unexpectedness), it is part of an ongoing conflict or series of attacks (continuity), it concerns national security, safety and well-being of the nation (composition), it was against a Western nation and people (elite nation, people or person), and it involves conflict and violence (negative). While Galtung and Ruge's study of news values has not endured without some criticism, it continues to be acknowledged as not only the foundational study on the subject but the most influential explanation of news values (Harcup and O'Neill, 2001).

The study of news values was continued by Gans (1980), whose examination of the US news media found that domestic news stories were deemed to be important or interesting based on two sets of criteria. Important stories are necessary as they fulfill the news media's obligation to provide society with the information necessary to function as informed citizens and simultaneously act as a watchdog vis-à-vis the various institutions of power and authority in society, a function referred to as the fourth estate. Important stories are determined by the extent to which they concern rank in government and other hierarchies, impact on the nation and the national interest, impact on large numbers of people and significance for the past and future (Gans, 1980). Interesting stories provide a measure of entertainment to audiences. Stories are deemed interesting if they are people stories, role reversals, human interest stories, exposé anecdotes, hero stories and 'gee whiz' stories (Gans, 1980, pp. 155–157).

An overriding function of the media in Gans' (1980) assessment is informing about disorder so as to contribute to maintaining order. He identifies four types of disorder: natural, technological, social and moral. Even the casual consumer of news media would immediately recognize the prominence given to stories about floods, earthquakes and fires (natural disorder), car, plane and train crashes (technological disorder), protests, acts of violence as well as violations of cultural norms (social disorder) and crime as well as other violations of the law (moral disorder). It is in the context of the latter two categories that Muslims tend to make the news. Muslims protesting against a war overseas or an insult to the Prophet Muhammad, the 'strange' dress worn by Muslim females, and certainly acts of violence and terrorism fall into the category of social disorder. Similarly, terrorism and other crimes constitute moral disorder. Equally important, however, is the role of journalists in maintaining order, which is done by defending social and national values such as equality, democracy and various personal freedoms. To the extent that Muslims publicly oppose or are seen to threaten such values, they can expect to be attacked by the news media as part of the media's defense of the social and moral order.

In their examination of Galtung and Ruge's (1965) study, Harcup and O'Neill observe that Galtung and Ruge 'ignored day-to-day coverage of lesser, domestic and bread-and-butter news', which, they argue, constitutes the majority of news stories (2001, p. 276). Harcup and O'Neill (2001) concede that news stories do frequently contain the factors identified by Galtung and Ruge, but that many news stories are in effect advertising in the form of government and corporate public relations spin masquerading as news. The reporting of Islam and Muslims has tended to fall into the former rather than the latter category. However, since 9/11 political discourse has become a major source of news media content concerning Muslims, particularly stories framed as part of a national security or national values agenda, such as those concerning terrorism, immigration and integration of Muslims.

Framing

It is from the seminal work of Robert Entman (1993) that framing has become both an enduring concept and a method of analysis in the field of media studies. Entman explains that framing essentially involves making certain aspects of reality known through 'selection' and thereby giving them prominence or 'salience' (1993, p. 52). He defines 'salience' as 'making a piece of information more noticeable, meaningful, or memorable to audiences' (Entman, 1993, p. 53). According to Entman, 'to frame is to select some aspects of a perceived reality and make them more salient in a communicating text, in such a way as to promote a particular problem definition, causal interpretation, moral evaluation, and/or treatment recommendation for the item described' (1993, p. 52). Frames are used to 'define problems', 'make moral judgments' and 'suggest remedies' (Entman, 1993, p. 52). The application of this model to the media coverage of the war on terror, for instance, would identify that the attacks in this context are covered so as to identify their source (Muslim militants), offer moral judgments (anti-Western/American aggression) and commend particular solutions (US drone strikes on suspected hideouts). In the lead up to the 1991 war against Iraq, Entman (1993) observes that media frames were employed to limit the options presented to the American public. Negotiations between Iraq and Kuwait were excluded from the media frames and only two options, war and sanctions, were included. Similarly, media frames of the Israel–Palestine peace process include only the option of negotiations between the conflicting parties and exclude options that call for a resolution based on international law or pressure derived from the boycott, divestment and sanctions (BDS) movement against Israel, as was employed against the apartheid regime in South Africa in the 1980s (Han and Rane, 2013).

The process of framing involves selecting for inclusion in a story certain aspects of an event or issue being covered, including facts, images, and sources or interviewees, and, as importantly, excluding other facts, images, and sources or interviewees. This process has significant implications for how audiences understand and respond to issues and events reported in the media. As Entman explains,

the frame determines whether most people notice and how they understand and remember a problem, as well as how they evaluate and choose to act upon it. The notion of framing thus implies that the frame has a common effect on large portions of the receiving audience, though it is not likely to have a universal effect on all.

(1993, p. 54)

Numerous studies have used framing to analyze media content concerning the representation of Islam and Muslims and its potential impact on audiences (see, for instance, Nacos and Torres-Reyna, 2007; Sardar and Davies, 2010; Morey and Yaqin, 2011; Powell, 2011; Han and Rane, 2013). Morey and Yaqin (2011) examine how Muslims are stereotyped and framed within Western political, cultural and media discourses. The frames used in the coverage of Islam and Muslims, according to Morey and Yaqin, are not merely descriptive and neutral but 'are almost always contained within a framing narrative whose parameters are defined by questions of belonging, "Otherness" and threat' (2011, p. 21). Powell's study of 11 terrorist attacks that occurred in the decade after 9/11 finds a pattern of media coverage dominated by fear of organized international terrorism associated with Islam, Muslims and Arabs directed at 'Christian America' (2011, p. 91). By contrast, her study finds domestic acts of terrorism to be portrayed as isolated incidents that pose only a minor threat and perpetrated by 'troubled individuals' (Powell, 2011, p. 91).While the US government's response to the 9/11 attacks was to launch a war on terror, the media were instrumental in not only framing subsequent acts of terror within this context but in sustaining a widespread fear that linked Islam and terrorism (Powell, 2011).

Agenda-setting

Traditional mass media such as newspapers, radio and television have always had power and potential to reach large audiences and inform about people, places and events that these audiences have not directly experienced. The mass media remain a primary source of information for most people. Almost a century ago, Walter Lippmann (1922), in his renowned work entitled *Public Opinion*, observed that much of what people know about the world around them is not derived from personal experience or direct interaction but indirectly through second-hand sources, most prominently the mass media. With the advent of global satellite news networks, the internet and social media, the reach and instantaneity of the mass media are even more apparent, and consequently the media have become potentially more influential. However, it seems that, out of the plethora of events and issues going on in the world around us, those that are covered by the mass media and thereby given prominence are the ones with which we concern ourselves most. This process is referred to as the media's agenda-setting function.

At first glance, the agenda-setting theory of McCombs and Shaw sounds rather like framing: 'In choosing and displaying news, editors, newsroom staff, and broadcasters play an important part in shaping political reality' (1972, p. 176). Agenda-setting is concerned with the prominence given to a story, which in turn tells audiences 'how much importance to attach to that issue from the amount of information in a news story and its position' (McCombs and Shaw, 1972, p. 176). The key factor for agenda-setting is the amount of emphasis the media place on an issue, as this, the theory explains, is likely to influence how much importance audiences will attach to the issue. McCombs and Shaw concede that the media imperfectly reproduce the reality of the issues they cover, which, as audiences 'tend to share the media's composite definition of what is important strongly suggests an agenda-setting function of the mass media' (1972, p. 184). In the context of this book, the agenda-setting theory helps explain why Western audiences associate Islam with terrorism and see Muslims as violent oppressors of women. There are certainly groups of Muslims who commit acts of terrorism in the name of Islam, while there are also Muslims who commit various human rights violations and oppress women. However, as we argue in this book, there is often a vast gulf between image and reality in the Western media reporting of the Muslim world.

Orientalism

Edward Said's (1978) concept of orientalism is widely used to describe and explain the Western media's portrayal of Islam and the Muslim world as a different, strange and threatening other (Nacos and Torres-Reyna, 2007; Morey and Yaqin, 2011; Powell, 2011; Amin-Khan, 2012). The orientalist perspective not only sees the Muslim world as antithetical to the West but also as static, lacking the capacity to make progress and development akin to that of the Western world. Said defines orientalism as

> a style of thought based upon an ontological and epistemological distinction made between 'the Orient' and (most of the time) 'the Occident.' Thus a very large mass of writers, among whom are poets, novelists, philosophers, political theorists, economists, and imperial administrators, have accepted the basic distinction between East and

West as their starting point for elaborate theories, epics, novels, social descriptions, and political accounts concerning the Orient, its people, customs, 'mind,' destiny, and so on.

(1978, pp. 2–3)

In reference to this central point concerning the difference or distinction between Islam and the West, Morey and Yaqin describe the image of Muslims in the Western media as 'unenlightened outsiders. Even Muslims who may live and work in the West, are portrayed as having an allegiance to values different from those recognized in Europe and North America' (2011, p. 1). The authors identify such an image of Muslims as being stereotypical and representative of an orientalist perspective. However, as we discuss in the next chapter, while a general characterization of Muslims as unenlightened is unfair and inaccurate, it is certainly true that Muslims in general do adhere to values that are different from those of Western countries. These values, combined with certain norms, beliefs and worldview, are central to the Muslim identity. Muslims are, in these respects, distinct from Westerners.

Historically, and still today, orientalism reflects the more general problem of understanding other cultures and our relationship with them (McLoughlin, 2007). It involves the West defining itself as different and in opposition to the East, particularly Islamic civilization. This process results, however, in discourses that often tell us more about the West's concerns, desires and aspirations than they do about the Muslim world (Said, 1978).

The seminal work on orientalism in media reporting is Said's (1997) *Covering Islam*, which contends that orientalism is the dominant approach in the Western media's coverage of Islam and the Muslim world. This is apparent in a portrayal of Muslims as a violent, strange and threatening 'other' that is fundamentally different from Westerners. Said (1997) argues that the most negative and irresponsible images of Islam are the result of media organizations using the label 'Islam' to describe and explain issues and events concerning which Islam is a peripheral factor at best. He adds that the 'Islam' label is used as a form of attack and provocation (Said, 1997, pp. xv–xvi). To appreciate Said's point, one need only read or watch one of the countless news reports about a Muslim group or party whose goal is to establish an 'Islamic' state based on 'Islamic' law. The 'Islamic' label is all that needs to be said in order to evoke fear, alarm or some other negative sentiment among audiences. So denigrated has the Islamic brand become that no further details are required.

A range of criticisms has been launched at orientalism over the years. It has been accused of encouraging anti-Westernism among Islamic fundamentalists, ignoring the history of positive interaction and exchange between Islam and the West, and holding Islam and Christianity to markedly different standards (McLoughlin, 2007). However, McLoughlin (2007) contends that such criticisms fail to consider the later work of Said, in which such issues are addressed. Moreover, he rightly argues that the various criticisms of orientalism do not detract from Said's central thesis, and nor does the negation of orientalism necessarily vindicate Islam (McLoughlin, 2007).

Moreover, the events of 9/11 have seen a resurgence of interest and a revitalized relevance of orientalism. Overt and covert forms of orientalism were central to America's response to 9/11, particularly the rhetoric and actions of the war on terror (Yamaguchi, 2012). Orientalist representations of Muslims in general and of Iraq and Afghanistan in particular as the 'other' were used to justify the war on terror (Khalid, 2011). Said, among many other scholars, has identified a resurgence of orientalist writing in the aftermath of the 9/11 terrorist attacks. Bernard Lewis is often cited as a leading figure of what has come to be described as new orientalism (Yamaguchi, 2012).

New orientalism is identical to the original, but tends to focus more on the failure of Islamic civilization in the context of modernity (Yamaguchi, 2012). Within this context, the central failures of Islam tend to be its perceived incompatibility with democracy, human rights and gender equality. Additionally, the Western media's coverage tends to be limited to stories concerning the control of oil, war and terrorism (Powell, 2011). In this respect, Powell (2011) finds the media coverage of the events of 9/11 and thereafter to be orientalist.

Old orientalism emphasized the superiority of the occident versus the inferiority of the orient. This conception was central to European colonization of the Muslim world, whereby European colonial powers sought to impose their own norms, values, systems and institutions on people they ruled. By the mid-20th century most of the colonized lands had acquired their independence, and so emerged the modern Muslim nation-states. Towards the end of the 20th century Islam experienced a resurgence in these Muslim-majority countries that was often characterized by a rejection of the West's colonial legacies. In this context of a more assertive Islamic identity, new orientalism evolved along the lines of a clash of civilizations (Amin-Khan, 2012), which is a theory that views religion and culture as being the fundamental bases of national alliances and international relations (Huntington, 1993). In Chapter 7, we examine the clash of civilizations theory in respect to a number of controversial issues that seemingly confirm this clash.

Similarly, Kumar (2012) finds orientalism to be central to contemporary international relations and manifested in racism, Islamophobia and redemptive violence. He describes the events of 9/11 as having a more profound impact on the contemporary world than the two world wars and the Cold War combined. Terrorism has become a central feature and focus of the post-9/11 world, but one that is not equally ascribed. New orientalism associates terrorism with the actions of the 'other' and never with our own. A case in point is Anders Breivik, who is responsible for bombing a government building and a mass shooting that resulted in the deaths of 78 people in Norway in 2011. Western media outlets initially suspected Islamic terrorists, but when Breivik, a Caucasian, Norwegian-born Christian, was identified as the perpetrator the descriptions shifted from terrorist to 'maverick', 'nutball' and 'crazy-loner' (Kumar, 2012, p. 233). Similarly, in 1995 media organizations initially blamed the Oklahoma City bombing on Middle Eastern terrorists. When it became apparent that the perpetrator was Timothy McVeigh, a Caucasian, American-born Christian, the media seldom described him as a 'home-grown terrorist' (Kumar, 2012, p. 233). Kumar contends that new orientalist thinking dictates that terrorists are foreign, while 'it appears as if "home" is congenitally incapable of breeding terrorists, let alone the ideological manure required for it' (2012, p. 233). New orientalism also redefines terrorism. While old terrorism was defined as violent and unlawful but a form of political resistance, new terrorism is violent and unlawful but irrational (Kumar, 2012).

The representation of Islam as the antithesis of Western civilization is the main signifier of new orientalism. Anti-Muslim racism or Islamophobia in Western societies 'has been considerably aided by the Western media's coverage of Muslims and the demonization of Islam along orientalist lines across Europe, America and Australia' (Amin-Khan, 2012, pp. 1595–1596). The consequence has been a 'racially embedded process of securitization' that involves not only external wars against Muslim-majority countries but also increased border protection against asylum seekers as well as the use of internal security forces against domestic Muslim communities (Amin-Khan, 2012, p. 1596). We address these issues in chapters 4 and 5 respectively. New orientalism emphasizes the multiple threats posed by Islam and Muslims, including the security threat of Muslim terrorists, the cultural threat of Muslim women's headscarves and face veils and the demographic threat of Muslim refugees (Amin-Khan, 2012).

Orientalism has also been spurred on since 9/11 by its opposite, known as occidentalism. Occidentalism is the mirror image of
orientalism, whereby the Islamic world views the West in negative,
stereotypical and oppositional terms (Joffe, 2007). Joffe (2007) sees
occidentalism as a relatively recent phenomenon, emerging in the aftermath of the 1967 Six Day War when Israel inflicted a humiliating
defeat upon the collective forces of Egypt, Jordan and Syria and effectively took control of the whole of historic Palestine as well as Egypt's
Sinai Peninsula and Syria's Golan region. Occidentalism developed in
response to the West's support for Israel and for pro-Western authoritarian regimes that ruled various Muslim countries. The inability of Islam
to become the dominant socio-political force in the Muslim world and
the loss of Palestine to Western-backed Israel inspired *salafist* groups and
movements in the Muslim world 'to demonstrate that the orient was not
weak and should emphasize difference by excluding the Occident from
its own political and social realm' (Joffe, 2007, p. 171). Occidentalism
was thereby manifested in a rejection of systems, institutions, values and
norms deemed to be 'Western' in origin. Joffe also observes the growth
of occidentalism among Muslim communities who migrated to various
European countries in the 1990s, a phenomenon he refers to as 'immigrant occidentalism' (2007, p. 168). This, he argues, is a consequence of
the Muslim migrant communities' sense of alienation and rejection by
their European host societies, a failure of social integration (Joffe, 2007).
Since 9/11, occidentalist thinking among Muslims has served to reaffirm
and reinforce orientalist approaches to covering Islam.

Chapter structure

This opening chapter has introduced four key concepts – news values, framing, agenda-setting and orientalism – which are central to this
book. We refer to these concepts in our examination of the various issues
we address throughout. Chapters 1 and 2 draw on the expertise of the
book's first author. In Chapter 1 Rane provides a general introduction
to Islam and the Muslim world. This chapter is particularly beneficial to
readers who are not familiar with the origins of Islam, beliefs and practices of Muslims, and views of Muslims on a range of religious, social and
political issues. It dispels the monolithic image of the Muslim world by
highlighting both the factors that unify and those that contribute to
the diversity of Muslim life. Rane also examines the question of Muslim
integration in the West in light of these factors. In Chapter 2 Rane
explains the concept of mediated Muslims, or the version of Islam that
is created by the Western media. He traces the representations of Islam

and Muslims from medieval Christian thought to the contemporary Western media. This chapter then discusses Western public opinion of Islam and Muslims and the extent to which the media have contributed to a fear of and prejudice towards Muslims, a phenomenon referred to as Islamophobia. Rane examines the scholarly research related to Islamophobia, its prevalence in Western societies and the implications of this for intercommunity and international relations.

Chapter 3 draws on the experiences of the book's third author, who worked as a foreign correspondent in various Muslim countries, including Afghanistan and Iraq. Martinkus compares media images with the reality of war and conflict, examining the realities of reporting from the Muslim world and the challenges faced by Western journalists covering Islam. He not only considers the dangers faced by journalists on the ground but also the complexities of reporting in a political context where the realities of the conflict contradict the propaganda campaign. Image and reality are juxtaposed, with the former referring to an incomplete, often contrived representation of issues and events, and the latter referring to a more complete representation including competing perspectives, images and information.

One consequence of war and conflict is the large numbers of people who are displaced and are subsequently forced to seek protection from other nations. Chapters 4 and 5 draw on the insights and experiences of the book's first and second authors. In Chapter 4 Ewart and Rane address the issue of asylum seekers in Western countries. This chapter focuses on the relationship between media coverage, political discourse and public opinion. It attempts to identify which of these factors drives the debate and what role the others play. In Chapter 5 Ewart and Rane examine the challenges of covering terrorist suspects, particularly the relationship between politicians, law enforcement and the media within the contexts of anti-terror legislation, public interest and the media's role as the fourth estate.

In Chapter 6, Rane and Martinkus examine the role of social and mass media in the Arab Spring in terms of both facilitating protests in the Arab world and informing Western publics about these events. This chapter discusses the central role of *Al Jazeera* as primary news source for both Arab and Western audiences. It also explains the relationship between social and mass media during the uprisings, and how the framing of these events influenced how Western publics and governments perceived and responded to them.

In Chapter 7, Rane discusses the clash of civilizations theory in the context of two cases: the publishing of offensive cartoons depicting the

Prophet Muhammad in a Danish newspaper in 2005 and the posting of a film on YouTube in 2012 that was deemed to insult Islam and its Prophet. In both cases, groups of Muslims across the globe reacted violently, confirming for many the inevitability of a clash between Islam and the West. This chapter examines the media coverage of these events and the public opinion of Muslims and Westerners to consider the validity of this claim. It also considers freedom of expression in Islam and the extent to which there is congruence with the Western conception.

Chapter 8 is based on extensive research conducted by Rane and Ewart, who examine the extent to which the media has evolved in the decade since 9/11. This chapter presents the findings of their analysis of the tenth anniversary coverage of 9/11 along with the findings of focus groups they conducted with Muslims and non-Muslims. The chapter contends that the media have moved on from 9/11, particularly in respect to the framing of Islam and Muslims. It also finds that public opinion has evolved; non-Muslims have become more discerning in respect to Muslims and are able to differentiate between the mainstream majority of Muslims and the extremist minority. The final chapter presents the book's major findings and concludes with insights on the implications for media studies and Islam–West relations.

1
Islam and the Muslim World

Largely as a consequence of intense media coverage since 9/11, Islam has been brought to the attention of people across the globe. However, most Westerners know little about the faith and its adherents. This chapter begins with a basic overview of Islam's main teachings and looks at the prevalence of Islamic beliefs and practices among Muslims around the world. Contrary to media representations of Muslims as a monolithic group, this chapter highlights the unity and diversity of Muslims in respect to culture, religiosity and ideology. The chapter also presents what Muslims really think about a range of social and political issues. We then examine the question of coexistence, with a focus on Muslim integration in the West.

A brief history of Islam

Islam is a monotheistic faith that has its origins in 7th-century Arabia. Islamic tradition tells us that Islam began in the year 610, when the Prophet Muhammad is said to have received the first revelation of the Quran, the holy book of Muslims. By the time of his death in the year 632, Muhammad had unified the Arab tribes under his rule and most had converted to Islam. Muhammad's close companions expanded Arab Muslim rule beyond the Arabian Peninsula, conquering the lands of the Persians and much of the Byzantine territory as well. Internal conflict resulted in the emergence of the first of many Muslim empires or caliphates, which were political entities that ruled over vast territories and were led by a *caliph*, who possessed both political and religious authority. The Umayyad Caliphate ruled from 661 until 750. During their reign, the Umayyads established an empire, with Damascus as its capital, that extended throughout the Middle East, westward across North Africa to Spain and eastward to India. When they were overthrown by the Abbasid Caliphate, the surviving Umayyads established another flourishing caliphate in Spain, with Cordoba as its capital. The Abbasids inherited the Umayyad's Middle Eastern territories, but by the mid-10th century the Muslim world rapidly became divided among multiple rulers until the last of these, the Ottoman Caliphate, was replaced by the Republic of Turkey in 1923. By this time, many of the Muslim lands that had formerly been Ottoman territories had met the same fate already experienced by much of the Muslim world, falling under the colonial rule of various European powers, particularly Britain and France.

While Islam's history is one of continuous political turmoil, the Islamic religion, guided by Islamic law (*sharia*) and its traditional custodians, the *ulema* (religious scholars), was a vital stabilizing and harmonizing force. Largely due to the social order that the *sharia* provided, coupled with the economic strength that Muslim empires acquired, the Muslim world boasted a glorious Islamic civilization characterized by high culture, great works of philosophy and literature, and advancements in the sciences, mathematics, medicine and technology that laid the foundations for the Renaissance in Europe. The Umayyad capital at Cordoba in Spain, the Abbasid capital Baghdad in Iraq, the Fatimid capital Cairo in Egypt and the Ottoman capital Istanbul in Turkey were once global centers of power, trade and scholarship, attracting the world's greatest minds, irrespective of race or religion. However, as the economic fortunes of the Muslim empires declined, by the 14th century their rulers' ability to patronize and support the arts and sciences led to the decline of Islamic civilization. Although the Ottoman Empire remained a potent force until the 17th century, much of the Muslim world outside the Ottoman domain was vulnerable to colonization by the ascending European powers at the time, beginning with Portugal and Spain and followed by the Netherlands, Britain, France and Italy in the colonial endeavor.

The Muslim world

It was not until the mid-20th century that most Muslim countries gained their independence from their European colonial rulers, which resulted in the emergence of today's modern Muslim nation-states. A combination of Islam and nationalism was often central to the Muslim struggles for independence. While some Muslim states, such as Saudi Arabia and, to a lesser extent, Pakistan, asserted their Islamic identity from the outset, others, such as Turkey, Tunisia and, to a lesser extent,

Indonesia, imposed a secular regime. Today, there are only a handful of Muslim countries that self-identify as Islamic states: these include Iran, Saudi Arabia, Pakistan and Mauritania. Most Muslim countries, particularly those in Central Asia (Azerbaijan, Kazakhstan, Kyrgyzstan, Tajikistan, Turkmenistan, Turkey and Uzbekistan), South and Eastern Europe (Bosnia-Herzegovina and Kosovo) and sub-Saharan Africa (Chad, Guinea, Mali and Senegal) are secular to the extent that the affairs of state and religion are officially separate. Many Muslim countries, however, have endorsed Islam as the state religion, including Algeria, Egypt, Iraq, Kuwait, Malaysia, Morocco and the United Arab Emirates. Effectively, this means that, while there is a separation of state and religious authority, many of the laws of the country, usually family and personal laws, are based on Islamic *sharia* law and Islamic courts operate to deal with such cases. In many Muslim countries there has been an ongoing struggle over the nation's identity and, in particular, the appropriate role of Islam in society and politics. In many Muslim countries, such as Algeria, Egypt, Indonesia, Malaysia, Morocco, Tunisia and Turkey, Islamic-oriented groups and political parties have struggled against the state to assert their rights and views, and in some cases, such as the Muslim Brotherhood in Egypt, have endured brutal repression.

Today there are currently 49 Muslim-majority countries. Globally there are over 1.6 billion Muslims, who comprise one-fifth of the world's population. A major study by the Pew Research Center estimates that the world's Muslim population will increase by about 35 per cent over the next 20 years. The Muslim population is expected to grow at twice the rate of the world's non-Muslim population. This means that the number of Muslims globally will rise to 2.2 billion and comprise one-quarter of the world's population. Currently the world's most populous Muslim nation is Indonesia, followed by Pakistan, India, Bangladesh, Egypt, Nigeria, Iran, Turkey, Algeria and Morocco. By 2030, Pakistan will be the world's most populous Muslim nation, followed by Indonesia, India, Bangladesh, Nigeria, Egypt, Iran, Turkey, Afghanistan and Iraq. Three-quarters of the world's Muslims live in Muslim-majority countries (in which over 50 per cent of the population is Muslim). All Muslim-majority countries are in the less developed regions of the world (with the exception of Albania and Kosovo, which are in Europe). Over one-fifth of the world's Muslims live in non-Muslim countries in the developing world, mainly in sub-Saharan African countries and certain developing countries in the Asia-Pacific and Central and South American regions. Only 3 per cent of the world's Muslims reside in the developed or Western world (Pew Research Center, 2011).

Only about 20 per cent of the world's Muslims live in the Middle East and North Africa, which has been the case for several decades and is expected to remain so into the foreseeable future. Sixty per cent of the world's Muslim population reside in the Asia-Pacific region. Within this region, Muslims continue to increase as a proportion of the population, up from 22 per cent in 1990 to 25 per cent in 2010, and are expected to increase to over 27 per cent by 2030 (Pew Research Center, 2011).

As far as the Western world is concerned, the largest numbers of Muslims are found in Europe. Over the next two decades, the Muslim population in Europe is expected to grow from 44 million in 2010 to 58 million in 2030, and will comprise 8 per cent of the continent's population. Several Western and Northern European countries will soon have Muslim populations that approach or exceed 10 per cent, including the United Kingdom (8.2 per cent), Austria (9.3 per cent), Sweden (9.9 per cent), Belgium (10.2 per cent) and France (10.3 per cent). Across Europe, the countries that are estimated to have the largest Muslim populations by 2030 are Russia (18.6 million), France (6.9 million), the United Kingdom (5.6 million), Germany (5.5 million) and Italy (3.2 million) (Pew Research Center, 2011).

In the United States, the population of Muslims is expected to double from 2.6 million today to 6.2 million in 2030. In Canada the Muslim population is expected to triple from just below 1 million in 2010 to almost 2.7 million in 2030. The Muslim population in Australia is expected to increase by 80 per cent over the next two decades, with the number of Muslims increasing from about 400,000 in 2010 to over 700,000 by 2030. The increase in Muslim populations in the Western world is due to a combination of high fertility rates and immigration, while the increase in Muslim populations in the broader Muslim world is a consequence of high fertility rates, the high proportion of Muslims entering the prime reproductive years, and improved health and economic conditions in Muslim countries, which have resulted in lower infant mortality rates and higher life expectancy (Pew Research Center, 2011). These figures alone make it clear that understanding Islam and Muslims is essential for the future of international relations and social harmony within Western countries.

Islam and Muslims

The term 'Islam' means 'submission' to God. A Muslim is one who follows Islam, which teaches that there is only one God and that Muhammad (d. 632) is a prophet of God. According to the Islamic tradition, Muhammad was the last in a long succession of prophets that included Adam, Noah, Abraham, Moses, Jesus and many others. Islam also teaches that that all human beings are accountable to God and, following a final judgment, will either be rewarded with a place in eternal heaven or punished by being sent to hell. The primary sacred text of Islam is the Quran, which Muslim tradition holds was revealed to the Prophet Muhammad over a two-decade period between the years 610 and 632. In the centuries following the death of Muhammad, narrations of his sayings and actions, known as the *Hadith*, became the second major source of Islamic teachings.

According to the Quran, Islam is not a new religion but a revival or renewal of the same basic teachings of the previous monotheistic faiths, namely Judaism and Christianity. The basic rituals of Islam are also found in earlier monotheistic religions. Islam is based on five pillars: a testimony of faith which states that there is only one God and that Muhammad is a prophet of God; prayers which are performed five times per day; almsgiving, charity or welfare tax of 2.5 per cent of annual savings, which is given to the poor and needy; fasting between dawn and sunset for the entire month of Ramadan; and a pilgrimage to Mecca at least once in a lifetime if possible.

The central teachings of Islam are almost 1500 years old, but to what extent do Muslims today still adhere to the beliefs and practices of the religion? The Pew Research Center (2012a) conducted over 38,000 face-to-face interviews in over 80 languages with Muslims in 39 countries, a sample that represents two-thirds of the world's Muslim population. The study found that Islam is very important in the lives of the overwhelming majority of Muslims globally. Islam is most significant in the lives of Muslims in Southeast Asia, South Asia, sub-Saharan Africa, and the Middle East and North Africa, but less so among Muslims in Southern and Eastern Europe and Central Asia. However, Islam tends to be more important in the lives of Muslims aged over 35 than for those aged 34 and under (Pew Research Center, 2012a). A majority of Muslims around the globe believe that there is only one correct interpretation of Islam. However, at least a third of the population in Chad, Ghana, Guinea Bissau, Iraq, Kenya, Lebanon, Mozambique, Palestine, Senegal, Tanzania and Uganda, as well as over half the population in Morocco and Tunisia, say that multiple interpretations of Islam are possible (Pew Research Center, 2012a).

Belief in God and the prophethood of Muhammad is almost universal among Muslims globally, and overwhelming majorities believe that the Quran is the literal word of God revealed to the Prophet Muhammad.

Other teachings of Islam, including the existence of angels, fate or pre-destination, the reward of heaven for the righteous and punishment of hell for the wicked, are accepted by a majority of Muslims around the world, and almost universally among Muslims in Southeast Asia, South Asia, and the Middle East and North Africa (Pew Research Center, 2012a).

In general, Muslims are observant of Islam's basic rituals, namely prayer, charity and fasting. In most Muslim countries a majority of the population perform the five-times-daily prayers. Prayer is particularly prominent in the lives of Muslims in sub-Saharan Africa, Southeast Asia, South Asia, and the Middle East and North Africa, but observed by far fewer Muslims who reside in Southern and Eastern Europe and Central Asia. Muslims also attend mosques regularly. A majority of Muslims globally attend the mosque at least once per week, specifically on Fridays to perform the Friday or *jumma* prayers. While there is no significant difference between men and women in the observance of the five-times-daily prayers, women are far less likely to attend mosques than men, especially in Central and South Asia, where cultural norms and local customs restrict women from attending mosques. By contrast, there is little difference between men and women in mosque attendance among Muslims in Southeast Asia, as well as those in Egypt, Morocco and many countries in sub-Saharan Africa (Pew Research Center, 2012a).

In all but three of the 39 countries surveyed, a majority say they engage in the Islamic tradition of almsgiving or charity, including nine out of ten Muslims in Southeast Asia, at least eight out of ten Muslims in South Asia, and at least seven out of ten Muslims in the Middle East and North Africa. Fasting during the month of Ramadan is the most observed of the Islamic rituals, with near-universal observance among Muslims in Southeast and South Asia and (with the exception of DR Congo) between 85 and 100 per cent observance among Muslims in the Middle East, North and sub-Saharan Africa. Outside these regions, fasting is observed by at least three-quarters of the Muslim population in Bosnia-Herzegovina, Kosovo, Tajikistan and Turkey. However, performance of the pilgrimage to Mecca is rare among Muslims. Generally, the further the region from Saudi Arabia, the fewer the number of Muslims who have made the journey. While 17 per cent of Muslims from the Middle East and North Africa and 13 per cent of those from sub-Saharan Africa have completed the pilgrimage, only 8 per cent of Muslims from Southeast Asia, 6 per cent of Muslims from South Asia and 3 per cent from Central Asia and Southern and Eastern Europe have done so (Pew Research Center, 2012a).

There are two major Muslim sects: Sunnis and Shia. Sunnis are the majority, constituting about 90 per cent of the world's Muslim population. The two differ mainly on issues of leadership and succession rather than on matters of Islamic belief or practice. Sunnis contend that lineage is not a criterion for a Muslim ruler, while Shias claim that a legitimate Muslim ruler must be a descendant of the Prophet Muhammad, specifically from the family of Ali and the Prophet's daughter Fatima. While sectarian differences and conflict between Sunnis and Shias are often a focus of media reports, most Muslims are either unaware of or unconcerned about such issues. In many of the countries surveyed, most respondents preferred not to identify as Sunni or Shia but as 'just a Muslim' (Pew Research Center, 2012a, p. 9). However, in many Muslim countries large pluralities of the Sunni population do not accept Shias as fellow Muslims, particularly in Egypt and Morocco, where half the population do not regard Shias as Muslims, and in Indonesia, Jordan, Pakistan, Palestine and Tunisia, where around 40 per cent of the population share this view. Interestingly, in those countries with significant Sunni and Shia populations, namely Iraq and Lebanon, around 90 per cent of the Sunni population accept Shias as fellow Muslims. The study posits that, in these cases, 'the experience of living side-by-side may increase, rather than decrease, mutual recognition between Sunnis and Shias' (Pew Research Center, 2012a, p. 89).

Aside from the major Sunni–Shia divide, Muslims tend to be unified in their basic beliefs and practices, specifically Islam's core articles of faith (belief in God, angels, previous sacred scriptures, previous prophets, day of judgment, heaven and hell) and the five pillars (testimony of faith in God and Muhammad's prophethood, prayer, charity, fasting and pilgrimage). However, Muslims are very diverse in terms of their cultures, languages, ethnicities, nationalities, geographical distribution, histories, education levels, economic development and political experiences. All of these factors have a bearing on the various approaches to Islam and multiple political, jurisprudential, theological and ideological groupings that have developed across the Muslim world.

Shortly after the death of the Prophet Muhammad, Shias, Kharajites and Sunnis emerged as the earliest Muslim political factions. Additionally, within the first century of Islam's founding, individuals began to emphasize living the austere life of the Prophet as a rejection of the luxurious lifestyle of the new Muslim rulers and practiced a more spiritual and mystical approach to Islam that developed into Sufism. Furthermore, in the following centuries, various schools of theology emerged, including the Mutazilite, Atharite and Asharite. Also, between the 8th and 9th centuries a number of schools of Islamic legal thought developed, including the Hanafi, Maliki, Shafi, Hanbali and Zaydi.

Today, numerous *sufi* orders as well as the major schools of Islamic jurisprudence continue to define and interpret Islam for their respective adherents. The modern world has also given rise to a number of other Muslim groupings. Saeed (2007b) identifies eight trends in contemporary Islam, and classifies Muslims as legalist traditionalists, theological puritans, militant extremists, political Islamists, secular liberals, cultural nominalists, classical modernists and progressive *ijtihadis*.

Legalist traditionalists stress adherence to classical Islamic law as developed by the classical jurists. Theological puritans, namely *salafists*, emphasize adherence to what they regard as correct, strictly monotheistic, Islamic beliefs. Militant extremists, such as Al-Qaeda, advocate the use of violence and terrorism for what they consider to be the defense of Islam and Muslims. Political Islamists, including the Muslim Brotherhood, are committed to establishing Islamic states in Muslim countries and an Islamic social order elsewhere based on what they consider to be Islamic values, laws and institutions. Secular liberals see faith as a more private rather than a public matter and advocate personal freedom, civil liberties and human rights. Cultural nominalists focus on culture rather than religion and are Muslim due to their family background rather than a commitment to Islam's beliefs and practices. Classical modernists emphasize the reform of Islamic law and theology from within the Islamic tradition and based on classical methods. Progressive *ijtihadis* are also concerned with the reform of Islamic law in order to respond to the realities of contemporary Muslims, but emphasize the spirit and principles rather than the letter of the law.

What Muslims really think

Morey and Yaqin describe the media portrayal of Muslims as 'a problematic presence, troubling those values of individualism and freedom said to define Western nations' (2011, p. 1). However, as the above-mentioned groupings indicate, there is a diversity of Muslim perspectives in response to the realities of modernity and life within a Western country. A number of major studies have been conducted that examine the views of Muslims concerning religious, social, moral and political issues as well as their perceptions of the West. Among these studies are the Pew Research Center's (2013a) Religion and Public Life Project on 'The World's Muslims: Religion, Politics and Society' and a Gallup World Poll study, *Who Speaks for Islam: What a Billion Muslims Really Think* (Esposito and Mogahed, 2007). Between 2008 and 2012, the Pew

Research Center conducted 38,000 face-to-face interviews in over 80 languages and dialects across 39 Muslim-majority countries, including a number with significant Muslim minorities, on the continents of Asia, Africa and Europe. Overall, Muslims around the globe are deeply committed to their faith and want it not only to guide their personal lives but also to inform the social and political order of their respective countries. A majority of Muslims consider Islam to be the one true faith, and belief in God is seen as necessary in order for one to lead a moral life and attain eternal life in heaven. Many Muslims support the implementation of *sharia* (Islamic law) as the official law of their country and think that their religious leaders should have at least some influence over political matters. However, such views are more prominent among Muslims in the Middle East, Africa, and South and Southeast Asia than they are among Muslims in Central Asia and Southern and Eastern Europe. Generally among Muslims, support for *sharia* varies little by age, gender or education. It is noteworthy that Muslims support the religious freedom of non-Muslims and that Islamic law should only apply to Muslims. In respect to the implementation of *sharia*, among Muslims who are supportive, higher proportions support it in the context of family and property matters than in cases of criminal and moral offenses and in the case of apostasy. However, in certain Muslim countries, namely Afghanistan, Egypt and Pakistan, over three-quarters of the population support corporal punishment for theft, stoning for adultery and execution for apostasy. Muslims tend to believe *sharia* to be the revealed word of God rather than a system of laws developed by man. As such, higher proportions of Muslims consider there to be only one true interpretation of *sharia* than those who accept the notion of multiple interpretations. Most Muslims do not think their country's laws are based on the *sharia*, and most view this negatively. The view that it is a bad thing that their country's laws do not follow the *sharia* is particularly high in Afghanistan, Bangladesh, Morocco, Pakistan and Palestine (Pew Research Center, 2013a).

In the practice of their faith, most Muslims identify no inherent tensions between Islam and modern society. Moreover, most do not consider the beliefs of Islam to contradict science and most Muslims believe in evolution. Muslims generally prefer democracy to authoritarian rule. Support for democracy is highest among Muslims in sub-Saharan Africa and Southeast Asia. Support for democracy varies little among Muslims in respect to religiosity, age, gender or education level. The majority of Muslims in Southeast Asia, South Asia, and the Middle East and North Africa tend to express support for religious leaders having at least some

influence in politics. This view is higher among those who are themselves more religious. As far as Islamic political parties are concerned,
the majority of Muslims around the world see them as the same as or
better than other political parties. Islamic political parties are viewed
most favorably in Afghanistan, Bangladesh, Egypt, Jordan, Malaysia,
Morocco and Tunisia. Overwhelming majorities of Muslims in all countries surveyed support religious freedom for non-Muslims. In no country
surveyed did fewer than three-quarters of the population support the
freedom of non-Muslims to practice their faith, and in most countries
the figure was above 90 per cent. Although many Muslims personally
enjoy Western television, films and music, most think that Western
popular culture has a negative impact on public morality (Pew Research
Center, 2013a).

An overwhelming majority of Muslims reject suicide bombing and
other attacks against civilians; they regard such actions as unjustifi-
able even in the defense of Islam. The majority of Muslims also regard
other acts of violence, such as honor killings, as never justified in Islam.
Muslims tend to have conservative views on moral issues. A majority of Muslims in the countries surveyed believe sex outside marriage,
homosexuality, euthanasia and abortion are morally wrong. Regarding
polygamy, sub-Saharan Africa is the only region of the Muslim world
where majorities of the population view the practice as morally acceptable. It is noteworthy that polygamy is more likely to be regarded as
morally acceptable by Muslims who also support the implementation of
sharia (Pew Research Center, 2013a).

Muslims tend to favor traditional gender roles. A majority of Muslims
around the world believe that a wife should always obey her husband.
In 13 of the 22 countries where the question was asked, a majority
of Muslims believe that a woman should have the right to terminate
her marriage. This view is particularly high among Muslims in Southern and Eastern Europe and Central Asia (except Tajikistan). Outside
these regions, high levels of support for a woman's right to divorce are
also found in Bangladesh, Lebanon, Morocco and Tunisia. However, this
does not mean that Muslim societies necessarily deny women various
liberties. Majorities of Muslims in Southern and Eastern Europe, Central Asia, Southeast Asia and South Asia (except Afghanistan), as well
as Lebanon, Palestine, Morocco, Tunisia and Senegal, favor a woman's
right to choose whether or not to wear a head scarf in public. Large
pluralities in Egypt, Iraq, Jordan and much of sub-Saharan Africa also
support this right. In 12 of the 23 countries where the question was
asked, a majority of Muslims say that sons and daughters should inherit

equally, which is a surprisingly high proportion considering that the Quran explicitly states that sons shall inherit twice the share of daughters (Quran, 4:11). Large pluralities in Bangladesh, Kyrgyzstan, Lebanon, Malaysia and Palestine also support equal inheritance. The Pew report notes that attitudes towards gender issues may be influenced by the existing laws of the country; in those countries where the law supports gender equality, Muslim views are similarly supportive (Pew Research Center, 2013a).

While most Muslims say that the way they live their life reflects the conduct (*sunna*) of the Prophet Muhammad at least a little, only a minority say that the way they live their life reflects the conduct of the Prophet a lot. This view is most prominent among Muslims in Afghanistan, Iraq, Pakistan, Malaysia and Thailand. Only small proportions of Muslims consider there to be tension between those who are more devout and those who are less devout. However, tension between Sunni and Shia Muslims is considered to be a very big problem by at least a fifth of the population in Afghanistan, Iraq, Lebanon and Pakistan, countries that have a history of Sunni–Shia conflict. Sunnis constitute a minority in Iraq and Lebanon, and are more likely than their Shia counterparts in Iraq and Lebanon, respectively, to view sectarian conflict as a major problem for their country (Pew Research Center, 2013a).

Not only do a majority of Muslims consider Islam to be the one true faith that leads to salvation, but many also believe converting others to Islam to be a religious duty. Few Muslims around the world believe that Islam has a lot in common with other faiths, and most have a social circle that does not include non-Muslim friends. Not only are Muslims unlikely to have Christian friends even in countries where Christians constitute a majority or significant minority, but a majority of Muslims would consider their children marrying a Christian to be unacceptable. Most Muslims do not think that interreligious conflict in their country is a significant problem. Rather, most tend to identify crime, unemployment, corruption and ethnic conflict as far more significant problems facing their country. However, in most Muslim countries minorities do see hostility between Muslims and non-Muslims, specifically Christians. With the exception of Bosnia-Herzegovina, Guinea Bissau and Mozambique, the majority of Muslims in the countries surveyed know little about Christianity. While many Muslims in sub-Saharan Africa, as well as parts of Southern and Eastern Europe and Central Asia, are likely to say that Islam and Christianity have a lot in common, most Muslims in the Middle East and North Africa, South Asia and Southeast Asia are likely to consider the two faiths to be very different. Interestingly, Muslims who know more about Christianity are more likely to say that the two faiths have a lot in common (Pew Research Center, 2013a).

Muslims in the West: The challenge of integration

Many of the views and beliefs of Muslims in the Muslim world are quite different from those of people in the West. Others are quite similar, however. In any case, the possibility of Muslims becoming integrated in Western countries has been an issue of significant debate over the past decade. The media provide numerous examples of Muslim hostility towards their own Western societies, including terrorist attacks in London and Boston and the murder of a filmmaker in the Netherlands for allegedly insulting Islam. We have also witnessed violent Muslim protests in response to the publication of cartoons in a Danish newspaper and the film *Innocence of Muslims*, both deemed to have insulted the Prophet Muhammad. Muslim integration is also questioned on the grounds of women choosing to wear traditional Muslim dress in public. The answer to the question of Muslim integration in Western societies lies in knowing what views Muslims in the West actually hold as well as understanding what happens to beliefs, norms and values in the process of cultural change and socialization that occurs when Muslims migrate to the West.

Inglehart and Norris (2009) conducted a ground-breaking study on this issue, making a number of important findings. First, the largest differences between Muslim migrants to the West and their host Western societies concern religiosity, gender roles and sexual norms. The authors identify a significant 25 per cent gap between the Muslim country of origin and the Western country of destination of Muslim migrants concerning religiosity, sexual liberalization and views on gender equality. Moreover, in respect to tolerance for homosexuality, divorce and abortion, Westerners are twice as liberal as Muslims in Muslim countries. In respect to democratic values, the gap is only 10 per cent between the two groups. In sum, with all other factors being equal, the difference in values that results from being raised in a Western society compared with a Muslim society is that the latter is likely to be ten percentage points more conservative in terms of sexual morality, ten percentage points more religious, eight percentage points less supportive of gender equality and three percentage points less positive towards democratic values (Inglehart and Norris, 2009).

However, when compared with their counterparts in the Muslim world, Western Muslims are 'at the center of the cultural spectrum', about half-way between the dominant values of their origin and their destination (Inglehart and Norris, 2009, p. 18). The authors acknowledge that 'self-selection' is part of the explanation: those who choose to migrate to a Western country 'may already have values that are relatively compatible with their future host country' (Inglehart and Norris, 2009, p. 18). Most importantly, Inglehart and Norris (2009) observe that, although one's social context has a stronger impact on values than individual-level religious identities, education, age, gender or income, the processes of enculturation and socialization are active in the case of Muslim migrants. As with other migrant groups, Muslim cultural values change in conformity with those of the Western society to which they have migrated. The reason a gap persists between Western Muslims and their host Western society is that the rate of cultural change among the Muslim migrants is often slower than the rate of change that is occurring in the host Western society. The authors explain that the cultural differences between Muslim migrants and Western publics are unlikely to disappear through generational change, as 'younger Westerners are adopting modern values even more swiftly than their Muslim peers' (Inglehart and Norris, 2009, p. 17).

Second, the study finds that Muslims tend to absorb much of the host culture. However, while Muslims largely embrace the procedural aspects of Western liberal democracy, they tend to resist aspects of the system that relate to tolerance of sexual liberation and gender equality. One's socialization in respect to gender roles, ethnic identity and religious values occurs early in life, becoming part of one's core identity and therefore more resistant to change (Inglehart and Norris, 2009). Importantly, the authors contend that such cultural differences do not necessarily lead to social tension or clashes. Rather, 'high levels of existential insecurity, xenophobia and intolerance are particularly intense and likely to lead to violence' (Inglehart and Norris, 2009, p. 18). In short, while cultural pluralism is a potential fault line, intercultural conflict is not inevitable. In large part, the reason European countries have perceived a greater problem with Muslim integration than Australia, Canada or the United States is that the former have historically been more homogeneous, while the latter have been established through immigration and therefore have always been more pluralistic (Inglehart and Norris, 2009).

Third, Inglehart and Norris (2009) discuss the persistence of cultural resistance among some sub-groups of Muslim migrants, even second and third-generation Muslims born in the West. When cultural norms are deeply ingrained from the country of origin they are often carried to the host country and retained. While host Western societies, like Australia or Canada, that advocate a settlement policy based on multiculturalism are less likely to find such cultural persistence to be problematic, other Western nations, such as France, that advocate an assimilationist policy are far more alarmed by the persistence of immigrant cultures. The experience of migration may strengthen ethnic and religious identities (Inglehart and Norris, 2009). This is especially likely when members of the migrant community feel alienated from the Western society, as many Western Muslims have felt since 9/11. The consequences have been that certain groups of Western Muslims have resisted integration into the society in which they live, increased their Islamic identity and even adopted revivalist or fundamentalist interpretations of Islam.

Conclusion

Islam will have a greater presence globally into the foreseeable future. Muslims are about to comprise one-quarter of the world's population, and, almost 1500 years since the advent of their faith, the overwhelming majority of Muslims remain committed to its central beliefs and practices. In general, the views of Muslims concerning social issues are more conservative than those of Westerners, but this should not be perceived as a source of conflict. Muslims are far more culturally, religiously and ideologically diverse than the Western media images portray. A limited understanding of this fact can leave audiences vulnerable to accepting that narrow media images of specific Muslim individuals or groups represent the majority. This juncture brings to mind broader historical and contemporary issues in Islam–West relations, including how ideas about Islam have developed in Western thought. Within this context one should examine the media's representation of Islam and Muslims along with the impact it has on Western audiences' perceptions of this religion and its adherents. This is the focus of the following chapter, in which we discuss these issues in relation to the concept of Islamophobia.

2
Media-Generated Muslims and Islamophobia

Much of what is known about Islam and Muslims in Western societies is derived from the mass media. Studies have shown that over three-quarters of people in Western societies rely on the mass media, mainly television, as their primary source of information about Islam and Muslims (Rane, 2010b). The scholarly consensus is that, in the aftermath of the 9/11 terrorist attacks, the sustained intensity of media coverage of Islam and Muslims resulted in an almost universal awareness of the religion and its adherents. That is not to say that most, or even many, people were then or are now knowledgeable about Islam or know Muslim people as a consequence of their media consumption; far from it. What it does mean is that a media version of Islam is widely known; what we are familiar with are media-generated Muslims. An important question, however, is how widely such images are accepted and what the implications are for intercommunity and international relations. This chapter explores Western public opinion and the extent to which there exist fear and prejudice towards Islam and Muslims, a phenomenon called Islamophobia. To assess the media's role in this phenomenon, we examine the dominant representations of Islam and Muslims that have been identified by a growing body of scholarly research. In order to understand the origins of the Western media's representations, we begin with the history of Western thought concerning Islam and Muslims.

Origins of Western images of Islam and Muslims

The representation of Islam and Muslims in the Western media cannot simply be explained in terms of how contemporary events involving Muslims are covered. National histories, particularly Muslim migration and settlement patterns, contribute to how groups within society are perceived and positioned within cultural, political and media discourses (Morey and Yaqin, 2011). Current representations of Islam and Muslims in Western media are also a product of much longer and broader histories that reside within the realm of civilization. The origin of frames and stereotypes of Islam and Muslims as the uncivilized other bent on the destruction of the West can be traced back to medieval Christian thoughts and images that informed the orientalism of the colonial and post-colonial era through to the war on terror (Morey and Yaqin, 2011). By the 11th century Islam was viewed by Europe as Christendom's 'main civilizational enemy' (Morey and Yaqin, 2011, p. 9). Such a perception only intensified when the Ottoman Empire captured Constantinople in 1453, and refused to abate two centuries later, when Ottoman decline resulted in their defeat at Vienna, or even by the 20th century, when most of the Muslim world was under European colonial rule. The portrayals of Muslims in Hollywood films also draw on historic depictions of Muslims as promiscuous and licentious from the 8th and 10th centuries, warring and violent from the 11th and 12th centuries, and barbaric and despotic from the 14th and 15th centuries. Films have helped make such representations 'part of Western popular imagination and consciousness' (Sardar and Davies, 2010, p. 239).

Various studies have concluded that the Western publics' views of Islam and Muslims are predominantly shaped by their representation in the mass media (Nacos and Torres-Reyna, 2007). The Western media are generally seen as orientalist, in that difference, inferiority and threat in relation to the West are the dominant images of Islam and Muslims (Said, 1997). Said (1997) traces the Western media's portrayal of Islam and Muslims to European colonial writings of the Muslim world. These orientalist portrayals 'have their origins in the defensive reactions of Christian orientals unwitting subjects of the new Muslim empire' that emerged in the 7th century (Tolan, 2002, p. 67).

A limited number of scholars have been dedicated to studying the history of Islam in Western thought. One of the earliest works is Norman Daniel's book *Islam and the West: The Making of an Image*, which was first published in 1960. Another is Richard Southern's *Western Views of Islam in the Middle Ages*, published in 1962. The most important recent contributions to this area have been made by John Tolan, particularly his book *Saracens: Islam in the Medieval European Imagination*. Tolan (2002) explains that the hostility towards Islam in the contemporary media today dates back to the earliest writings about Muslims by medieval Christians. While Spanish and Eastern Christians were less ignorant about Islam than their more northern European brethren, both were hostile. They failed to recognize Islam as a monotheistic faith, instead regarding it as idolatrous. Medieval Christian writing about Islam is based on a combination of prejudice, misinformation and ignorance derived from a 'feeling of rivalry, contempt and superiority' (Tolan, 2002, p. xvii). Indeed, the terms 'Muslim' and 'Islam' were seldom even used by Christian writers for the first 900 years following Islam's advent.

Christian writers struggled to comprehend the essence and central teachings of Islam, or even that it represents a monotheistic religion within the same family of Abrahamic faiths to which both Judaism and Christianity belong. The early Christian writers referred to Islam simply as the law of Muhammad or law of the Saracens. Muslims were referred to in terms of ethnicity, namely Arabs, Turks, Moors and Saracens, or by Biblical references, such as Ishmaelites or Hagarenes (Tolan, 2002, p. xv). The earliest Christian texts about Islam, written between the 7th and 13th centuries, are particularly important, Tolan contends, as they form the seminal works to which the writers about Islam and Muslim continued to refer until the 20th century (2002, p. xix). It is also noteworthy that many of the early Christian writings to which Tolan (2002) refers present discourses about Islam and Muslims that are still found in Islamophobic discourse today. For instance, the assertions that Islam is not a religion and that all Muslims are violent extremists were part of early Christian discourses and are also identified as 'central themes that run through the Islamophobia network's messages' according to the most recent report on Islamophobia by CAIR (Council on American-Islamic Relations) (Tolan, 2002; CAIR, 2013, p. 37).

Several themes emerge from Tolan's (2002) study of medieval Christian thought about Islam. First, there was little interest in understanding Islam on its own terms, based on Islamic texts. Early Christian writings about Islam and Muslims were not based on any study of Islamic sources; rather, the dominant approach was to construct a narrative about the religion and its adherents based on Biblical references. The task that Christian writers set for themselves was to fit Islam into existing Christian perceptions of God's plan, 'divine history and divine geography' (Tolan, 2002, p. 4). The emergence and spread of Islam and the success of Muslims in conquering the Near East, North Africa and Spain were interpreted by Christians as punishment from God for the sins of Christians. Tolan (2002) identifies a preoccupation with sexual sins as the dominant explanation for God's dissatisfaction with Christians and hence his use of the Muslims as a means of chastisement. This discourse essentially positioned Christians as God's favored ones and placed them at the center of his divine plan. This narrative also precluded Muslims from a place among God's chosen ones, denying the possibility of attributing their success to God's favor.

Second, Islam was seen as heresy based on a corrupt version of the true religion. Muhammad was often portrayed as the Antichrist and was especially condemned for his multiple marriages and engagement in armed conflict. Islam was presented as 'a creed devoted primarily to the worldly delights of sex, wealth and power' (Tolan, 2002, p. xx). Muslims in general were dehumanized, portrayed as violent, barbarous and uncivilized. These arguments were used to dissuade Christians from converting to Islam, which was the main objective of medieval Christian writings about Islam. The military successes of Muslims, coupled with the power, wealth and prestige they accumulated, along with their mastery of the arts and sciences made Islam attractive to the Christian masses (Tolan, 2002).

Third, the differences between Islam and Christianity were constantly emphasized, while any similarities or common ground were either ignored or distorted so as to reinforce the dominant narrative of Islam's deviance, inferiority and illegitimacy. For instance, that Jesus is revered in the Quran as a great prophet of God but not the son of God was used by Christian writers as proof that Muhammad must be the Antichrist, for his religion preached the denial of Christ's divinity. Moreover, the fact that the Quran also confirms the virginity of Mary and the immaculate conception of Jesus was defiled by an alleged saying attributed to Muhammad, that he would have Mary as his wife in the next world and would have the honor of deflowering her (Tolan, 2002). In Tolan's words, 'even those elements of Islam that resemble Christianity (such as reverence of Jesus and his virgin mother) are deformed and blackened, so as to prevent the Christian from admiring anything about the Muslim other' (2002, p. 93). This approach is echoed in the Western media's portrayal of Islam until today.

Western media representations of Islam and the Muslim world

Negative media coverage of Islam and Muslims was certainly present prior to 9/11. Since the Gulf War of 1991, and even as far back as the Iranian Revolution of 1979, Islam and Muslims have attracted considerable, negative media attention. The tendency of the media to associate Muslims with terrorism also existed prior to 9/11. Morey and Yaqin argue that the Western media present a 'limited and limiting conceptual framework surrounding Islam in public discourse' within which the perceived 'negative', 'threatening' features of Muslim belief and behavior are 'constantly promoted and reinforced' (2011, p. 20). The dominant stereotypes of Muslims include 'the bearded Muslim fanatic, the oppressed, veiled woman, the duplicitous terrorist who lives among "us" the better to bring about our destruction'; such stereotypes have been reinforced since 9/11 (Nacos and Torres-Reyna, 2007, p. 2).

The Western media's preoccupation with the extremes in the Muslim world precludes any awareness of mainstream Muslim life and lends legitimacy to extremist Muslims as the representatives of Islam. Those who rely on the mass media for their understanding of Islam and Muslims are unlikely to gain a view of the complete picture, or even the main picture. The statements and actions of a minority of Muslims are deemed newsworthy and dominate the popular understanding of Islam (Rane, 2010b).

Elizabeth Poole finds that, in the British press, Muslims are presented not as an accepted part of society but as an out-group or 'other', in accordance with orientalist thinking (Poole, 2002). Australian journalist and media commentator Peter Manning also finds orientalist and stereotypical coverage in the Australian press of events in Indonesia, Lebanon, Syria, Israel and Palestine. Among his major findings are that Arabs and Muslims overseas are portrayed as violent, 'without reason, humanity or compassion'; Sydney Arab men are portrayed as 'sexual predators'; and Middle Eastern asylum seekers are presented as 'tricky, ungrateful and undeserving' (Manning, 2006, p. 37). Focusing on the American context, Fawaz Gerges argues that negative media representation of Islam and Muslims, coupled with the influence of certain lobby groups and foreign-policy elites, exerts significant influence on the American public, which in turn fosters a hardline foreign policy towards political Islam (Gerges, 1999, pp. 72–89).

While most analyses of the representation of Islam and Muslims in the mass media tend to focus on factual or news media, predominantly newspapers and television news, fictional media are equally important in the context of this discussion. Jack Shaheen's (2003) study *Reel Bad Arabs: How Hollywood Vilifies a People* demonstrates that Hollywood films portraying Arabs and Muslims frequently allude to or are based upon actual events or issues, giving fictional films a factual or authoritative character. In his analysis of more than 900 films portraying Arabs and Muslims, Shaheen contends that the films repeatedly dehumanized Arabs and Muslims, portraying them as heartless, brutal, uncivilized, religious fanatics, violent and terrorists. He argues that, because of their repetitious nature, such portrayals have a negative impact on public discourse and policy. Films that offered audiences a humane and humanized understanding of Islam and Muslims were very few (Shaheen, 2003). It should be noted, however, that a more balanced and sophisticated portrayal of Arabs and Muslims is presented in more recent Hollywood films such as *Syriana*, *Body of Lies* and *Traitor*, which portray not only the complexities of Middle East politics but also present a diversity of Arab and Muslim characters and their approaches to Islam.

Since 9/11, further research has continued to show not only a massive increase in the volume of media coverage of Islam and Muslims, but also an increase in the pejorative nature of this coverage. The dominant image of Muslims in the Western media is of a people who are violent, intolerant, oppressive and threatening. A number of studies have demonstrated that, post-9/11, the media frames used in the coverage of Islam and Muslims are based on orientalist depictions of a religion and people as a different, strange, inferior and threating 'other' (Poole, 2002; Manning, 2006; Steuter and Wills, 2009; Kumar, 2010; Powell, 2011). Since 9/11, media and political discourses have tended to associate Islam with violence and values inimical to those of Western societies (Martin and Phelan, 2002; Celermajer, 2007; Steuter and Wills, 2009; Powell, 2011). These studies have consistently found that terrorism, violence and the threat of Islam tend to be the dominant media frames used in the coverage of Muslims. Numerous studies have identified that Western news media conflate Islam and terrorism through portrayals of Muslims as terrorists and Islam as a religion that condones terrorist acts (Norris, Kern and Just, 2003; Ryan, 2004; Papacharissi and de Fatima Oliveira, 2008).

Views of Islam and Muslims in the West

The ways Muslims are framed by the media are found to obstruct the cultural understanding of Islam and Muslims among Western audiences (Morey and Yaqin, 2011). Nacos and Torres-Reyna (2007) conclude that, as a consequence of the media coverage of the 9/11 attacks and subsequent acts of terrorism, fear and apprehension of violence and terrorism by Muslims has become part of the American psyche. The authors explain that 'the typical coverage of Muslim and Arab Americans before and after 9/11 did not provide readers, listeners, and viewers with a representative picture of these minorities' (Nacos and Torres-Reyna, 2007, p. 121). The authors note that the negative portrayal of Muslims can be largely attributed to a focus on extreme rather than moderate voices from within Islam and Muslim communities. Nacos and Torres-Reyna

(2007) identify a correlation between the prominence given to Islam and Muslims on the news media agenda and their prominence in public consciousness. They also explain that, with the framing of Islamic and Muslim issues within the context of violence and terrorism, the news media significantly contributed to a majority of Americans expressing a fear of Islam and Muslims (Nacos and Torres-Reyna, 2007).

A World Public Opinion study found that 46 per cent of Americans believed that Islam 'does not teach respect for the beliefs of non-Muslims', with the same percentage believing that Islam is more likely than other religions to encourage violence among its adherents (2005, p. 4). Yet in the same study, when asked about Muslims as people, views are more favorable. While fewer than a third have an unfavorable view of Muslims, approximately half say they do have a favorable view. Furthermore, and perhaps most importantly, it was found that 'Americans reject the idea that there is an inevitable clash of civilizations between Islam and the United States' (World Public Opinion, 2005, p. 4).

Muslims in Europe are viewed more unfavorably than Jews. However, negative views of Jews across the board were increasing, while negative views of Muslims were in fact decreasing in a number of countries (Pew Research Center, 2008). In the West, attitudes towards Muslims are found to be mixed, with majorities in the United Kingdom, France and the United States having favorable views. Yet countries such as Spain, Germany and Poland express pejorative sentiments, with over 50 per cent of the population in Spain and Germany and 46 per cent in Poland having unfavorable views. Older and less educated people tend to express more negative opinions, as do those who are from the right of the political spectrum.

Additionally, the Pew Research Center (2010) found that knowledge about Islam is still comparatively low, with over 55 per cent of Americans saying they know nothing or not much about Islam and only 9 per cent saying they know a great deal. This coincides with other studies which show that Americans reported having more knowledge about Islam in the years following 9/11 compared with the preceding years (Nacos and Torres-Reyna, 2007). It is important to note that other studies that tested respondents' knowledge of Islam found that those who actually possessed higher levels of knowledge also tended to express more favorable views of Muslims than those who were found to have lower levels of knowledge. Additionally, those who were most informed about Islam tended to identify commonalities with their own faith, while those who were least informed about Islam tended to see Islam as very different from their own faith (Nacos and Torres-Reyna, 2007).

Indeed, in the years following the 9/11 attacks, studies have shown that around 60 per cent of Americans see Islam as very different from their own faith, while fewer than one-third see Islam as having much in common with their own faith (Nacos and Torres-Reyna, 2007).

Those who watch television news more frequently express higher levels of fear and anxiety in respect to Islam and Muslims, and are more likely than those who rely less on television news to think that another terrorist attack on the United States is imminent (Nacos and Torres-Reyna, 2007). High levels of fear also correlate with high levels of support for the restriction of civil liberties of Muslims. The 7 July 2005 bombings in London resulted in higher levels of public anxiety about home-grown terrorism, which, in the United States, manifested in an increase of negative perceptions of American Muslims and a widespread belief among Americans that members of the American Muslim community were planning a terrorist attack (Nacos and Torres-Reyna, 2007).

However, a significant proportion of Americans were often reluctant to express negative sentiments about Islam or Muslims due to a desire to be racially tolerant and politically correct. Consequently, public opinion polls taken in the years following the 9/11 attacks show a high proportion of respondents expressing no opinion on questions about Islam and Muslims. It is noteworthy, however, that there has been a significant decline in the proportion of Americans unwilling to express negative views of Islam and Muslims. Increased media coverage of Islam and Muslims over the past few decades has resulted in Americans forming a negative opinion about Islam and Muslims. Nacos and Torres-Reyna (2007) explain that, in the aftermath of the first World Trade Center bombing in 1993, 80 per cent of Americans were unable to express either a favorable or an unfavorable opinion about Muslims. Throughout the 1990s and by the turn of the century, Americans had become aware of further acts of terrorism by Muslims, including the 1996 attack on the US military housing in Saudi Arabia, the bombing of US embassies in Kenya and Tanzania in 1998, and the 2000 attack on the USS *Cole* in Yemen. By early 2001, prior to the attacks on 9/11, the proportion of Americans who remained undecided about Muslims had dropped to 60 per cent. Following the attacks on the United States in 2001 and then on London in 2005, only 20 per cent of Americans were still unwilling or unable to express an opinion about Muslims. In specific reference to Islam, after the first World Trade Center bombing in 1993, 56 per cent of Americans claimed not to have enough information to form an opinion about the religion. However, by 2002, this figure had dropped to 35 per cent and by 2005 it had dropped further to 25 per cent. Moreover, by 2006, only 10 per cent of Americans were unwilling or unable to express an opinion about Islam (Nacos and Torres-Reyna, 2007).

In the immediate aftermath of 9/11, the American public had not generally made the connection between Islam and terrorism. However, by 2003, a majority of Americans had come to perceive the threat posed by Islamic fundamentalism to be extremely important. Significantly, most Americans attribute this threat to a minority rather than the majority of Muslims. Polls conducted since 9/11 have consistently shown that between one half and two-thirds of Americans see the Islamist threat as a conflict with a small, radical group, while only around one-third of Americans view the conflict with the majority of Muslims in terms of a clash of civilizations. While two-thirds of Americans did not see America as being at war with the Muslim world, over 70 per cent thought that Muslims consider themselves at war with America (Nacos and Torres-Reyna, 2007).

It is important to note that audiences are not passive but active in their engagement with media content. As such, media content has varying levels of influence on audiences, depending on their age, religion, cultural background, socio-economic status, educational level and life experiences. Essentially, media engagement and its potential influence are generally a negotiated process. For example, American opinions about Islam and Muslims are found to differ according to demographics, including age, ethnicity, religion, educational level and political orientation. Blacks, people aged under 50, Black Protestants, White Catholics, people with at least a college education and Democrats tend to have more favorable views of Muslims. By comparison, Whites and Latinos, people aged over 50, people with only a high school qualification, White Protestants and Republicans tend to have more unfavorable views of Muslims (Nacos and Torres-Reyna, 2007).

Americans' opinions of their Muslim compatriots also deteriorated in the years following 9/11. A year on from the attacks, over two-thirds of the public thought that Muslim Americans sympathized with the 9/11 terrorists, 44 per cent thought that American Muslims had not done enough to help authorities bring terrorists to justice, and 44 per cent thought Muslim Americans posed a threat to the moral character of the country. However, concerning the civil liberties of Muslim Americans, most Americans opposed measures by the government and security forces to violate the rights of Muslims. Almost half of the respondents to Nacos and Torres-Reyna's (2007) study opposed all suggested security measures that would violate the civil liberties of Muslims. Fewer than one-third favored infiltrating Muslim organizations, surveillance of mosques and Muslims having to register their whereabouts with authorities. Fewer than one-quarter favored the profiling of Muslims and those of Middle Eastern appearance (Nacos and Torres-Reyna, 2007).

Since 9/11, it has been commonplace for non-Muslims and the Western media to claim that Muslim leaders are not doing enough to denounce terrorism. Such a perspective ignores a plethora of statements made by Muslim political, religious and community leaders across the globe. A basic internet search reveals hundreds of statements by Muslim religious scholars, organizations and governments condemning suicide bombing, terrorism and extremism. Charles Kurzman (2012) has compiled a list of over 70 such statements, while Sheili Musaji's (2011) compilation consists of over three times this number. As Nacos and Torres-Reyna point out, 'the problem was that the news media did not report it prominently – or not at all – when Muslim leaders did speak out against the attacks of 9/11 or against terrorism in general' (2007, p. 29). This dilemma arises as a consequence of news values that prioritize stories that convey negativity, conflict and controversy over those that promote conciliation, peace and harmony. As a result of the fear evoked by such standards of newsworthiness, the phenomenon of Islamophobia has become an increasing concern since 9/11.

Islamophobia

There is much scholarly debate on the origins of Islamophobia and even how to define it. Lopez (2010) and Ciftci (2012) identify citations of Islamophobia in a number of works from the late 19th and early 20th centuries. Lopez claims that the first known work to use the word Islamophobia was in an article by French African Maurice Delafosse that dates back to 1910. Delafosse states: 'France has no more to fear from Muslims in West Africa than from non-Muslims... Islamophobia therefore has no *raison d'être* in West Africa' (cited in Lopez, 2010, p. 562). Other works of the late 19th and early 20th centuries include the first explicit definition of Islamophobes by Alain Quellian as those 'who consider Islam an implacable enemy of Europeans' (Lopez, 2010, p. 562). A 1997 report on Islamophobia stated that 'a deep dislike of Islam is not a new phenomenon in our society' (in Allen, 2007, p. 126). Regarding its origins, most scholars consider orientalism and the process of 'othering' as the historical basis of Islamophobia.

As the term suggests, Islamophobia refers to a phobia or fear of Islam and Muslims. The Runnymede Trust's report *Islamophobia: A challenge for us all*, published in 1997, is one of the first explicit uses of the term, and its definition is much used in scholarly debate. The report defines Islamophobia as an 'unfounded hostility towards Islam', of which the 'practical consequences of such hostility [result] in unfair discrimination against Muslim individuals and communities, and to the exclusion of Muslims from mainstream political and social affairs' (in Lentini, Halafoff and Ogru, 2011, p. 411). A more recent report by the Center for American Progress defines Islamophobia as 'an exaggerated fear, hatred, and hostility toward Islam and Muslims that is perpetuated by negative stereotypes resulting in bias, discrimination, and the marginalization and exclusion of Muslims from America's social, political, and civic life' (Ali et al., 2011, p. 9). Also noteworthy is what is not defined as Islamophobia. CAIR's 2013 report on the phenomenon explicitly states:

> It is not appropriate to label all, or even the majority of those, who question Islam and Muslims as Islamophobes. Equally, it is not Islamophobic to denounce crimes committed by individual Muslims or those claiming Islam as a motivation for their actions.
>
> (CAIR, 2013, p. ix)

Contributing factors

There is a general consensus that mass media and, increasingly, social media play an instrumental role in stimulating and intensifying Islamophobia. There is also an increasing identification of specific groups and individuals who, through generous funding, are central to the propagation of Islamophobia. For these individuals and groups, the media, like politicians, are tools by which to disseminate their message. According to the Center for American Progress report on Islamophobia, a small, tight-knit network consisting of five key individuals and their organizations have spread Islamophobia in the United States through effective advocates, media partners and grassroots organizing (Ali et al., 2011). The report claims that, between 2001 and 2009, over $40 million has flowed from seven foundations (Donors Capital Fund, Richard Mellon Scaife Foundation, Lynde and Harry Bradley Foundation, Newton and Rochelle Becker Foundation and Newton and Rochelle Becker Charitable Trust, Russell Berrie Foundation, Anchorage Charitable Fund and William Rosenwald Family Fund, and Fairbrook Foundation) to Frank Gaffney, Center for Security Policy; David Yerushalmi, Society of Americans for National Existence; Daniel Pipes, Middle East Forum; Robert Spencer, Jihad Watch and Stop Islamization of America; and Steven Emerson, Investigative Project on Terrorism. The report highlights that the writings of these individuals have informed anti-*sharia* bills that have been passed in various states in the United States. These writings were also cited by the Norwegian terrorist Anders Breivik, who confessed to killing over 70 people and told the court that his violent act was 'necessary' to repel 'ongoing Islamic colonization of Europe' (Ali et al., 2011, p. 1). Specifically, Robert Spencer was cited 162 times in Breivik's 1500-page manifesto (Ali et al., 2011). Moreover, Pipes, Spencer, Emerson and others regularly appear in print and on broadcast media as 'experts' on terrorism, Islamic and Muslim issues. Their views are legitimized and endorsed by large media organizations such as Fox News, the *Washington Times* and *The National Review* (Ali et al., 2011).

CAIR's 2013 report on Islamophobia in the United States cites an 'inner core' consisting of 37 groups 'whose primary purpose is to promote prejudice against or hatred of Islam and Muslims' as well as an additional outer group of 32 organizations 'whose work regularly demonstrates or supports Islamophobic themes' (2013, p. vi). The report estimates that almost $120 million was provided to the inner core between 2008 and 2011. While this report also highlights the work of specific individuals, namely David Yerushalmi, as central to the drafting of the anti-*sharia* bills in 29 states in the United States, it also notes that Islamophobia has been dealt a setback as 'multiple federal government outlets agreed to review their training on Islam and remove biased or inaccurate materials' (CAIR, 2013, p. vi). Although the report identifies a decline in Islamophobia in the United States from a score of 6.4/10 in 2010 to 5.9/10 in 2012, among the most concerning findings is that 'Islamophobic rhetoric remains socially acceptable' (CAIR, 2013, p. vii).

Manifestations and impacts

Vilification, abuse and discrimination against Muslims have far-reaching negative effects for intercultural and international relations. Islamophobia is considered by Muslim governments and Muslim organizations in Western countries as a serious problem. The world's largest international organization after the UN, the Organization of Islamic Cooperation (OIC), which is comprised of 57 member states, has a dedicated Islamophobia Observatory. This initiative of the OIC was established 'to raise awareness of the dangers of Islamophobia and counter it by monitoring all its forms and manifestations, in addition to initiating a structured dialogue to project the true values of Islam' (Organization of Islamic Cooperation, 2008, p. 2). The OIC's Islamophobia Observatory has issued five major reports since its creation in 2005, the most recent of which highlights the prominent role of the media in propagating national discourses of an Islamic threat. The report states:

Western media, including the social media, continued to play a key role in promoting and disseminating an anti-Muslim culture. The lack of objectivity and biased reporting combined with continuous focus on the issue of 'Islamic extremism' steadily consolidated negative stereotyping of Muslims. It was revealing how the Norway attacks by Breivik were initially presumed and reported to have been committed by a Muslim although no evidence whatsoever to corroborate this fact had been made available. Furthermore, the amalgam between the acts of a few extremists and the Islamic religion as a faith and set of principles and teachings has exacerbated tensions and augmented suspicion and marginalization of Muslims who were portrayed as being guilty by association. Misinformation about Islam being a backwards religion that sanctioned violence and decadence was rampant in the media fuelling negative stereotyping, discrimination and violence against Muslims.

(Organization of Islamic Cooperation, 2012, p. 3)

Turkey's ruling party, the Justice and Development Party (AKP), has specifically addressed Islamophobia in its vision 2023 document in the following words:

As we saw in the cartoon crisis several years ago and now with the reprehensible film about our beloved Prophet, there is an urgent need for an international initiative and joint effort to fight against the rising tide of Islamophobia and to establish peace and harmony between different cultures and civilizations. Islamophobia is a very dangerous trend that poisons relations between Islamic and Western societies. Just like anti-Semitism, Islamophobia is a form of racism and a crime against humanity. In this regard, we began a comprehensive initiative to classify Islamophobia as a hate crime and will pursue it to the end.

(AKP, 2012, p. 62)

The manifestations of Islamophobia vary from the overt – physical violence, hate speech, large demonstrations of discrimination – to the covert – media framing, exclusion, subtle forms of discrimination. Nacos and Torres-Reyna (2007) document a plethora of examples of assaults against Muslims that occurred in the aftermath of the 9/11 attacks. Additionally, the leading television news networks in the United States aired a total of 16 segments that reported on the plight of Muslims in the immediate aftermath of the 9/11 attacks. Two decades prior to 9/11, the Salman Rushdie affair put the United Kingdom on notice that the country's Muslims were not sufficiently British. The social exclusion of Muslims intensified after 9/11. The media reinforced negative attitudes towards Muslims, and in the aftermath of the terrorist attacks over 300 assaults against Muslims were reported (Harb and Bessaiso, 2006).

The moral panic involved in Islamophobia evokes responses to Muslims based on overgeneralizations and stereotypes that remain resilient in spite of what the majority of Muslims may say or do. Ciftci (2012) finds that there are four interrelated dimensions which affect the values and practices against Muslims: exclusion, discrimination, prejudice and violence. Of these, violence against Muslims and Muslim institutions is most easily and readily seen, particularly in the media. Similarly, Larrson's (2005) post-9/11 study of Muslims in Sweden identifies a number of overt forms of Islamophobia. It was found that the media, police and other state organizations reported that Muslim institutions (mosques and prayer halls), as well as individuals with a cultural background in Muslim cultures (but not necessarily Muslim themselves), were targeted and discriminated against, even to the extent of having violence used against them. The 2012 OIC report on Islamophobia makes specific reference to bans on the construction of minarets in Sweden as an example of such Islamophobia in Europe (2012). Other issues raised in the report include *hijab* bans, broader social and political campaigns against Islam and Muslims, and discrimination in the workplace, educational institutions and airports.

Factors limiting Islamophobia

While Australia imports much of its discourse about Islam and Muslims from the broader Western world, there are a number of factors that have a mitigating influence on Islamophobia. Before discussing these factors, it is important to provide some context. Perhaps as a legacy of the White Australia Policy (the Immigration Restriction Act which prevented non-Europeans from migrating to Australia), combined with the current anti-Muslim sentiment through much of the West, 'Muslims have suffered sustained vilification, attacks and resistance' in recent history in Australia (Bouma, 2011, p. 438). Examples of Islamophobia include difficulties in obtaining city council approval to build mosques, schools or other facilities. The recent denial of permission to build an Islamic school in Camden, New South Wales, is one example of this – much coverage of which can be seen in the news. Certain objectors were quoted as saying that the building of the said school would bring an unwanted element and threats of violence, and some of these beliefs were supported and promoted by right-wing Evangelical Christians. Additionally, isolated attacks on mosques and Muslim individuals are other manifestations of Islamophobia in Australia. Perhaps the most extreme case was an arson attack on a mosque in Brisbane in the aftermath of the 9/11 attacks, which completely destroyed the building.

However, some argue that the multicultural policies which have been in place since the late 1960s have had a moderating effect on the level of Islamophobia within Australian society (Bouma, 2011). Comparatively, Australia has been found to be more accepting and, although not exempt from the Islamophobic discourse, it is somewhat less Islamophobic than other nations, such as those in Europe or the United States (Bouma, 2011, p. 434). Bouma suggests that in a country of immigrants, where approximately 25 per cent of Australians were born overseas and nearly 50 per cent have one or more parents born overseas, 'Islamophobic discourse does become more difficult to sustain in the face of disconfirming reality' (2011, p. 434).

A number of factors contribute to a mitigation of Islamophobia. Among these are higher levels of education, personal interactions with Muslims in day-to-day life, and the degree to which one perceives the media to be credible. Lentini et al. state that 'the more knowledge individuals have about Muslims, including personal contact, the more likely they are to form positive opinions about them' (2011, p. 411). Earlier studies by the Swedish Integration Board in 2005 and 2006 found that those who have a more positive attitude towards Muslims and Islam are: women more than men, residing in urban areas rather than rural, and more highly educated (Bevelander and Otterbeck, 2010). In general, it was found that a more negative attitude was associated with increased age as well as in those who were unemployed. Politically, it was found that those who identified more as right-wing had less positive attitudes than those who identified more as left-wing. These findings are consistent with those in the Australian context cited above.

Among the more positive consequences of 9/11 has been recognition on the part of governments that support is needed for a better understanding of Islam and Muslims within society. This has been particularly apparent in the university sector, where governments of various Western countries have supported the establishment of academic centers for research and teaching of Islamic and Muslim issues. In Australia, for instance, a $7 million National Centre of Excellence for Islamic Studies was established in 2007 across a consortium of universities that included the University of Melbourne, Griffith University and the University of Western Sydney. McLoughlin observes that, in the post-7/7 context, the UK government viewed universities as potential sites where threats to security could develop, but also as providing opportunities 'for engineering good citizenship' (2007, p. 273). This led to a focus by the UK government on how Islamic studies at the tertiary level 'might illuminate the practice and interpretation of Islam in contemporary contexts, including those of multicultural Britain' (McLoughlin, 2007, p. 274). Another limiting factor in this context, with respect to Islamophobia, is that the investment in Islamic Studies at the tertiary level has produced public servants, policy makers and journalists who have at least a basic understanding of Islam and Muslims. Moreover, there is now a larger pool of academics who are experts on Islam and the Muslim world and whom journalists can consult in order to present more accurate, balanced and objective coverage on such issues.

A study by Dunn (2005) shows that only one-fifth of the Australians surveyed had a knowledge of Islam that was 'reasonable or better', and that half of those he surveyed knew 'a little' about the faith. One-third of respondents were completely ignorant of Islam's teachings. The respondents' lack of knowledge of Islam was related to feelings of being threatened by Islam, with 61 per cent of those with a little knowledge of Islam feeling threatened, dropping to 46 per cent among those with a reasonable or better knowledge of Islam. Demonstrating the importance of direct contact with Muslims and a basic understanding of Islam in counteracting misconceptions, Dunn's study reports that fewer than half of the respondents knew any Muslims.

Similar research has also found positive correlations between higher levels of interaction with Muslims, acceptance of Muslims as part of Australian society, and opinions that Muslims do not pose a threat to the country. A survey conducted among Australians in 2006 asked respondents about their sources of knowledge, understanding of Islam, interaction with Muslims, degree of acceptance of Muslims, perceptions of Muslims as a threat, and their evaluations of the media and political discourse on Islam and Muslims. The major findings were that 79 per cent rely on the mass media as a primary source of information about Islam and Muslims, and of those 62 per cent rely on television news and current affairs programs. Over half of those surveyed did not have a basic understanding of Islam. While two-thirds of respondents had never met or rarely interact with Muslims, 33 per cent interact with Muslims occasionally, often, or constantly as work colleagues, classmates, neighbors and friends. Among the most surprising finding was that 78 per cent of respondents said they are comfortable with Muslims as part of Australian society and two-thirds did not regard Muslims as a threat to the country. Most significantly, the study found that those who interacted more with Muslims and those with higher levels of education were more likely to accept Muslims as part of Australian society and less likely to view Muslims as a threat (Rane, 2010b).

Part of the explanation for these findings is a perception among respondents that the media lack credibility. Almost two-thirds of those surveyed recognize the media representation of Islam and Muslims as sensational, biased or inaccurate, rather than accurate, objective or fair. Moreover, the potential for media content to negatively impact on inter-community relations is undermined by higher education levels and interaction between Muslims and the wider society. It seems that, in spite of the media being a primary source of information, the potential for pejorative representations of Muslims to generate Islamophobia is limited to a minority of the population (Rane, 2010b).

Conclusion

The Western media's coverage of Islam and the Muslim world is both negative and a distortion of reality. This is not to deny that Muslims are committing acts of violence and terrorism in the name of Islam, or that such incidents should be covered by the news media. However, as shown in the previous chapter, the overwhelming majority of Muslims reject the killing of civilians as unjustified in Islam. The projection of an image of Islam that does not reflect the beliefs and practices of the overwhelming majority of its adherents dates back to medieval Christian writings. These ideas influenced orientalist thought during the era of European colonial rule of the Muslim world and have continued into modern times. Western media portrayals of Islam and the Muslim world have been instrumental in evoking a fear of Islam and discrimination against Muslims. While this phenomenon of Islamophobia is a major concern of the OIC, Muslim governments and Muslim organizations in Western countries, there are a number of factors that mitigate the media's influence on audiences, including higher levels of education, interaction with Muslims and perceptions of media credibility. However, it seems that the further audiences are from the context of news stories, the more reliant they are on the media and therefore potentially more vulnerable to media influence. As such, media coverage of specific issues in the Muslim world may be influential in shaping audiences' attitudes and opinions. It is the matter of image versus reality in war and conflict, and the challenge of reporting from the Muslim world, to which we now turn.

3
Image and Reality of Reporting War and Conflict in the Muslim World

This chapter documents the realities of being a Western journalist covering the war in Iraq during the pivotal years of the conflict from 2004 onwards as the security situation further deteriorated. The Iraq war was immensely divisive in the Middle East; it was looked upon as an exercise in US imperialism and a thinly veiled grab for resources justified with exaggerated and still unproven claims of weapons of mass destruction and spurious links to Al-Qaeda in the wake of 9/11. The March 2003 invasion was intensely covered by the Western media, with thousands of media personnel present during the invasion period, either embedded with the invading coalition forces or working independently. This chapter is written in the first person, primarily by the book's third author, John Martinkus, who gives a detailed account of his personal experiences. It presents a close examination of how social and political contexts in the field and at home impact on a journalist's ability to report highly contentious issues when the reality of these sharply contrasts with the image that governments and media seek to proclaim.

The Iraq war

By the time I arrived in January 2004, commissioned to write a book on Iraq's reconstruction, the war had been declared won and many Western and Australian media organizations were in the process of withdrawing their personnel from Iraq. For Western journalists, the freedom of movement and engagement with the Iraqi population was in a state of flux. An ever-closing window on the society we were trying to report on. The increasingly sophisticated strategies of kidnapping, televised beheadings and increasing targeting of Western individuals and organizations by suicide and truck bombs, by those resisting the occupation, led to the easy demonization of extremist Islam that was used by the Western media almost as a justification of the initial involvement and (unfounded) reasons to invade in the first place. But what it also did was drive a wedge between the Iraqi populace and the foreign organizations such as NGOs and the media, disconnecting them from the Iraqi people. It was in that environment that bias and anti-Islamic stereotypes were allowed to flourish. There were institutional issues, issues with access to the US military and issues of the dominant narrative in Western media that had been largely supportive of the 2003 invasion. As the following two case studies reveal, there were also serious and basic security issues involved in Western journalists trying to cover that conflict.

The pre-determined nature of the coverage of much of the Western media in Iraq at that early stage in 2004 was summed up by this exchange between the author and a Fox News correspondent while waiting to receive the all-important coalition press card in Baghdad's green zone in 2004. Fox News correspondent to US Marine sergeant waiting in a queue: 'you know there is a lot of good stories here that people aren't reporting'. To which the author interjected 'and a lot of really awful ones too', and the marine sergeant laughed, to the embarrassment of the Fox reporter. Like the Australian News Limited reporters who made increasingly infrequent visits to Baghdad, and often only then within the security bubble of a ministerial visit, there was an increasing disengagement with the conflict as the narrative of victory turned to one of grinding and daily bloody violence. So what happened after that? A degree of silence, then a declaration of victory, all comfortably framed within the justification of our initial involvement in what was effectively an occupation and a grab for resources. To stray from that narrative meant, effectively, professional suicide, and that is what working Western journalists had to deal with. The following descriptions are offered to illustrate what it was actually like to try and cover this huge and divisive war from the perspective of a practitioner in the Western media.

Friday the 15th of October 2004 was the first day of Ramadan in Iraq. Everything was closed and I spent the day translating tapes in my room at the Al Hamra hotel. I was booked to leave on Sunday the 17th and to be honest I couldn't wait. Three weeks in Baghdad had been long enough. The daily attacks on US convoys, mortar attacks and car bombs, attacks on places like the Sheraton Hotel and the suicide bombing of the green zone café and market in the previous few days were signs of the growing strength and audacity of the resistance. It was my third trip to Iraq that year and as I had been reporting the space within which

Western journalists could work independently had shrunk dramatically every time I returned. At the start of the year in January, February and March I had traveled the length and breadth of the country unarmed, in a car, and down south to Basra and back to Baghdad by rail. I had driven several times to Fallujah and through Ramadi and had also traveled by road to Karbala and north to Kirkuk, Sulaimaniyah and Erbil. At that time there were only some parts of the country, mainly in the Sunni triangle, where extra caution was needed.

By the time I returned in June and July the situation had deteriorated immensely. Travel by road through the west to Jordan was out of the question as the whole area from the western outskirts of Baghdad through Fallujah to Ramadi was outside of the control of the occupying forces. On that trip I remember driving out to Abu Ghraib jail to follow a story and film some interviews and was greeted by an incredulous US army military reserve captain who could not believe I had simply driven out there in a local taxi. They were under near constant attack every night and at that stage had started to be supplied by helicopter even though they were only 30 kilometers from Baghdad. By the middle of the year it was not safe to travel outside of Baghdad. By the time I returned for a third stint for the year in September and October there were substantial parts of the capital itself where it was no longer safe to travel. This included the sprawling Sadr city slum which had risen up in the Shia revolt led by Muqtadr Al Sadr in April of that year and was then still firmly controlled by the militiamen of Muqtadr's Mehdi Army. The other area where it was getting almost impossible to work was the whole western area of Baghdad where attacks on foreigners, both troops and contractors, was making it exceedingly dangerous for journalists. The space that we were able to occupy and function in as journalists trying to report on the situation in the country had become confined to several fortified and guarded hotel complexes, the green zone and wherever in the city our drivers and translators felt safe enough to take us that day. The only other way to report on the growing violence was to embed yourself with US military units which had the negative effect that as a reporter you would never speak to an Iraqi who wasn't getting a gun pointed at them or who wasn't a direct employee of the US military.

It was a frustrating time for a journalist because as the general deterioration of security in Baghdad and across the country became the story our ability to effectively tell that story was diminished by restrictions placed on us by ourselves, our organizations, and the US military. As we were trying to deal with a fluid situation, new dangers and hazards presented themselves daily. There was a fine line between getting the story and getting killed as danger came from many directions.

About two o'clock in the afternoon I drove out of the Al Hamra compound to go and shoot some footage. Within minutes I was carjacked by insurgents with a car in front and behind blocking me off and armed men getting out and forcing their way into our vehicle. They ordered my driver to go to western Baghdad, then largely out of coalition control. Over the next 24 hours I was alternately bound, blindfolded, interrogated and threatened with death at gunpoint. Finally I was ordered to make a video condemning the occupation of Iraq and Australia's role in it. Ironically I was questioned over my links with a certain tribal sheik in Fallujah, whom I had interviewed months before and had tried to publish a story about his father's mistreatment as a detainee in Abu Ghraib prison after he had been detained in a routine cordon and search operation conducted by US forces. I honestly answered my captors that I had tried to tell that story but the *Age* newspaper, whom I had a loose relationship with as a freelancer, had refused to publish it. Also my captors declared they had checked my story out on the internet and it was the review by Scott Burchill published in the *Age* on 28 August 2004 that contributed to their decision to release me as it spoke about my 2004 book on the conflict. To cut a long story short, myself, my translator and my driver were released because we demonstrated that we were trying to fairly report the conflict. When I returned to Australia and tried to explain this to the media the dominant narrative of insurgents as monsters and an inhumane 'other' took over.

Two days after being released I arrived back at Sydney airport greeted by a press pack. As Australia's first hostage in Iraq there was an immense amount of media attention. As soon as I walked out of the departure gates at customs I was overwhelmed by a group of photographers, TV cameras and journalists. My boss Mike Carey was there along with my girlfriend, my brother, my colleague Mark Davis from Australia's Special Broadcasting Service (SBS) and a large group of reporters. I walked the short distance outside so I could light a cigarette and then stopped to answer questions, which were rapidly fired at me. I was asked what I thought about those who had taken me hostage. I tried to be fair. 'They're fighting a war but they're not savages. They're not actually just killing people willy-nilly. They talk to you, they think about things' (Roy, 2004).

I was asked why I was not killed and other hostages were. I replied that 'From their perspective there was a reason to kill [British hostage Kenneth] Bigley, there was a reason to kill the Americans; there was not a reason to kill me [and] luckily I managed to convince them of that'. I was also asked about the then Australian Foreign Minister, Alexander Downer's comments about where I was when I was kidnapped. I angrily replied, 'Alexander Downer doesn't know his geography very well.... I was actually across the road from the Australian embassy when I was kidnapped. He should apologize to me, actually – personally'. I wanted to get away from them and I think I started to walk away when a reporter asked me what I thought was a question that revealed just how far removed the rhetoric about the Iraq war was in Australia from the reality of the Iraq that I had just come from. 'Do you think Iraq is on the road to reconstruction?' To which I replied almost laughing at the absurdity of the question. 'No it's on the road to shit'.

The next day I had to go into SBS to prerecord an interview for that night's edition of *Dateline*, the program I worked for, regarding the kidnapping. As I got in to the taxi I could hear the radio. It was announcer John Laws talking about Downer's latest comments regarding what I had said the previous night at the airport. He was referring to me as 'a so-called journalist' and saying that I 'obviously sympathized with terrorists'. What Downer had actually said was in response to a page one article in *The Australian* newspaper that morning:

ALEXANDER DOWNER: I just could not believe he said those things. I was just appalled. For me, I mean, that is exactly what people should not do. They should never unintentionally or intentionally in this case, let us be charitable and say unintentionally give comfort to terrorists in this way. It's a terrible thing to have said. I was absolutely astonished when he said that...

RADIO ANNOUNCER: Well, you'd say there was a reason to kill Bigley, there was a reason to kill the two Americans, there was no reason to kill me, that's what he said.

ALEXANDER DOWNER: Well, I mean, exactly. I just...I...just is pretty close to the most appalling thing any Australian has said about the situation in Iraq.

(*Herald Sun*, 2004a)

I had been asked a straightforward question as to why other hostages had been killed and why I wasn't. The fact was I had not been killed was because I was not associated with the coalition forces as the other high profile hostages who had been killed were. It was a simple grim reality of the situation in Iraq that if the insurgents deemed you to be part of the coalition or working for them they saw you as a legitimate target.

It was my understanding of this reality that contributed to my ability to negotiate my way out of that situation. But that wasn't what the Foreign Minister wanted people to understand. He wanted to paint me as a supporter and sympathizer of terrorists, a charge that was rapidly multiplied by a swathe of conservative commentators. The most hysterical of these was a series of opinion pieces written by right-wing commentator Andrew Bolt of the *Herald Sun*. His assertion ran as follows:

> John Martinkus could have been beheaded but was safely released. In Iraq's propaganda war, some journalists are better alive than dead. Australian journalist John Martinkus said *he was going to be* killed by the Iraqi terrorists who grabbed him on Sunday – until he convinced them he was on their side. "I was not hurt and treated with respect once they established my credentials as an independent journalist who did not support the occupation," the SBS filmmaker told Reuters. An SBS producer, Mike Carey, confirmed on 3AW yesterday that Martinkus told the terrorists he sympathized with them – 'as you would' to save your life. As I sure would, too.
>
> And then, added Carey, his captors got onto the internet to check him out. Did they? I guess they liked what they saw, then, or Martinkus would be as dead as the two Macedonian brickies who were beheaded in Iraq that very weekend. In fact, it would have been easy for the terrorists to think Martinkus, brave as he is, was more useful to them as a sympathetic reporter than a dead infidel.
>
> (*Herald Sun*, 2004b)

Two days later, spurred on by the condemnation of my comments, Foreign Minister Alexander Downer intensified his attacks:

> Just when I feared I'd been too hard on SBS journalist and activist John Martinkus, he opens his mouth. Martinkus, unlike many other hostages, was freed this week by the terrorists said to have snatched him in Baghdad on Sunday. And on Wednesday I noted that he said he would have been killed if he hadn't persuaded his captors he was on their side and hated the American 'occupation'. Once the terrorists checked out his anti-American writings on the internet, they let him go, seeming to believe he'd be more useful to them alive – as useful as too many Western correspondents are. They didn't have to wait long for a reward. On arriving back in Sydney, Martinkus declared that freed Iraq was 'on the road to s – '. The terrorists are winning. But, worse, he seemed to excuse the terrorists who recently, on video,

sawed off the heads of three screaming Western civilians. 'They're fighting a war but they're not savages,' he protested. 'They're not actually just killing people willy-nilly. They talk to you, they think about things. There was a reason to kill (British hostage Kenneth) Bigley, there was a reason to kill the (two) Americans (kidnapped with Bigley). There was not a reason to kill me.' I think we've now heard what that reason not to kill Martinkus was.

(Senate Submission, 2004)

It seemed suddenly I was guilty of such things as describing insurgents as disaffected Iraqis. The underlying tone of the criticism was that because I had tried to describe the 'terrorists' as people who had their own reasons for fighting against the occupation I was therefore supportive of them.

When I had arrived in the office that morning I could sense an extreme sense of disquiet. To be honest my immediate superiors were scared. They were scared of such condemnation by Alexander Downer and they were scared for their own positions. On the surface they were supportive but in reality they were not going to back up the logic of what I had said, they were simply going to try and quiet down the issue and avoid a confrontation with the foreign minister. Phil Martin, then head of news and current affairs, began 'speaking on my behalf' and unbeknownst to me had already told the ABC that morning that I would not be commenting further on the issue. His defense of my statement was along the lines that I was exhausted, which was true but it also ignored the fundamental reality of what I had said. In the office I was told not to speak to the press and I agreed, thinking that the interview I would do with Mark Davis for that night's program would be enough.

Such was the outcry about my perceived support for terrorists that when I was interviewed that afternoon for *Dateline*, Mark Davis addressed the question directly to me:

MARK DAVIS: Well, you're very aware of the fate of others...
JOHN MARTINKUS: Of course. Of course.
MARK DAVIS: And that would have been wearing on you at the time. You've described your captors, you said that they're not – they're not monsters, but it's pretty monstrous to be slashing the throats of truck drivers and engineers which they have done and I'm assuming that it's the same group or an associated group.
JOHN MARTINKUS: Yes, it is a monstrous thing and there's no way anybody could support that kind of behavior and you mentioned

some comments I made when I arrived back yesterday at the airport and I think some of them have been used out of context. All I was basically trying to say there was I wasn't – I wasn't killed because they didn't see me as a target. They didn't see that – they realized that I didn't – they realized that I didn't work with the Americans. From their perspective, anybody, Iraqi or a foreign national, who works with the coalition is a combatant, is a justified target in their campaign to basically terrorize the foreign presence there into leaving.

(SBS Dateline, 2004)

I felt I had to tell the whole story one more time in print just to get it on the record and to finally end this insidious speculation that the government was driving through friendly media outlets to discredit me. I chose to publish this in the *Bulletin* magazine the following Monday because I had worked for them often in the past and trusted them. I sat down to write the piece back in my Melbourne home exactly a week after being kidnapped in Baghdad. It was very hard to write as I was still vividly remembering all the details and how terrified I had been. When I gave it to the *Bulletin* I remember the assistant editor Kathy Bail calling me with some changes recommended by the editor Gary Linnell. He wanted to move the section where I cursed one of my captors to the intro to, I suppose, make me seem more antagonistic to those who kidnapped me. I agreed but have always regretted that as it changed the tone of the piece and was not my intention and as a few friends remarked to me later, it did not sound like me at all.

I also published a clarification called 'A message to Alexander Downer' alongside the story 'John Martinkus responds to remarks made by the Foreign Minister about the circumstances of his kidnapping'.

Foreign Minister Alexander Downer and others seem intent on painting me as someone who condones kidnapping and murder. Some clarification is necessary. In no way do I justify such actions, in any circumstances. I survived because my captors came to believe they had no reason to kill me. It was my position as an independent journalist which saved me. To note this is in no way to justify their decision to murder others, which I have unreservedly condemned. I was also incorrectly accused of being in the wrong area. In fact, I was kidnapped in the area the Australian government chooses to house its diplomats.

(*Bulletin with Newsweek*, 2004)

This I naively thought would be the end of the matter but unfortunately it wasn't. The perception that I was a left-wing activist or that I was sympathetic to terrorists was something that was raised again and again by those in the media who had followed the government of the day in condemning my statements and ridiculing my experience in order to detract from the central truth of what I was saying about the deteriorating situation in Iraq in 2004.

What the furore surrounding my kidnapping revealed to me was that in October 2004, after the fourth electoral win of the Howard government, prominent individuals in the Australian media had become so supportive of and defined by their close association with the Howard government that objective reporting of issues such as the Iraq war had ceased to exist. There was never a serious dialogue in the Australian press about what was happening in Iraq or Australia's role in that war. By 2005, as the situations in Iraq deteriorated into a civil war and the Taliban resurgence occurred in Afghanistan, the commentary and analysis offered by many Australian media outlets mirrored what the governments of the United States and Australia were saying. The issues raised by journalists in Iraq and Afghanistan in 2004 and 2005 were precisely those which were being addressed in the counter-insurgency doctrines that were being discussed and implemented in 2007 and 2008 at the highest levels of the US military. But at the time to even broach the topic of what was motivating the Iraqi insurgents was enough to bring down a wave of condemnation for being seemingly sympathetic with terrorists from the kind of right-wing opinion writers who proliferated in the Howard era.

While the government and its sympathetic mouthpieces in the Australian media were loudly condemning my statements and questioning the circumstances of my kidnapping, the Australian Federal Police and a representative of Britain's MI5 came to the offices of SBS in Sydney to seek advice regarding the case of kidnapped Care Australia NGO worker Margaret Hassan, who had been abducted on 19 October. I told them everything I knew about the insurgents who had kidnapped me and who they seemed to have loyalties to in order to help them formulate a negotiation strategy for her release. Tragically she was later killed by those who had abducted her. According to the International Committee to protect journalists 57 journalists have been kidnapped in Iraq since 2003. Seventeen of those have been killed, 35 including myself have been released and the whereabouts of five is still unknown.

On 25 October 2004, Australian troops near the Australian embassy in Baghdad were directly targeted for the first time in a car bomb attack on their armored vehicles near where I was kidnapped. Three soldiers were wounded (*Age*, 2004a). In a revealing statement of what Foreign Minister Alexander Downer thought of journalists in Iraq he claimed the media had been tipped off about the forthcoming attack and were at the bomb site within two minutes of the attack (*Age*, 2004b). But the reality was the main hotel housing foreign journalists in Baghdad, the Al Hamra, was across the road and the journalists would have heard the massive blast. It had already been announced the Australian Embassy would be relocating to the relative safety of the heavily fortified green zone across the Tigris River.

The war in Iraq got worse and worse. The Western media, in many ways, withdrew. There were still the big US organizations covering it but, as the next case study shows, they had retreated into fortified compounds. Most of the on the ground reporting was done by Iraqis employed by Western media organizations, which was reflected in their higher mortality rate, victims of both the insurgents and the coalition forces. I was temporarily black-banned by the US military for reporting a story on US soldiers burning Taliban corpses in 2005. Finally after three months waiting I got approval in 2007 to go back and embed with US forces. It was the only way I could get to the fighting but it was compromised and came at a cost.

Working in Iraq at the height of the 2007 surge

By August 2007 the US military presence in Iraq peaked at 167,000 troops as part of President Bush's surge strategy. It was a time of intense Western media scrutiny of Iraq as well as heightened levels of violence and death. How did reporters living in a city that was in the midst of bloody sectarian and insurgent violence report on the conflict? I will explore the themes of framing, media bias and the attempts by the US military to manage the message coming out of Iraq with the embedding system and how that manifested itself at this time of heavy fighting and casualties.

Ali Al Saleem airbase was about an hour's fast drive from Kuwait city. It was the logistical and supply hub for the wars in Iraq and Afghanistan. At any one time there were up to 4000 troops in transit, waiting for flights in and out of theater, accommodated in rows and rows of white air-conditioned tents and cordoned off by concrete blast walls and razor wire in the middle of the desert.

There was a McDonalds, a Subway, a Pizza Hut and a Burger King all housed in separate containers and arranged as a kind of main street where during the day Kuwaiti traders would come and set up stalls where you could buy anything from cheap watches to hookah pipes and hand woven carpets. There was even a stall where young soldiers could stick their heads through a painted board and be photographed as an Arab riding a camel in the manner of a fairground exhibit where you are photographed as a cowboy or in 19th-century dress. But in the middle of the summer of 2007 it was mostly too hot to do anything with the temperature close to 50 degrees centigrade and soldiers trudged up and down the rock pathways laid to keep the dust down, which became so hot in the desert sun the heat came through the soles of your boots.

In between the rows of tents at certain intervals were containers with the sides cut out and benches inside. These were for smoking and despite the oven-like atmosphere the men and women with little else to do but wait to get in or out of their 15-month tours to Iraq and Afghanistan sat and smoked and talked. One large black sergeant on his way back into Iraq after his one two-week home leave in the middle of his tour asked what kind of a reporter I was: 'You are not one of those who are going to come over here say we are winning are you?' I assured him I wasn't. He continued: 'I just been back in the [United] States and I heard so many people talking about this war and how it is all about money and you just look around here' pointing to the Kellogg Brown and Root run dining hall near where we were. He further exclaimed:

Who is making money here? Damn well is not the US government paying for all this. You know how much it costs them every time someone gets killed? $440 000 dollars! You think if this was about money they would pay that for the three and a half thousand already dead? Think about how much that is worth.

He continued on about how much this whole war was costing and who was benefiting. In a place like Ali Al Saleem, the logistical center of two wars, it was easy to see his point. Halliburton and Kellogg Brown and Root (KBR) ran the place and ordinary soldiers were moved in and out like cattle.

The sergeant's theories on why the war continued came to an end when a tall, skinny, very sunburnt soldier from the 1st cavalry started butting in:

I tell you I did not sign up for this shit. I enlisted in artillery and now they got us working as MPs [military police] at camp Bucca. I've had shit thrown at me, I've been pissed on. The other day I had to shoot someone in the face with a shotgun. No that is not what I signed up for.

This soldier had that nervous rapid talking manner of the severely stressed when to interrupt them is almost to invite violence. I exchanged glances with the sergeant who indicated just to let him talk.

Camp Bucca was the main detention camp for Iraqis suspected of involvement in the insurgency. It was at Umm Qasr near Basra and this soldier was saying they currently had 15,000 inmates and they were extending the camp to hold 20,000. The detainees were both Sunni and Shia and the tall skinny soldier outlined the fighting between the two groups and detailed how he had seen a man get his eyes gouged out with a metal 'shiv' (a handmade knife sharpened on a rock). He was waiting for his flight back to the States: 'No way man I did not sign up to be a prison guard', he said before describing again how he had shot the Iraqi in the face with his shotgun for throwing feces at him just a few days ago.

There are other soldiers who don't want to talk. One in particular spent close to two days sitting in the same container chain smoking. When I finally got him to say something he told me he had only three weeks to go until his eight years were up. In the US Army if you sign on for four years you can still be called back anytime in the next four if your unit is being redeployed, which now most of them are. If you serve the full eight you can't be called back. This soldier had just finished his third full deployment to Iraq: 'They got nothing on me. I am walking out of this army and never coming back'.

If anybody has any doubts about how unpopular the long 15-month deployments were among US troops, they should have a read of the graffiti in the toilet blocks at Ali Al Saleem. There are obscene cartoons of George Bush and Dick Cheney and General Petraeus as well as countless misspelt ravings by departing troops of their hatred for Iraq and the Army. You can see the faded ones underneath that date back a few years. They try to wash them off but new ones keep appearing. 'Impeach Bush' is a common one but the ones regarding Cheney and Petraeus involve pictures and sexual acts too explicit to go into here.

Unaccompanied journalists, particularly those from obscure networks such as Australia's SBS, rated pretty low on the US military transport priority listings, lower than military sniffer dogs and above only the Bangladeshi and Indian contract laborers brought in for the construction of bases they don't trust the Iraqis to do. After a few days on the base I managed to get a seat on a US embassy plane full of civilian employees, who jumped when the plane fired flares as it began its steep descent to Baghdad airport to avoid missiles. Once there I was told no transport to the green zone was available and I was directed to another transit holding camp of tents surrounded by blast walls. Inside the reception office a former Marine gunnery sergeant working for Halliburton, who ran the camp, told me they could put me on a transport vehicle sometime during the night. He yelled when he spoke and told me he had landed with the Marines in Da Nang in Vietnam. There are a lot of these types working for Halliburton. Beside me an overweight American girl in civilian clothes was explaining why she was there. 'I just had to come and see where he died'. She was talking about her father and she was on a kind of pilgrimage. Outside in the blazing heat some sweating Bangladeshis inside a concrete bomb shelter pleaded with me to help them use the Iraqi recharge card on their mobile. They weren't allowed to have phones, one of them told me (security reasons) and they just wanted to text message their families and tell them they were safe.

After hours of waiting, following a midnight roll call, the armored buses arrived with their Humvee escort. Very thin black Africans, that I later found were Ugandan laborers, formed a chain to load the luggage and everybody donned their body armor and climbed on board. The passengers were a mix of Iraqis, Egyptians and Lebanese working for the Americans as translators, black African and South Asian laborers along with a few non-American white civilians and a smattering of low-ranking military personnel, basically everybody without priority for a helicopter. The buses were guarded by contractors carrying several guns each and decked out in the trademark outdoor gear complemented by body armor. It took an hour crawling through Baghdad suburbs to arrive in the green zone where men with automatic weapons surrounded the buses as we climbed out.

The green zone, then officially known as the international zone, was not the same as it used to be. Back in 2004 you could walk around the area or there was a shuttle bus service you could ride unescorted to whatever military or government building you wanted. There was an outdoor market, that never really recovered from the June 2004 suicide bombing, as well as several bars and restaurants you could go and indulge in any number of bizarre conversations with the contractors or young officials working for Paul Bremers Coalition Provisional Authority (CPA). Rocket and mortar attacks were rare and ineffective and just added to the buzzing excitement of the place. That had all changed by 2007. The international zone was a bleak series of fortified buildings each with their own different detachments of security. One building may be guarded by ex-Peruvian Special Forces in the plain khaki of Triple Canopy. Another was guarded by short Nepalese in blue and yet another by the Americans of Blackwater. The actual perimeter of the zone was protected by 18-feet high blast walls as well as the ever-present dirt-filled Hesco car bomb barriers that are guarded by US troops, but within that area is a patchwork of different contractors and security guards each with different regulations and requirements. Nobody trusted anybody else and movement was very difficult involving many searches, identity checks and delays.

Mortar attacks were now regular and increasingly accurate. From the underground basement filled with containers that served both as offices and living quarters for the Press Office I heard the pre-recorded alarm 'incoming approaching' followed by a siren. Grabbing my camera I headed outside. But the Peruvians were having nothing of it. Despite being assigned to guard the press center, they refused to recognize my press credentials, my passport or my written orders and would neither let me out of the building nor back inside. Filming anything was absolutely out of the question and until a Spanish-speaking reporter from New York arrived I was caught in the security limbo of arguing with guards who didn't speak my language and in fact interpreted my increasing agitation as a sign of guilt.

Filming at all inside the zone was forbidden, as it was on most US bases in Iraq. The reason is security and the belief that anyone with a video camera is secretly casing the place for an insurgent attack. Orders put in place for security reasons were not questioned by anyone. The threats inside the zone were constant and the area around what served as the Iraqi Parliament was pockmarked with the impacts of mortars, marching in lines towards the building, and on the building itself.

The contractor who was supervising the Peruvians outside the Parliament was typical of the type: ex-military, early forties and with a Special Forces background, short graying hair, baseball cap and body armor as well as radios and weaponry. He looks like an aging action star. He claims the Peruvians are good trusted soldiers: 'we have had a lot to do with them; we trained them', he said, referring to when he was in the US military and they trained Latin American Special Forces. That's where these connections and contracts come from. He did not like the press and just wanted to talk about how wrong the press got the Abu Ghraib story in 2004: 'these people understand force; they respect that and that is what the press got so wrong', he says, gesturing towards the Iraqis being searched. He calls the area around the Parliament more of an orange zone: half way between the green zone and the red zone out-side. The problem for him, he explained, is that he was guarding the Parliament. The Iraqi government was actually in control of this area but they employed his company Triple Canopy to provide security. Pre-sumably the Iraqi army was not trusted enough to provide their own Parliament's security. To him, the bad part of his job was that he has to allow Iraqis in: 'and we just have to presume they are all potential bombers'. It is not hard to argue with him considering a suicide bomber did get in to the Parliament that year but as the starting point of any exchange with those he is supposed to be guarding it was easy to see how accidents happen and innocent Iraqi civilians get killed.

To those in charge of security it benefited no one to let the insur-gents know when they are actually on target. It also benefited no one to allow the media to reveal how besieged the seat of power for the US-backed Iraqi government had become. The actual physical realities, the blast walls, the Hesco barriers, the razor wire, floodlights, sand-bagged machine gun emplacements and the streets inside the zone devoid of traffic except for three car convoys of armored SUVs bristling with weapons *inside* the zone, weren't really discussed let alone shown on television. The reason why you were not allowed to film inside the zone was always given as security but I think part of it was a reluctance to admit just how bad things had become and how tenuous the position of the international zone was.

I had been stuck inside the press office for a few days sharing the dormitory room with several other journalists who were waiting for embeds. There seemed at the time to be a network of freelancers who were taking advantage of embedding system to kick start their careers. They would go on these long and sometimes uneventful, sometimes dangerous, embeds and make a living writing stories and shooting pic-tures and footage. They would spend their whole time in Iraq within the military network of bases and if they ever met an Iraqi, he or she would either be working for the Americans or have a gun pointed at them by the US troops while on patrol. To many of these young freelancers the US military embed system meant they could cover the war on the cheap, for as long as they stayed within the embed system and followed the rules, they would be fed and to a basic level given accommodation. But the downside of this kind of reporting was that their entire view of the conflict was through the prism of the US military and everything was seen as it looked from a US base or through the window of a Humvee. They were entirely dependent upon the US military for everything from security, food and for most even their ticket out of the country. In fact, as happened to me, most of these freelancers who arrived in Iraq as part of the US embedding system would not have even had Iraqi visas, which meant that if they were to leave the protection of the US military they could be detained by Iraqi authorities for not having a valid visa. It was a serious disincentive to either try to report independently or break the many rules associated with embedding.

There used to be a gate where we as journalists would queue to get into the press conferences. In 2004, I was always nervous using that gate. There would be delays and you were left standing exposed in a line. There were several car bombs at that gate and some shootings from passing cars. The military responded by placing more and more barriers along the footpath to cover those who were queuing. But no matter how far they extended the barriers there was always a point where the barriers finished and those entering or leaving were exposed. When I left the green zone through that gate this time in July 2007 I had to run the deserted last 100 meters where even the guards would not go and dash into the waiting vehicle, expecting sniper fire from the buildings across the street. Short of demolishing the buildings and relocating the people the entrance will never be safe. But even if they did that there will always be a point where the zone finishes and the real Iraq began and in the summer of 2007 there seemed to be nothing the US military could do about that.

In the car waiting for me outside the green zone was CNN's Baghdad Bureau Chief Australian, Michael Ware. He was armed with a loaded pistol. Behind his car was an armored SUV with his security detail of armed foreign contractors and trusted Iraqi armed guards. We sped off away from the entrance and drove the short distance to a street adjacent to one of the exterior walls of the green zone. Then we were weaving between another series of concrete barriers and passing through a checkpoint manned by Iraqis and foreign contractors. Because the situation in Baghdad had deteriorated so much in late 2004, 2005 and 2006 most of the remaining foreign news media based in Baghdad had banded together and rented all the large upscale houses in this street that backed on to the green zone. They had then pooled their security details to basically guard what effectively became the media's own compound. Concrete blast walls were erected to block the street to prevent car bomb and suicide attacks and to keep kidnappers at bay. Watchtowers and machine gun posts were established and manned by both foreign and Iraqi contractors paid for by the big media networks. It was the only way the big television networks such as CNN, Fox, CBS, ABC (United States) and BBC could keep their operations going through the years of bloodshed in Baghdad without basing themselves permanently within US military bases. Basically what they had been forced to do is band together and fortify the whole street that they occupied, which if they were ever under full scale attack was situated to allow them to escape straight across the wall back in to the fortified international zone.

To give an indication of what life was like to be a foreigner that year in Baghdad, here is how Michael Ware responded to a question put to him by CNN host Wolf Blitzer following comments by Senator John McCain in March of that year when he said life in Baghdad was getting better and that there were some neighborhoods that were safe enough to walk around in:

> No. No way on earth can a Westerner, particularly an American, stroll any street of this capital of more than five million people. I mean if Al-Qaeda doesn't get wind of you or if one of the Sunni insurgent groups do not descend upon you or if someone doesn't tip off a Shia militia then the nearest criminal gang is just going to see dollar signs and scoop you up. Honestly Wolf you'd barely last twenty minutes out there. I don't know what part of Neverland Senator McCain is talking about when he says we can go strolling in Baghdad.
>
> (CNN, 2007)

Michael Ware had been based in Baghdad since the invasion in 2003, first as the Baghdad Bureau Chief for *Time* magazine then for CNN. He was in charge of running their operations from Baghdad and reporting the conflict himself. The way CNN was operating at that time and for much of the preceding three years was to only venture out in armed convoys of two and often three cars to prevent kidnapping, roadside bombs or being stranded by breakdowns. They had to meticulously plan every trip, even just to the neighboring green zone, to lessen the chance of apprehension by or attack from insurgents who were actively targeting their compound. Almost all the reporting from the field by the foreign journalists based there was done on embeds with the American forces. The risks for foreigners in Baghdad had made the kind of independent reporting we had done back in 2004 simply impossible. This reality and the expense involved in maintaining that level of security for foreign journalists meant that most organizations, including my own SBS, walked away from trying to report on the situation in Iraq from the ground. It was simply too expensive. At the time of this visit in mid-2007 the monthly budget for the CNN house in Baghdad to be kept secure was running in the order of $40,000 US dollars. The only way I had managed to get approval from SBS to return to Iraq was by agreeing to spend the majority of the trip embedded in the US military system.

The situation for journalists on the ground had evolved beyond what acclaimed veteran Middle East correspondent for *The Independent* newspaper, Robert Fisk, referred to as 'mouse journalism' when he wrote of how reporters working in Baghdad in 2005 had to basically hide themselves in order to remain there (Fisk, 2006). By 2007 almost all of the footage being used by wire services to report the daily bombings and attacks in Baghdad was coming from Iraqi cameramen, who were often killed by both US forces and the insurgents or sectarian militia. A graphic example of this is the case of two Iraqi Reuters reporters, Saeed Chmagh and Cameraman Namir Noor Eileen, whose deaths on 17 July 2007 in Baghdad were famously filmed by the Apache helicopter gun camera and leaked by Wikileaks. Foreign reporters were confined to their fortified offices and it was the Iraqis who were collecting the material. Going on embeds with the US forces was by 2007 the only reasonably safe way to move around the country but doing that within the military system was frustratingly slow and random, which is the reason why I had ended up staying for a few days at the CNN house. I had been stuck in the Press office inside the green zone and they were telling me it would take at least a week to organize a ride on a helicopter to Diyala province where I was to begin my embed with a unit. When I told Mick Ware of my problems he decided to come along to Diyala as well. I told him it had taken me three months to organize my embed but he simply made a call to the Public Affairs officers and not only organized for him and his crew to do an embed in Diyala but also organized a helicopter to take his team and myself to Diyala the next day. It said something for the enormous influence and respect he had acquired as one of the few reporters who had stayed covering Iraq the whole way through the war that what took months of waiting for me he could achieve with a simple phone call.

For the CNN reporters who regularly rotated through Baghdad, life in the fortified compound had become a fishbowl-like existence. One described it to me as being in a very heavily armed big brother household with very ambitious people living in each other's pockets. The advantage of being outside of the green zone was that their Iraqi employees and sources of information could come and go more easily and they could conduct interviews and live crosses from the roof. Travel outside of the compound was rare and highly organized when it did occur with multiple vehicles, differing routes and weapons present and body armor on at all times. Often the only time they were able to move around freely was on US bases and the only time they were able to walk in the streets was while on patrol with US troops. Each organization had security advisers who were former military contractors from the United Kingdom, Australia or South Africa who would be costing the media organizations sometimes several thousand dollars a day. Their job was to try and advise journalists and in many cases protect them and often tensions would arise due to the different mindsets required by the roles of a journalist and a security contractor.

July 2007 was a critical discourse moment in the waging of the Iraq war. The extra 30,000 surge troops had arrived in Iraq and the tours of all those serving in Iraq had just been extended by three months to 15 months. This meant that there were more than 160,000 US troops in Iraq. There had never been and never would be more US forces in the country than at that time. Violence was high with attacks on US troops and civilians a daily occurrence. In an Associated Press report on 27 July the fact only 64 US troops had died so far in Iraq that month was held up as a measure of progress given more than 100 US troops had died in each of the preceding three months (Burns, 2007). Still it was reported that on the previous day at least 78 people had been killed or found dead the previous day from car bombs, truck bombs and death squads. Meanwhile US General David Petraeus pleaded for more time to allow the surge strategy to work as the violence to the north of Baghdad increased as militants moved out of the city to the province of Diyala where major operations were being conducted, which is why we were going there.

At the small public affairs office at the US base outside Baquba, the capital of Diyala, there was a picture of a young-looking pale-faced guy in an outsized Black Helmet. It was a memorial picture of the 29-year-old Russian photojournalist Dimitry Chebotayev who had been sent out from this same office on 6 May to go on patrol with members of the US military first cavalry. He had been in Iraq for two months primarily for the Russian language edition of *Newsweek*. An Associated Press report describes what happened next: 'Chebotayev climbed into a Stryker and the troops headed out around noon to another street to cut off the insurgents' (2007, para 3). As the vehicles inched down a trash-strewn road, a thunderous blast consumed one of them in a huge ball of gray debris that flipped the eight-wheeled, 37,000-pound troop carrier upside down and tore out its interior.

As troops scrambled to recover casualties, gunmen fired from a large yellow-domed mosque across the street, sparking a firefight that saw rounds ping off the wreckage. The strykers blasted small chunks of concrete off the mosque with 40 mm grenades and heavy caliber guns. Later, three insurgents wearing armored vests – probably stolen from police – were found dead in the mosque. That night, Chebotayev's remains were loaded onto a Black Hawk helicopter on a darkened runway and blessed by an Army chaplain. The aircraft pulled straight up and disappeared into a starry sky, the first step of the journey back to Russia.

I had read the reports of that incident and how the massive improvised exploding device (IED) had also killed the other six soldiers in the huge Stryker armored vehicle as well. What was happening in Iraq was an evolutionary process in the way the war was being fought. The United States was continually armoring up their vehicles such as the Humvee or using heavier vehicles like the massive Stryker and the Iraqi insurgents in turn were constructing bigger and more lethal roadside bombs or IEDs. Such was the power of this explosion that it killed everyone in the vehicle. I looked at his photo in the office less than two months after his death and thought of the force of that explosion that it could flip a 16,800 kilogram vehicle. By contrast a 2013 model Toyota Land Cruiser weighs 3300 kilograms. He would not have had a chance. Such was the nature of the war that when you were getting in to those vehicles to patrol those roads it produced this kind of sheer animal fear and dread with the knowledge that there was nothing you could do if your vehicle was hit by such a device. Journalists would talk amongst themselves about which vehicle in a convoy was best to be in. The first would always get hit they would say. Then it was the last that would always get hit, then the second last. The truth was it was just dumb luck most of the time and that realization just added to the feeling of dread and inevitability that sooner or later it would be the vehicle you were in.

Up to and including Dimitry Cherbotayev's death, at least 101 journalists and 38 media staffers had been killed in Iraq since the war began in 2003 (Committee to Protect Journalists, 2007). Seven of those were killed while embedded with coalition forces. There were no journalists embedded at Forward Operating Base Warhorse in Diyala when we arrived, even though there were major operations being conducted by paratroopers from the US 82nd airborne and the 1st Cavalry Division in trying to clear insurgents out of their strongholds in the Diyala River Valley, or the DRV, as the US military referred to it. One of the first things that struck you when you walked around the base was the lengthy honor roll that was painted on a section of concrete blast wall in the center of the base. It listed all those who had died in the operations launched from this base. Of the 1st Cavalry soldiers who had taken over the base the previous November, 80 had already been killed seven months into their 15-month deployment. For the 300 or so 82nd airborne troops who had deployed in the first half of the year to Warhorse, 21 had been killed. It was, as was grimly repeated to me by several officers and men, the highest casualty rate of any other unit serving in Iraq. I had specifically requested on my embed form to be sent to the US units that were doing most of the fighting and to my surprise (and contrary to many previous experiences with the military) they had complied. The huge scale of the war in 2007 and the vitriolic debates back in the US media about the surge and the future of the war in Iraq had almost made the US military more open in its dealings with the media. The military seemed to want to tell their story about how hard they were fighting and what they thought was being achieved but the closer you got to what constituted the front line in the villages and palm groves of the Diyala River Valley, the more the sheen came off any attempt to spin the story or play up the achievements as these soldiers were too busy trying to stay alive.

The CNN team and I went out on patrol and covered the war. It was hot, 50 degrees, and exhausting. Sleeping on the concrete at the end of the day you didn't need blankets as the warmth from the day's sun seeped through your clothing. But we never ever met an Iraqi who was either not having a US gun pointed at him or her. The only other Iraqis we met were employed by the US forces or those we saw on video material provided by US information officers. Basically *jihadi* tapes found during raids on houses. It confirmed all the dominant stereotypes of extremist Islam. It added to the imbalance of Western media coverage because we were fundamentally scared for our lives. A fear reinforced because, through circumstance, we were forced to seek refuge and protection with those who were targeted and naturally, over time and shared experience, identified with the coalition forces. We completed the operation in Diyala and all got back to base safely. Then we had to negotiate our way out of there.

The CNN crew quickly arranged their flight back to Baghdad. They were keen to get out of the embedding system and back to their fortified house in the capital and to send their report. For me the journey was more complicated. Having arrived with the US military and with no Iraqi visa in my passport I was obliged to leave the country in the same way I had arrived. That is, on a US transport to Kuwait. It turned out to be quite a simple trip. One of the public affairs officers pointed out to me that most transports going back to Kuwait flew from the large Balad airbase which was relatively close to Diyala. I put myself on a transport list to Balad and within two days I was waiting in the middle of the night to see if I could board a darkened Chinook for the short flight to Balad. Then after an eight-hour wait in the Balad terminal I was given a place on a C-130 flight all the way back to where I had started at Ali Al Saleem airbase in Kuwait. Finally, after another 48-hour wait to reprocess my passport with a Kuwaiti visa I was able to board a bus and be deposited back at Kuwait international airport and finally able to secure a seat on a flight to Dubai and to be finally free of the US military system. The whole trip had taken three weeks and the only time I was allowed to film unobstructed by the security regulations associated with the US bases I had transited through was that 36-hour period when I was on patrol. Throughout this whole trip, with the exception of a few days at the CNN house, the only Iraqis I had been able to speak to were either direct employees of the Americans, usually translators who lived on the bases because their lives were under threat, or those scared villagers having their houses 'cleared' by the American troops. In mid-2007, when the whole war effort was hanging in the balance, there was the narrow window in which reporters for Western news organizations were able to access the war and try to report on the progress of the surge strategy.

The Baghdad foreign press corps that Michael Ware and the CNN team returned to in August 2007 was analyzed in a journal article written for the April/May edition of *American Journalism Review* of that year. It contends:

> The relentless violence in Iraq has seriously compromised coverage of arguably the most important story in the world today. Certain facets of the conflict remain exasperatingly elusive or, at best, thinly reported. The media's vital role as eyewitness has been severely limited; the intimate narrative of victims, survivors and their persecutors is sorely lacking in places like Anbar province, where the insurgency continues to inflict havoc.
>
> (Ricchiardi, 2007, para. 2)

The report goes on to quote many of the American journalists then working in the country, including Michael Ware. As well as discussing the extraordinary dangers and exorbitant security outlays required to work in Baghdad by 2007, the report went on to estimate that there were no more than 50–60 foreign journalists working in Iraq at any one time. The report goes on to identify the three fortified zones in which journalists were based. The CNN house was on the same street as the Al Hamra Hotel compound, which was attacked frequently and in front of which I had been kidnapped. The *New York Times* compound was near the Palestine Hotel across the river from the green zone. By 2007, only the big organizations were maintaining a permanent presence as most smaller outlets had either left or occasionally sent in a correspondent who either embedded for the duration of their visit or stayed at one of the three secure locations where they, as I had done for SBS, piggy-backed on the security provided by the larger organizations.

The extraordinary amounts of money that were required to maintain a secure compound in Iraq at that time is another topic for examination in the report. It states that 'some media organisations like the *New York Times* and CNN have spent millions to build fortresses and maintain a private army of hired guns' (Ricchiardi, 2007, para. 11). The type of reporting that was possible under those circumstances also was affected by what the journalists could and couldn't do. Gone were the days of simply interviewing Iraqis about what was going on. Interviews could only be arranged in secure locations or done by proxy using a local staff member. Official statements and interviews could be obtained in the big bases or the green zone but the simple logistics of getting physically to the green zone often entailed the risk of kidnapping or suicide bomb attacks at the checkpoints and entry point as the journalist was waiting to be searched before entering. Peter Osnos, a senior fellow for media at the Century Foundation who covered the Vietnam War for *The Washington Post*, told the *American Journalism Review* that 'American Journalists have never seen a war like this before – the extraordinary danger, the vast expense and the extraordinary set of circumstances. Every inch of terrain is a potential battlefield … People underestimate how dangerous it is' (Ricchiardi, 2007, para. 15).

Danger to the journalists on the ground was reflected in the downturn in coverage of the Iraq War in the second quarter of 2007, which was recorded by the Pew Research Center report (Pew Research Center, 2007). The report found:

> Taken together the news hole devoted to the three story lines of the war – The debate over policy, events in Iraq itself, and the situation with veterans and families on the home front – fell in the second three months of the year by roughly a third, to 15 per cent of the index, down from 22 per cent of the news hole in the first quarter.
>
> (Pew Research Center, 2007, para. 2)

The report also noted that the areas of the media that declined most in their coverage of the Iraq war in this period were Network News in the United States, which declined from devoting 33 per cent of its news coverage in the first quarter to 19 per cent in the second quarter. Similarly, Cable TV in the United States declined from running 23 per cent of its coverage on the war to 14 per cent in the second quarter. One explanation for this is the huge outlay required to keep the coverage flowing from Iraq was reaching its limits. Another factor undoubtedly would be the two mediums that required visuals would be starved of pictures from their correspondents who, isolated in their fortresses with security consultants telling them it was not safe to go out, could not get out to report. The security situation was dictating what the networks and reporters were able to get and as such the demand was declining.

Meanwhile dissatisfaction with the sense of disconnect between the reality of the war in Iraq and the perception of that war in the political debates in the United States regarding its trajectory came from a surprising quarter, the soldiers themselves. On 19 August seven serving US soldiers from the 82nd Airborne penned an opinion piece in the global edition of the *New York Times,* the *International Herald Tribune* (2007). The piece, called 'The Iraq war as we see it', called the political debate in Washington 'surreal' (*New York Times*, 2007, para. 1). They bluntly stated 'The claim that we are increasingly in control of the battlefields in Iraq is an assessment arrived at through a flawed, American-centered framework. Yes we are militarily superior, but our successes are offset by failures elsewhere' (*New York Times*, 2007, para. 4). It was an extraordinarily frank recognition by the soldiers close to the end of their 15-month deployments that was a direct rebuke to the many pundits and politicians then claiming the surge was a success and should be continued. The strategy of arming both Sunni militia and Shia in the police and Iraqi army had led to a situation in which the battle space was 'crowded with actors who do not fit neatly into boxes: Sunni extremists, Al-Qaeda terrorists, Shiite militiamen, criminals and armed tribes. The situation is made more complex by the questionable loyalties and Janus-faced role of the Iraqi police and Iraqi Army, which have been trained and armed at U.S. taxpayers' expense' (*New York Times*, 2007, para. 6).

The piece was a blistering assessment of the complexities faced by the soldiers on the ground. The very fact the soldiers themselves felt compelled to risk punishment by speaking out reflected that they felt their experience was not being understood by the public and policy makers back in the United States. Their compulsion to deliver their own assessment in the opinion pages of the *New York Times* reflected poorly on how effectively the war was being covered in the press and on television.

As they noted in their piece, one of their number was shot in the head while they were writing it and in a sad postscript, another two were killed less than a month later when their truck rolled over and crushed them (Stout, 2007). As the war in Iraq ground on through the summer of 2007, the press offered the general public a glimpse of a small part of the wider tragedy and bloodshed. The press corps was so targeted and under threat itself, it was severely limited in what it could report despite the sacrifice and risk of some notable journalists. As Michael Ware told *The New York Observer* in 2008:

> This is the Vietnam War of our generation. This conflict is going to have repercussions that far exceed that of an Indo-Chinese, essentially, civil war. Yet for a litany of reasons, which may or may not be legitimate, from cost to security to audience fatigue, the media has dropped the ball on this conflict. It is a tragic indictment on the Fourth Estate.
>
> (Haber and Koblin, 2008)

Conclusion

The 2003 invasion and occupation of Iraq resulted in massive death and destruction to the country as well as extensive instability in the already volatile Middle East region. Unsanctioned by the United Nations, the US-led invasion was met with widespread opposition from the international community as well as from politicians and publics in countries that had committed troops as part of the coalition forces. The justifications for the invasion – Iraqi government possession of weapons of mass destruction – remain unsubstantiated to this day. While the invasion resulted in the removal of a brutal dictator, it is difficult to accept that even this outcome was worth the massive devastation to the lives of millions of Iraqis and their country. Given the controversial nature of the invasion, ongoing social, economic and political failures and continuing security threats within the country, governments that were party to the invasion and responsible for the ensuing catastrophes were desperate to construct an image of progress and success.

This, however, sharply contradicted the reality that journalists observed on the ground. This chapter has not only highlighted the security threats faced by journalists in reporting war and conflict but, perhaps more importantly, has presented a detailed account of the challenges journalists face in upholding fourth estate principles when reporting reality that contradicts the political context and prevailing media discourse. The next chapter examines the political and human consequences of war and conflict: large numbers of people fleeing their homeland and seeking refuge in foreign, often Western, countries. Again, the contrasts between image and reality, as well as the competing interests of political expedience and journalistic ethics, are brought to the fore.

4
Asylum Seekers

Given the extent of pejorative political, media and public discourse on asylum seekers, particularly where Muslims are concerned, it is ironic that migration and particularly asylum seeking have a special place in the Islamic tradition. At the advent of Islam in 610, many of the early converts to the new monotheistic faith were severely persecuted by the polytheistic Meccans. Muhammad instructed the weakest and most vulnerable of his followers to emigrate from Arabia and seek asylum under the protection of the Christian king of Abyssinia (modern-day Ethiopia). Moreover, in the year 622 the rest of the Meccan Muslim community, including Muhammad himself, migrated to a town called Yathrib (later named Madina) almost 280 miles (about 450 kilometers) to the north, where they were given asylum by the people of the town. This migration, known as the *hijra* in Arabic, marks year one on the Islamic calendar, as it was from this point in time and space that the religion of Islam began to take shape in terms of its characteristic rituals and laws (Rane, 2010a).

This chapter is concerned with the growing numbers of people around the world who have been forced to seek refuge in other countries. A large proportion of these asylum seekers are Muslims fleeing war, conflict and political repression in their own countries. Particularly since the turn of the century, however, some Western media have represented asylum seekers unsympathetically, as undeserving and opportunistic and as potential criminals and terrorists. The policies of certain Western governments have violated the rights of asylum seekers and attempted to deter them from applying for asylum. Public opinion in many Western countries has also hardened and concern about the arrival of asylum seekers is widespread. This chapter examines the relationship between media coverage, public opinion and policy making in respect to the asylum seeker debate and attempts to explain the direction of influence and implications for intercommunity relations.

Global asylum seeker trends

Over the past 50 years, international migration has become a growing phenomenon. There are now over 200 million people (3 per cent of the world's population) who reside in a country other than the one in which they were born (Pew Research Center, 2012b). In terms of the religious affiliation of international migrants, Christians comprise 49 per cent (over 100 million people), while Muslims account for 27 per cent (over 60 million people). However, within specific faith groups, the most mobile are Jews, with 25 per cent having left the country in which they were born. In comparison, only 5 per cent of all Christians and only 4 per cent of all Muslims have done so. While 31 per cent of the world's Muslim migrants have settled in Europe, 34 per cent have migrated to the Middle East and North African region. Forty-five per cent of the world's 60 million Muslim migrants originated from the Asia-Pacific region, while one-third emigrated from the Middle East and North African region. Numbering over five million, Palestinians are the largest Muslim migrant group, having been successively displaced by Israel's occupation of their country since 1948. The top ten countries of origin for Muslim migrants are Palestine, Pakistan, Bangladesh, India, Afghanistan, Turkey, Morocco, Egypt, Iraq and Kazakhstan. The top ten destination countries for Muslim migrants are Saudi Arabia, Russia, Germany, France, Jordan, Pakistan, the United States, Iran, the United Arab Emirates and Syria (Pew Research Center, 2012b). Hence, Muslims are more likely to migrate to another Muslim-majority country than a Western country.

However, this chapter is concerned with a specific type of migration, asylum seeking. An asylum seeker is:

> an individual who has sought international protection and whose claim for refugee status has not yet been determined. As part of internationally recognized obligations to protect refugees on their territories, countries are responsible for determining whether an asylum seeker is a refugee or not. This responsibility is derived from the 1951 Convention relating to the Status of Refugees and relevant regional instruments, and is often incorporated into national legislation.
>
> (UNHCR, 2013a, p. 5)

Once an asylum seeker's claims have been processed and determined under the 1951 Refugee Convention, such an individual is termed a refugee. The key criterion in determining an applicant's refugee claim is whether the person:

> owing to a well-founded fear of being persecuted for reasons of race, religion, nationality, membership of a particular social group or political opinion, is outside the country of his nationality, and is unable to, or owing to such fear, is unwilling to avail himself of the protection of that country.
>
> (UNHCR, 2013b, para 3)

In the year 2012 alone, 479,300 applications for asylum were lodged in 44 industrialized countries, including 38 European countries, the United States, Canada, Japan, South Korea, New Zealand and Australia. This marks the second highest number of asylum seeker applications since the turn of the century. Since 2010, the number of asylum seeker applications has continued to increase, but overall they remain lower than in the 1990s and early 2000s. In 2012, almost three-quarters were lodged in Europe, 22 per cent in the United States and Canada, 3 per cent in Australia and New Zealand, and 1 per cent in Japan and South Korea. Over the past five years the United States has received the largest number (313,500) of asylum claims of any country, followed by France (232,700), Germany (201,300), Sweden (153,900) and Canada (139,200). Almost three-quarters of those seeking asylum have come from Asia (46 per cent) and Africa (25 per cent). The top ten countries from which asylum seekers fled in 2012 are Afghanistan (36,634), Syria (24,755), Serbia and Kosovo (24,340), China (24,109), Pakistan (23,229), Russia (21,856), Iraq (19,584), Iran (19,068), Somalia (17,794) and Eritrea (11,860) (UNHCR, 2013a).

Some of the 44 industrialized countries have responded to the arrival of asylum seekers far less humanely than others. Australia is one industrialized country that has adopted increasingly extreme policies aimed at deterring asylum seekers from reaching its shores at the expense of human rights and obligations under the 1951 Refugee Convention. Over the past five years, Australia has received just over 50,000 applications for asylum, ranking it 15th among the 44 industrialized countries overall, 19th in terms of per capita rankings, and 15th in terms of GDP rankings (UNHCR, 2013a). Most of Australia's asylum seekers are coming from Muslim-majority countries, including Iran, Afghanistan, Pakistan, Iraq and Egypt (UNHCR, 2013a). Since the trend of Middle

Eastern asylum seekers began in the late 1990s and early 2000s, the government's policies have included the outright refusal to allow boats carrying asylum seekers to land on Australian shores, excising the migration zone to restrict the lodgment of claims and access to legal rights, mandatory detention in isolated facilities that have been implicated for various human rights abuses, offshore processing in detention centers in Nauru and Papua New Guinea, and, most recently, a policy of using the Australian Defense Forces to prevent asylum boat arrivals. Australian political leaders have also dehumanized asylum seekers through the routine use of such labels as 'illegals', 'queue jumpers' and 'boat people' as well as claims that asylum seekers bring disease, pose a security risk, present a demographic threat and are an economic burden (Phillips, 2013, p. 1). Furthermore, a large segment of Australian media have not challenged the government's policies and have unquestioningly repeated the political rhetoric on asylum seekers (Klocker and Dunn, 2003; Pedersen, Watt and Hansen, 2006). Consequently, about three-quarters of the Australian public say they are concerned about asylum seekers coming to Australia by boat, and 58 per cent favor the policy of asylum seekers being processed offshore rather than in Australia (Oliver, 2013). This policy views asylum seekers as a threat to Australia's sovereignty.

Media, policy making and public opinion

Seminal studies concerning media, public opinion and policy making include those of Walter Lippmann (1922), Bernard Cohen (1963, 1973, 1995) and Katz and Lazarsfeld (1955). The early writings of Lippmann (1922) explain the relationship between the public and government policy, finding that the public often lack the ability to form independent opinions that do not take cues from government officials or elites. These findings are consistent with those dating back to the early 1990s on 'policy feedback', which found that government policy tends to shape public opinion (Pierson, 1993). More contemporary studies have confirmed such findings and additionally demonstrated the significant role of political discourse in the propagation of misperceptions and misunderstanding of issues such as asylum seekers (Klocker and Dunn, 2003; Pedersen, Watt and Hansen, 2006) and events such as the 1991 Persian Gulf War (Morgan, Lewis and Jhally, 1991) and the 2003 US invasion of Iraq (Kull, 2003). Entman's (1991) work on framing is instructive in this regard as it demonstrates that public opinion arises from how the media frame particular issues and events, rather than from the public's direct contact with the actual issue or event. In this context, the media play a critical intermediary role between political discourse and public opinion. However, while the general consensus over the past couple of decades has tended to view public opinion as not significantly impacting on the making of public policy (Weakliem, 2005), a number of other studies have challenged this conclusion. Various studies have found that the public are capable of deriving perspectives that do not parallel those put forth by government officials or the media (Holsti, 2004; Zaller, 1994), while others contend that political leaders are responsive to the views of constituents and that public opinion influences policy making (Burstein, 1998; Erikson, MacKuen and Stimson, 2002).

The mass media have played a much more central role in politics over the past several decades. The advent of various forms of social media and online news sites has further enabled a comprehensive and efficient dissemination of information about policies and policy making. Consequently, the public now have an enhanced capacity to scrutinize government and to potentially influence policy making. However, when considering the issue of Muslim asylum seekers we should recall our discussion in Chapter 2 and appreciate that public opinion concerning Muslims is prior-informed by anti-Muslim sentiments that have a long history, dating back to medieval Christian images of Islam and European colonial orientalism. We now turn to the three key factors of public opinion, policy making and media coverage in specific regard to the asylum seeker debate.

Public opinion on asylum seekers

Following the events of 9/11, there was a considerable rise in anti-Muslim sentiment throughout the Western world. Public attitudes towards asylum seekers were also hardening, and Muslim asylum seekers in particular have attracted significant negative attention from the public during the past decade or so (Allen, 2004; Poynting and Mason, 2007). This is not to suggest that asylum seekers were not considered as problematic prior to 9/11 (Boswell, 2000), but antipathy towards them increased considerably after the 9/11 terrorist attacks. In their study of public attitudes to Muslims in Canada and Australia post-9/11, Poynting and Berry summarize the types of responses Muslims around the world experienced:

> In the aftermath of these attacks, backlash violence against those perceived to be Muslim escalated dramatically, resulting in assaults, arsons, even racially motivated murders across the world, and

especially in nations aligned with the United States. Even in Canada, one of the Western nations that did not support the 2003 US invasion of Iraq, anti-Muslim violence as well as anti-Muslim practices by the state mushroomed.

(2007, p. 151)

Importantly, McLaren and Johnson (2007) remind us that it is possible that members of the public view asylum seekers and immigrants as one and the same, and so they include asylum seekers and immigrants in their study of public attitudes towards British immigration policies. These researchers identify that the key drivers of public concerns about immigration policy in Britain focus on the 'economy, crime and symbols of Britishness' (McLaren and Johnson, 2007, p. 727). The research tells us that there is considerable angst among the public about asylum seekers being a drain on the economy and being associated with crime. Negative attitudes towards asylum seekers develop even before their arrival, as Coole (2002) noted in her study looking at news media coverage of the death of an asylum seeker in Glasgow.

While it has been generally accepted that anti-immigration sentiments are attributable to economic and immigration factors (Boomgaarden and Vliegenthart, 2006), Poynting and Berry show that there are more complex factors at work. They argue that 'through "ethnic targeting", "racial profiling" and the like, the state conveys a sort of ideological license to individuals, groups and institutions to perpetrate and perpetuate racial hatred' (Perry and Poynting, 2006, p. 10). These types of public responses to asylum seekers are, as Boomgaarden and Vliegenthart suggest, driven by 'some perception of a cultural threat and accordingly a public problematization of immigration' (2006, p. 413).

Negative public attitudes towards asylum seekers are not isolated to Europe and the United Kingdom. The problematic perspective Australians have about asylum seekers has been well documented (Romano, 2004; Pedersen, Watt and Hansen, 2006). Despite the perceived magnitude of the 'problem', asylum seekers arriving by boat comprise fewer than 1 per cent of all immigrants arriving in Australia, and asylum applications account for only 0.2 per 1000 inhabitants (Parliament of Australia, 2011). The perception that 'boatloads' of Muslims are trying to get into Australia has caused considerable public angst, although relatively few individuals seek asylum there, compared with the number of people who seek asylum in various European countries.

Apart from public opinion surveys (Forest and Dunn, 2007) about attitudes Australians have towards asylum seekers, there have been no sustained or in-depth attempts to explore the responses of Australian communities in which refugees have been relocated, or in which detention centers are hosted, to their presence. This is despite poll data showing that 74 per cent of Australia's population are concerned about unauthorized asylum seekers coming to Australia by boat; the proportion of those who are 'very concerned' increased from 43 per cent in 2009 to 52 per cent in 2010 (Hanson, 2010) and has remained at this level in 2013 (Oliver, 2013).

Responses to the arrival of Muslim asylum seekers arriving in Australia include fear, anxiety and opposition from the majority of Australians. In a study of Australians' attitudes towards asylum seekers, understanding of reasons for seeking asylum, and information sources about asylum seekers, McKay, Thomas and Kneebone (2012) identify that members of the public were concerned about the cultural threat posed by asylum seekers to their way of life. They reveal that 'attitudes and opinions towards asylum seekers were more influenced by the interplay between traditional Australian values and norms, the way that these norms appeared to be threatened by asylum seekers, and the way that these threats were reinforced both in media and political rhetoric' (McKay, Thomas and Kneebone, 2012, p. 113). In writing about the death of 40 asylum seekers after their boat was washed onto rocks near Australia's Christmas Island in December 2010, McKay, Thomas and Kneebone highlight that the 'political divide was mirrored by a divide in community attitudes and opinions towards asylum seekers' (2012, p. 116).

Opinion polls published by major news organizations following the incident indicated that a majority of respondents wanted increased patrolling of Australia's borders in response to the deaths and that only a small minority (11 per cent) thought Australia should increase its intake of asylum seekers so that similar events would not occur in the future (McKay, Thomas and Kneebone, 2012). They also show that survey respondents' attitudes towards Muslim asylum seekers were particularly extreme, focusing on the danger these asylum seekers presented due to a perceived link with terrorism. One of their important findings is that 'most respondents had limited accurate knowledge about asylum seeking issues, with knowledge highly dependent on media reporting of the issue' (McKay, Thomas and Kneebone, 2012, pp. 127–128). They conclude that 'attitudes towards asylum seekers at the time were influenced by a complex interplay between political rhetoric, media reporting, personal experiences, socio-demographic factors and the way that survey respondents conceptualized traditional Australian values, and what could potentially pose a threat to these values' (McKay, Thomas and Kneebone, 2012, p. 127).

Political discourses and policy responses to asylum seekers

Givens and Luedteke (2005) identify that there is a key link between public opinion about immigration and policy responses. Critical incidents in the United Kingdom, Europe and the United States, including the building of mosques, legal challenges to wearing Islamic-style head covering, and a broader debate over the extent to which Muslims can integrate into Western societies (Sells and Qureshi, 2003; Tayob, 2006; Gottschalk and Greenberg, 2007; Cherti, 2010; Fernando, 2010), have had a substantial influence on policy making in relation to asylum seekers. Relatively little attention has been paid as to how public opinion might be changed and how this may lead to alternative government policies more consistent with the various legal, social and moral obligations Western countries face. A less well-understood phenomenon is known as 'policy mood' or the potential of government policy to shape public opinion, attitudes and values (Pierson, 1993).

The presence of asylum seekers is a major political issue for numerous European nations, Canada, the United States and Australia. While Boswell draws attention to the European Union's emphasis on policies that ensure 'liberal democratic and human rights based values' in the treatment of asylum seekers, there have been increasing challenges to that approach in some European countries, particularly with the rise of political parties whose mandate is to oppose immigration (2000, p. 537). While we mentioned earlier in this chapter that there was a crisis associated with asylum seekers in the two decades before 2001, Boswell explains that the crisis associated with asylum seekers in the late 1990s was different from the previous decades because of 'the combination of high numbers of refugees, unemployment in receiving countries, and the impact of globalization on notions of both identity and state legitimacy' (2000, p. 539). She suggested that the future direction of asylum policy in Europe would be rendered highly uncertain because of these factors. This theme of uncertainty in relation to asylum policy has characterized the years since 2001 in Europe and has also pervaded the political discourse about asylum seekers in Western countries.

Asylum seekers have attracted significant political attention in the Netherlands, and much of that interest has been negative, both pre- and post-9/11. The policy landscape for post-9/11 responses to asylum seekers was set in train before 2001, as Alink, Boin and t'Hart (2001) reveal in their study of policy responses to the 1985 influx of hundreds of Tamil asylum seekers into the Netherlands. In examining the connections between the reactive political responses to public pressure about asylum seekers, they found the political responses to the Tamil asylum seekers set off a negative chain reaction:

> The Dutch government viewed the Tamils as bogus asylum seekers, i.e. economic refugees, and expected a swift and negative decision concerning their asylum applications. In the meantime more asylum seekers arrived and the application procedure became overloaded. The media reported daily about the chaotic situation; MPs and community organizations clamored for measures.
>
> (Alink, Boin and t'Hart, 2001, pp. 291–292)

In reacting to the combination of media coverage and negative public responses to asylum seekers, the Dutch government introduced new legislation whereby asylum seekers were unable to apply for financial assistance to support them while they waited for their asylum claims to be processed. More importantly, as Alink, Boin and t'Hart point out, this response, along with the pressures on the country's asylum processing system 'combined with ample media attention and critical public opinion, heralded a period of political micromanagement of the admission implementation process' (2001, p. 292). In this instance the confluence of a number of factors led to the intervention of political actors in asylum policy.

Post-9/11, these types of negative responses to Muslim asylum seekers continued in the Netherlands (Ruigrok and van Atterveldt, 2007). For instance, there was a rise in the popularity of anti-immigration parties in the Netherlands post-9/11 (Boomgaarden and Vliegenthart, 2006). The increase in anti-immigration parties and public support for them is not confined to the Netherlands, as Givens and Luedtke (2005) note. They refer to immigration in Europe as being 'one of the most salient political issues' (Givens and Luedtke, 2005, p. 1). They elaborate: 'Not only has the immigration issue dominated headlines and public attention, but it has also had dramatic political effects, leading to new political cleavages and the rise of new political parties in the once "frozen" European political landscape' (Givens and Luedtke, 2005, p. 1). This has led to more restrictive immigration policy, as the issue has become one that has high salience, attracting much media attention.

Public sentiments of anger, fear and insecurity towards Muslim asylum seekers have led some Western governments to construct asylum seekers as threats to the national interests and security. For example, Poynting and Berry describe the impact of political discourse in reference to Muslim asylum seekers as having 'effectively lent "permission to hate" to those inclined to commit hate crime against Muslims' (2007, p. 167).

Other researchers have also identified that politicians have conflated Muslim asylum seekers with the threat that they allegedly propose to national security. For example, McKay, Thomas and Kneebone find that 'constructed socio-political stereotypes, particularly around the link between Islam and terrorism, created the perception that asylum seekers pose a "threat" to Australian national identity and security' (2012, pp. 127–128). This has also been a theme of political discourses about asylum seekers in Scotland, as Coole shows that, when discussing the resettlement of refugees in Glasgow between 2000 and 2002, authorities recognized that many of the refugees, who were from Afghanistan, Iraq and Iran, could not speak English, had 'very different cultural and religious beliefs to the majority in Scotland' and that these individuals 'would pose problems and challenges for housing authorities, social work departments, police forces and communities in Scotland' (2002, p. 840). However, she makes the important point that authorities gave no consideration to the ways in which they could respond to and manage negative media coverage about the refugees. In Canada the presence of asylum seekers has led to reactive policy responses. Bradimore and Bauer find 'an intricate relationship between political and media discourses on the arrival of the boat and its passengers' and that those 'tell a similar story' (2012, p. 654). They also show that, when the public debate about the arrival and subsequent treatment of the refugees ceased early in 2010, the political debate continued for some time. This crucial point remains pertinent today across Europe and North America and in Australia.

The effect of political discourses that focus on the threat asylum seekers pose can be seen in harsh punitive policies that are implemented in response to public concerns about the presence of these groups. In the United Kingdom, such policies, including detention, have been introduced to assuage public fears about the threat asylum seekers pose to national security (Malloch and Stanley, 2005). In examining the links between legislative and discursive representations of asylum seekers, Banks finds that they are positioned as being 'dangerous and deviant' (2008, p. 43). He argues that the political discourses associated with asylum seekers have facilitated the introduction of 'increasingly restrictive and draconian legislation and policy' (Banks, 2008, p. 43). This means that current immigration policy in the United Kingdom can only make sense if asylum seekers are constructed in the aforementioned ways. In Australia, the Howard government's policies regarding asylum seekers attracted significant research attention. Extensive research documents the detrimental impact the Howard government policies had on both the health and well-being of asylum seekers, as well as the inconsistency of such policies with international humanitarian obligations towards those in need of protection (Tazreiter, 2004; Brennan, 2006; Gelber and McDonald, 2006; O'Doherty and Augoustinos, 2007; Babacan, 2009).

While the political responses to asylum seekers, and Muslim asylum seekers in particular, have thus far been manifested in negative ways, McLaren and Johnson (2007) acknowledge that politicians in Britain have attempted to address the public hostility towards Muslim immigrants. However, they warn that

> given the fairly overwhelming expression of fear about the values and commitments of Muslims in particular and hostility to the notion that those who do not share the customs and traditions of Britons can be British, along with the unchangeable fact of multiculturalism in Britain, the issue will very likely need to be addressed more definitively.
>
> (McLaren and Johnson, 2007, p. 727)

One way of doing this, McLaren and Johnson suggest, would be for politicians to pay more attention to these issues when formulating policy. While some British politicians have tried to reconstruct debate about Muslim asylum seekers, Prime Minister Cameron has focused on a perceived inability of Muslims to integrate successfully, and this has been a theme repeated by German Chancellor Merkel. Both have positioned this as evidence of the failure of multiculturalism (BBC, 2010, 2011).

Another enduring theme in the political discourse about asylum seekers is the construction of them by politicians as illegitimate. Nikels (2007) contends that previous work in this area reveals that politicians in Europe 'tend to categorize them in two groups: genuine/political and bogus/economic refugees and asylum seekers' (p. 41). Not surprisingly, given the broader framing of asylum seekers by politicians, Nickels says this results in political actors and the media agreeing that 'access to the asylum system must be restricted to people in "genuine" need of protection' (2007, p. 56). The discourse about bogus asylum seekers is, according to Welsch and Schuster (2005), more salient in the United Kingdom than it is in the United States. Lynn and Lea (2003) reveal that the opposite of this discourse – the need for asylum as being legitimate or genuine – is very rarely used by those talking about asylum seekers.

As an indication of the dominance of discourses that delegitimize asylum seekers, policies aimed at deterring their arrival and lodgment of claims have gained credibility. However, researchers have responded with compelling evidence of fundamental flaws in such policies. For instance, Afghan and Iraqi asylum seekers have next to no understanding of Australian government policy or Australia in general, and they rely primarily on friends and family for their information about the asylum process. Most importantly, once they become aware of or experience the harsh treatment associated with mandatory detention, they remain undeterred and continue to seek asylum in Australia as their only option and the only hope for their children to live in safety and security (Richardson, 2010). Crock and Ghezelbash (2010) argue that, while the Australian government should deter asylum seekers from attempting a dangerous voyage by boat to the country, there has been a misconception in the way the issue has been constructed. Importantly, they make the point that policy changes do not always have a bottom line effect on the legal or physical systems associated with detaining asylum seekers.

Policies that focus on deterrence, Crock and Ghezelbash (2010) suggest, are visible and easy to explain, and accordingly have multiple uses: as well as ostensibly acting to 'deter' irregular migrants, they flag to the domestic electorate that the government is doing something proactive. Deterrent policies 'work well for those condemned to communicate in sound-bites' (Crock and Ghezelbash, 2010, p. 241). This point alludes to the significant role of the media in this process. It is to this factor we now turn.

Media representations of asylum seekers

There is a significant body of research that highlights the negative media portrayal of Muslim asylum seekers. Within this body of work there are only a few examples of where particular media outlets have been critical, challenged the prevailing political discourses or attempted to set an alternate agenda on the issue. The overwhelming findings from the research indicate that not only do news media represent these issues negatively, but they also uncritically repeat prevailing political discourses about asylum seekers, thus reinforcing public animosity towards asylum seekers. There is also some evidence that the media reflect public sentiment about the characteristics of asylum seekers.

In Glasgow, the death of a Turkish asylum seeker in 2001 highlighted the negative tone of media coverage in British newspapers and the aforementioned link between media coverage and public attitudes. In writing about the responsibilities of reporters covering these types of events, Coole suggests that news media representations of asylum seekers 'often voice the views of the public majority, thus assigning a pre-conceived character to asylum seekers' (2002, p. 849). She shows that, while the actions of local police in building relations with the refugee communities in Glasgow and activities organized by the local council initially attracted some positive media coverage, it was the murder of Firsat Dag, a Turkish Kurd, in August 2001 that changed the direction and tenor of media coverage. In relation to the nexus between media and public opinion, Coole's study presents an interesting contrast to the majority of research findings, which suggest that news media report asylum seekers negatively and tend to support the views of those who are concerned about the impacts of asylum seekers on their communities. She finds that journalists in Glasgow responded atypically to Firsat Dag's death, becoming 'sympathetic to the plight of asylum seekers as lost souls seeking refuge in a civilized and compassionate country' (Coole, 2002, p. 839). Coole shows that, in representing the community in which the attack occurred, reporters framed local residents 'as racist and hostile to asylum seekers, and were even blamed for creating an antagonistic atmosphere in which violence towards asylum seekers could thrive' (2002, p, 839).

Negative media representations of asylum seekers in the UK press has been a sustained theme of much of the research around immigration and asylum seekers post-9/11. Malloch and Stanley (2005) identify that in the United Kingdom there is a close relationship between these negative media representations of asylum seekers and harsh punitive policies such as detention. These researchers found that media representations of asylum seekers, in which they were framed as posing a danger to the community, directly contributed to the policy responses implemented to deal with asylum seekers in the United Kingdom. While there is evidence that prior to 9/11 immigrants and refugees were being represented by some news media as a threat to security, post-9/11 this theme became an enduring one that was increasingly taken up by news media in various European countries.

Banks (2008) reminds us that there is another prominent theme that characterizes news media coverage of asylum seekers, whereby British citizens are represented as the innocent victims who are being exploited by asylum seekers. An equally powerful theme in news media coverage is the framing of news about immigration through an economic lens and that there is 'public sensitivity for the relationship between the two aspects in the media and consequently people were more likely to turn towards the right of the political spectrum' (Boomgaarden and Vliegenthart, 2006, p. 413). Through statistical analyses Boomgaarden and Vliegenthart (2006) identify that there is a substantive relationship between the prominence of stories about immigration in national newspapers and voters' intentions to support anti-immigration parties. Similarly, Nickels' study of asylum seekers in Luxembourg's two leading newspapers over seven years identified that the discourses about asylum seeking are strongly influenced by external factors and events and that 'the framing of asylum discourse in Luxembourg is more reactive than pre-emptive, especially as far as the media are concerned' (2007, p. 56).

In their study of discourses on asylum seekers over a ten-year period, Bradimore and Bauer (2011) found an intimate relationship between politics and the media:

> The media are inseparable from the political process. However, if media and political debates rely mostly on each other for information and knowledge, they then establish a closed discursive circle that silences dissent and stifles oppositional intervention. This is particularly problematic when discourses are based on information and knowledge that are obviously biased, selectively sequenced, and prioritized, as well as when important facts are omitted and critical voices are silenced. Not breaking this cycle can have detrimental material consequences. (p. 657)

In discussing attitudes and media coverage of asylum seekers in Canada, Esses, Medianu and Lawson suggest that 'positive attitudes toward immigration in Canada are based on a weak foundation, and negative portrayals by the media can rapidly degrade these attitudes' (2013, p. 521). In their examination of study participants' reactions to Canadian news media articles and cartoons about asylum seekers, the researchers identify that negative media coverage works to dehumanize immigrants and refugees and can lead to 'extreme' behaviors by resident populations towards asylum seekers. This, Esses, Medianu and Lawson (2013) suggest, works to maintain existing attitudes towards these groups, increases antagonistic attitudes towards policy that allows the entry of asylum seekers and immigrations, and reifies the need for negative policies around asylum seekers.

Australian news media have also taken up the international discourses about asylum seekers, particularly the discourse that suggests Muslim asylum seekers are potential terrorists (Marr and Wilkinson, 2003; Pedersen, Watt and Hansen, 2006). Asylum seekers are represented in Australian news media as illegitimate, illegal, threatening and possessing values deeply inconsistent with those of a Western liberal democracy (Klocker and Dunn, 2003; Pedersen, Watt and Hansen, 2006; Every and Augoustinos, 2008). McCleary (2011) examines media framing of maritime asylum seekers (MAS) in Australia's 2010 federal election campaign and finds that politicians cited as sources in Australian press 'constructed MAS predominately through a negative reinterpretation of the humanitarian framework, whereby such a construction denotes the MAS as "undeserving" of the protections of the state' (p. 64). Similarly, in exploring policies aimed at deterring asylum seekers who arrive in Australia or attempt to travel to Australia by boat, Crock and Ghezelbash find that the issue consistently attracts the attention of the news media and that 'the stronger and more sustained the flow of boats, the more shrill the headlines and (it would seem) the more pronounced become the reactions from government' (2010, pp. 238–239).

We have identified three studies that present somewhat of a counter to the majority of the research findings on media representations of asylum seekers. Each of these studies identifies that there has been positive media coverage of the issue by different sections of the media and in different countries. Finney and Robinson's study (2008) analyzed local newspaper reportage of asylum seekers settling in Cardiff and Leeds, and identified that, within a framework of national moral panic over asylum seekers, it was possible to take a much more positive approach to reporting on asylum seekers. They explain that the *South Wales Echo* 'has shown that it is possible and commercially viable to challenge pervasive national discourses that draw on stereotypes and play on fears' (2008, p. 409). Staff at that newspaper took a more 'personalized' and 'humanitarian-focused' approach to reporting asylum seekers, which, Finney and Robinson (2008) conclude, has significant ramifications for policy success and community cohesion. Importantly, their work also highlights that the discourses around asylum seeker settlement in local newspapers are not all the same and that, indeed, they are 'framed and constructed differently by the local press in different places' (Finney and Robinson, 2008, p. 410).

Coole (2002) suggests that one response to negative media coverage would be for journalists to provide audiences with more nuanced accounts of asylum seekers, including facilitating media access for all communities, rather than focusing on a limited number of voices who express limited views. While the mainstream news media present simplistic representations of asylum seekers to audiences, McKay,

Thomas and Blood point out that the processes by which these portrayals are rendered are 'complex, as they both shape, and are shaped by, broader opinions about asylum seekers and national identity' (2011, p. 610). In studying media representations and public perceptions of asylum seekers arriving by boat in Australia, McKay, Thomas and Blood focus on a particularly salient example, that of the Sieve 36, a boat carrying asylum seekers which exploded near a reef off the North West coast of Australia in 2009. Theirs is one of the few studies to examine news media audiences' responses to media coverage of asylum seekers. The authors examined print and online news stories about the incident and then looked at letters to the editor and online comments on stories about the Sieve 36. Significantly, they conclude 'that while the reporting toward asylum seekers is generally negative, it is no longer reliant on the stance of the Government. Rather, there were a broader range of perspectives evident in the reporting of the SIEV 36 incident' (McKay, Thomas and Blood, 2011, p. 622). Despite this, the newspapers involved in the study blamed the Howard government's harsh asylum policies and the Rudd government's weaker policies for the event. McKay, Thomas and Blood's analysis reveals that the story was not framed through the humanitarian lens, but rather through the frames of asylum seekers seeking economic advantage in coming to Australia, and the newspapers' audiences responded to the asylum seekers as posing a potential security threat. They identify that, although 'media reports were not overtly racist in their remarks, the online comments posted by readers to articles had strong racist undertones and were often derogatory and demeaning to asylum seekers' (McKay, Thomas and Blood, 2011, p. 622). While a majority of news stories they analyzed are positive in terms of their representation of asylum seekers, they were featured alongside polls that presented significantly negative public opinion results. Thus, we are again led back to the assumption that media coverage, public opinion and policy making are strongly connected in respect to the asylum seeker debate.

The research shows that political responses to asylum seekers are driven by public opinion and that this has been played out in countries around the world, particularly post-9/11. However, when it comes to the interplay between media, public opinion and policy making, McKay, Thomas and Kneebone sum up the difficult task of changing the interactions between these factors:

Altering negative attitudes and opinions regarding asylum seekers will necessarily require a significant shift in political rhetoric and media reporting. We appreciate that these shifts are not easy to achieve. Political parties have played a central role in creating these negative public attitudes, and must now respond to the public's ideals, opinions, and expectations in maintaining a 'hard line' approach towards asylum seekers. These shifts will also be difficult for the media.

(2012, p. 130)

While it remains a challenge to conclude from the available research whether public opinion drives government policy on asylum seekers, it is clear that there are complex dynamics at work in the spaces where these factors intersect. Internationally, the literature we have focused on in this chapter reveals generally negative policy, public opinion and media coverage towards asylum seekers.

Few studies to date have addressed the critical question of how Western values and ideals are being impacted by both the presence of Muslim asylum seekers and refugees and government policies on asylum seekers. We know little, apart from Mummery and Rodan's (2007) study, about how interventions might work to change public opinion, media coverage and policy and the responses they garner for a more positive policy and national debate that reflect the values of liberal Western countries. Coole (2002) suggests that one response to negative media coverage would be for journalists to provide audiences with more nuanced accounts of asylum seekers, including facilitating access to media for all sections of communities, rather than focusing on a limited number of voices who express limited views.

With the exception of studies such as Richardson (2010), there has been little systematic empirical research about the circumstances, motivations, expectations and knowledge of those seeking asylum. As Coole (2002) and Mummery and Rodan (2007) suggest, these factors should be made more explicit publicly, as they have the potential to contribute to changing public opinion about asylum seekers and leveraging policy changes. While the literature suggests that public opinion influences policy making (Weakliem, 2005), on the issue of asylum seekers further research is needed as to how public opinion might be changed and how this may lead to alternative government policies that are more consistent with the various legal, social and moral obligations Western countries face. In the future, the world will confront increasing challenges with asylum seekers, as climate change increases the number of people who are forced from their home countries to seek refuge elsewhere. Boswell (2000) warned that at the turn of the century 'pressure on asylum systems, negative media coverage and growing public antipathy towards asylum-seekers suggest that the future of the liberal universalist approach is far from assured' (p. 539). The challenge of asylum seekers is much more than one of economic interests or national security.

Conclusion

This chapter shows that there are multifaceted elements at work in the processes associated with public opinion formation and political responses to asylum seekers. It is equally clear that certain media coverage of these issues and the subsequent political responses tend to be relatively simplistic. It is where the three combine that the interplay becomes more difficult to fully understand, and there is an opportunity here for more research. The question of the social and political drivers of asylum seeker policy, and the barriers to a policy that is more consistent with international obligations, universal standards of human rights, and national self-perceptions and values of generosity, tolerance, humanitarianism and a fair go, has thus far been largely neglected. Further research is needed on the potential for governments to develop asylum seeker policies that are more consistent with legal, social and moral obligations.

It does appear that in some contexts, when the media does not sufficiently fulfill its role as the fourth estate, political responses to asylum seekers may exploit pre-existing fears, anxiety and misconceptions, if they are present among publics, which seems to further entrench negative attitudes towards asylum seekers and consequently reinforce certain government policies towards asylum seekers. However, despite what may appear to be a gloomy picture of the negative interplay between media, public opinion and policy on asylum seekers, there is some indication in the literature that change is possible where media coverage and public opinion question and challenge government policy and political discourse. Responses to asylum seekers are a reflection on the state of liberal democratic values and identity, which, it seems, will continue to be tested as engagement with the Muslim world increases. Central to the challenge of Islam–West relations is the question of terrorism. It is to this issue that we turn in the next chapter.

5
Covering Terrorism Suspects

There is a long tradition of armed struggle in Islam that dates back to the time of the Prophet Muhammad. At its advent, Muslims fought numerous battles with the polytheists of Arabia for the preservation of Islam and for the establishment of the Islamic social order across the Peninsula. Like Islam's spiritual struggle in respect to prayer and charity and other physical struggles to lead a morally upright and righteous life, armed struggle was another form of *jihad* practiced by the early Muslims. Over time, the definition of *jihad* became narrowed and synonymous with fighting or holy war. By the 9th century self-defense against armed aggressors ceased to be a necessary criterion for a call to *jihad* and the concept came to be used for offensive wars against non-Muslims for political purposes of empire-building. By the 14th century, the concept was invoked to legitimize armed struggle against Muslim rulers deemed not sufficiently Islamic. During the era of European colonial rule, various Muslim groups fought for independence under the banner of *jihad* (Rane, 2009). Today, *jihad* is linked to a new phenomenon, terrorism.

The first Muslims to use terrorism as *jihad* were Hezbollah, a Shiite group based in southern Lebanon which mobilized in response to Israel's occupation of their country. Hezbollah began using suicide bombings in the early 1980s in order to drive out foreign forces. This tactic was adopted by Hamas in Palestine in the 1990s in a futile attempt to liberate their country from Israeli occupation. By the late 1990s, Al-Qaeda arrived on the scene and made suicide terrorism its hallmark. By the turn of the century, ideological affiliates of Al-Qaeda, among others, in the Middle East, South Asia and Southeast Asia also adopted the tactic, as did a handful of Western Muslims, who came to be referred to as 'home-grown' terrorists. It is this latter group on whom this chapter focuses.

It is pertinent to first provide a definition of terrorism. There is no internationally accepted or UN-approved definition of terrorism. The Federal Bureau of Investigations (FBI) in the United States defines two types of terrorism, international and domestic, as follows:

'International terrorism' means activities with the following three characteristics:

- Involve violent acts or acts dangerous to human life that violate federal or state law;
- Appear to be intended (i) to intimidate or coerce a civilian population; (ii) to influence the policy of a government by intimidation or coercion; or (iii) to affect the conduct of a government by mass destruction, assassination, or kidnapping; and
- Occur primarily outside the territorial jurisdiction of the U.S., or transcend national boundaries in terms of the means by which they are accomplished, the persons they appear intended to intimidate or coerce, or the locale in which their perpetrators operate or seek asylum.

'Domestic terrorism' means activities with the following three characteristics:

- Involve acts dangerous to human life that violate federal or state law;
- Appear intended (i) to intimidate or coerce a civilian population; (ii) to influence the policy of a government by intimidation or coercion; or (iii) to affect the conduct of a government by mass destruction, assassination, or kidnapping; and
- Occur primarily within the territorial jurisdiction of the U.S.

(FBI, 2013)

In Australia, terrorism is defined in Commonwealth legislation, specifically the Criminal Code Act 1995, as 'an action or threat of action where the action causes certain defined forms of harm or interference and the action is done or the threat is made with the intention of advancing a political, religious or ideological cause' (Australian Government, 2013, para. 8). The Act further defines terrorism as when an action is done or the threat is made with the intention of:

(i) coercing, or influencing by intimidation, the government of the Commonwealth or a State, Territory or foreign country, or part of a State, Territory or foreign country; or

(ii) intimidating the public or a section of the public; and where the action

    (a) causes serious harm that is physical harm to a person; or

    (b) causes serious damage to property; or

    (c) causes a person's death; or

    (d) endangers a person's life, other than the life of the person taking the action; or

    (e) creates a serious risk to the health or safety of the public or a section of the public; or

    (f) seriously interferes with, seriously disrupts, or destroys, an electronic system including, but not limited to: (i) an information system; or (ii) a telecommunications system; or (iii) a financial system; or (iv) a system used for the delivery of essential government services; or (v) a system used for, or by, an essential public utility; or (vi) a system used for, or by, a transport system.

The Criminal Code Act makes it an offense if a person commits a terrorist act, provides or receives training connected with terrorist acts, possesses a thing connected with terrorist acts, collects or makes documents likely to facilitate terrorist acts, or does any act in preparation for or planning of terrorist acts. The penalty for engaging in a terrorist act is life imprisonment (Australian Government, 2013).

This chapter examines several aspects of the media and terrorism, including media coverage of terrorism, terrorists' use of media and the impacts of anti-terror laws on journalists. Because journalists around the world have, since the 9/11 terror attacks, had to negotiate new terrain when covering terrorism-related events and terrorism trials, this chapter looks at the role of the media as the fourth estate through an analysis of several Australian case studies, including the Holsworthy Army Barracks plot, the case of Dr Mohammad Haneef, and the case of the Benbrika terrorist group. These cases were selected as they have received far less attention in the international media than similar cases that have occurred in the United States, the United Kingdom and other European countries. Public access to information about these cases has in some instances been restricted by the wave of anti-terror laws that were introduced in many Western and non-Western countries post-9/11. While these cases are situated in an Australian context, the lessons learned from them are more broadly applicable to Western media and journalists covering terrorism stories. This chapter considers the coverage of these cases by some news media within the context of the passing of anti-terror legislation and the subsequent impact that the prevailing discourse has had on Muslim communities in terms of social inclusion and exclusion.

Media coverage of terrorism

There is a broad body of research dealing with media coverage of terrorism. This body of work largely falls into three areas: the use of news media to condemn or promote terrorism, the role of the media in promoting fear of terrorism, and examinations of the way media frame and present stories about terrorism. Louw (2003) argues that war has become a public relations exercise for government and a media opportunity for terrorists. He identifies that 'those attacking the World Trade Centre deployed an understanding of terrorism as a "media event", and a grasp of how US politics (and warfare) has been "mediaized" ' (Louw, 2003, p. 211). His insights into the Pentagon's responses to the public relations problems caused by the 'war on terror' are of value to public relations practitioners and journalists.

Damphouse and Shields (2007) examine some of the impacts and consequences of major terrorism events, and related media coverage, on the way the US government pursues such cases. While their study concentrates on the policy changes that occur as a result of terrorist events and their consequences for officials involved in the 'investigation and prosecution of terrorist activities', they also reveal the increased focus that is brought to bear on public officials by the media during terrorism trials (Damphouse and Shields, 2007, p. 192). Their study shows that the 'desire by federal actors to appear proactive in light of this scrutiny results in changes to investigative and prosecutorial strategies, and those changes have several intended and unintended consequences' (Damphouse and Shields, 2007, p. 192).

Terrorist groups have had some success in using various forms of media for situational awareness during terrorist attacks. One of the most significant recent instances of terrorists using media to gather information and use it for strategic and tactical advantage was evidenced in the 2008 Mumbai bombings. The case was exceptional as it marked a change in the way terrorist groups use news media, including social and mass media, to monitor the event (Oh, Agrawal and Rao, 2011). The terrorists involved in the Mumbai attacks tracked the social media activities of individuals caught up in the attacks via Twitter and traditional media coverage of the attacks as they occurred. Oh, Agrawal and Rao found that the terrorists 'monitored live media and Web sites as the attacks took place, using that information for situational awareness and to change strategies' (2011, p. 33). India's intelligence agencies later identified

> that the terrorist group collected situational information on the fly through live media and websites. They opportunistically utilized such information to make decisions of where and how to mount their attacks, and whom to kill with precision.
>
> (Oh, Agrawal and Rao, 2011, p. 34)

The terrorist group used Twitter posts made by individuals hiding in the hotel they attacked to improve their decision-making in relation to the use of their hand-held weapons. Oh and colleagues suggest that controls on social media are needed during terrorist attacks in order to prevent terrorists from using the information. Moreover, live news broadcasts coupled with social media 'could potentially aid terrorists who were monitoring those media reports and online postings through satellite phones and other communication methods' (Oh, Agrawal and Rao, 2011, p. 38).

Kaplan (2009) presents an interesting counterpoint to Oh and colleagues' argument, suggesting that the focus on terror groups' use of mobile technologies and the monitoring of social media is a form of technological determinism. She found that attention was diverted away from more important issues, such as the complex relationships between Pakistan and India, and thus the context for why the attacks occurred was lost in the outrage at the terror group's use of mobile technologies and monitoring of traditional news media and social media.

Earlier work by Bassiouni (1982) suggests three effects of media coverage of terrorism. First, media attention to terrorism encourages further acts of terrorism. Second, when the media focus on terrorism events, the motivation of others to engage in terrorism is weakened. Third, Bassiouni proposes that the media have an effect akin to immunization, which leads to increased tolerance of terrorism by the public. He found that terrorists tailor their acts and how they carry them out to garner media coverage, not only for the act but also as a way of inspiring fear among populations. This means that the 'media thus unwittingly further terrorist objectives by publicizing an event that has been staged by the perpetrator for the very reason of obtaining media coverage to produce a social impact which would not otherwise exist' (Bassiouni, 1982, p. 17). Nacos (2009) also says that mass media coverage of terrorist events is an important element in the dissemination of terrorist groups' messages and tactics.

Altheide (2006) focuses on the media's role in promoting terrorism through its emphasis on fear and uncertainty. He suggests that the media's role in facilitating the promotion of fear has become 'more pronounced since the United States "discovered" international terrorism on 11 September 2001' (Altheide, 2006, p. 287). He identifies that politicians use symbols to create connections in the minds of the public that conflate Iraq and Muslims with terrorism and then use the resultant fear to justify 'expanding domestic social control' (Altheide, 2006, p. 287). In an analysis of the portrayal of terrorism during elections, Oates (2006) looks at news programs from Russia, the United Kingdom and the United States, discovering that the media are instrumental in the flow of emotive messages during elections. She reveals that the 'fear factor' seems to be a tempting card to play, offering political leaders means of entrenching their positions (Oates, 2006, p. 425). This is supported by another study, which identifies that anxiety is created by exposure to television images of national threats and terrorism. Slone (2000) examines psychological responses to televised images of national threats and terrorism among Israeli audiences, finding that responses vary according to participants' religion and gender, but that generally the images used induce anxiety among those exposed to the material.

Much of the work on media reportage of terrorism has been approached through examinations of news frames. One of the key studies in this field (Papacharissi and de Fatima Oliveira, 2008) provides insights into how newspapers in the United Kingdom and the United States frame terrorism stories. In the United States, newspapers tend to frame terrorism through a military perspective, while in the United Kingdom newspapers emphasize 'diplomatic evaluations of terrorist events' (Papacharissi and de Fatima Oliveira, 2008, p. 52). Similarly, Erajavec and Volcic, in a study of the discourses used by newspapers in the former Yugoslav countries in reports about the 'war on terror', found that these discourses were used to justify their 'nationalisms and the past military actions against the Muslims in former Yugoslav wars, and with that, they assert their belonging to an antiterrorism global discursive community' (2006, p. 298). In a study of Russian journalists and self-censorship in relation to coverage of the 'war on terror', Simons and Strovsky (2006) identified that in the early stages of the 'war on terror' security services provided stories to Russian media to create moral panics, with the key message being one of fear of imminent attack by terrorists. However, this was followed by the provision of stories that were aimed at 'settling society's frayed nerves with "good" news stories that give the impression of progress in "winning" the war against terror' (Simons and Strovsky, 2006, p. 208).

Nacos and Torres-Reyna (2003) found that 9/11 had the effect of forcing the news media to provide audiences with a more comprehensive and nuanced picture of Muslim and Arab minorities. Theirs is a significant study because it shows that some news media took alternative approaches to coverage of Islam and Muslims, rather than the usual approach of demonizing Islam and Muslims, which van Atteveldt, Ruigrok and Kleinnijenhuis (2006) identifies as typical of the Dutch press in an analysis that spanned from 2000 to 2005. Karim (2006) observes that the continued representation of the violent Muslim performs a propaganda function. Unlike Nacos and Terres-Reyna (2003), Karim says that media coverage tends to brush aside alternative voices for a reliance on sources who confirm pre-existing stereotypes of Islam.

Journalists and anti-terror laws

Post 9/11, a number of Western countries introduced legislation specifically aimed at dealing with terrorists and planned terrorism attacks. Several international incidents have recently highlighted the problems that this legislation poses for journalists, academics and citizens, particularly in relation to restrictions on media reportage and public access to information. These problems are not restricted to Western countries. For example, in Ethiopia the impacts of the country's anti-terror laws, enacted after bombings in the country's capital Addis Ababa in 2008, have been most evident with the arrest of Ethiopian journalists among journalists from other countries (Thurston, 2012). In 2011 the Ethiopian government used these laws to arrest two Swedish journalists, who were found guilty of 'helping and promoting the outlawed' Ogaden National Liberation Front (Maasho, 2011, para. 1). The pair were sentenced to 11 years in jail. Human Rights Watch said the conviction of the two men demonstrated that 'the country's anti-terrorism law is fundamentally flawed and being used to repress legitimate reporting' (2011, para. 1). Human Rights Watch has identified that there are 29 journalists, members of the opposition and other individuals on trial under Ethiopia's anti-terror laws (MSNBC, 2011).

In 2010, Turkey's restrictive anti-terror laws, introduced in 2006, were the focus of criticisms by international agencies including Reporters Without Borders, when a Turkish photographer and newspaper editor were charged with 'exposing an official on anti-terrorist duties to a terrorist organization' (Reporters Without Borders, 2010, para. 3). The charges related to the photographing of a Turkish army colonel who was giving evidence in a terrorism investigation. The photographer was charged for taking the photo and the newspaper's managing editor for publishing it. This incident highlighted the restrictive nature of Turkey's anti-terror laws, particularly in respect to the media's ability to inform their audiences.

In Western countries, anti-terror laws have also led to problems for journalists and academics. In 2012, academics at Boston College in the United States were ordered by a US court to hand over interviews undertaken by several of its academics with former members of the Irish Republican Army (IRA) (CBS, 2012). The transcripts were related to the murder of a woman in Ireland in 1972, which was purportedly undertaken by the IRA. The academics had made commitments to the interviewees that their identities would not be revealed, but the court overrode those promises. This case highlighted the impact of anti-terror laws in the United States on academics' right to undertake this type of research, and on their ability to uphold the ethical commitments they make to interviewees.

These cases raise significant concerns about the media's ability to act as the fourth estate – that is, acting as a check and balance on the executive, the judiciary and the government. These cases also bring into question the media's ability to report terrorism-related stories without fear, and they highlight the willingness of governments to use, and at times abuse, anti-terror laws in order to stifle, prevent or control media reportage and, consequently, public access to information about terrorism. Australia has had several high-profile terrorism-related cases, which have raised issues about access to information, freedom to report and restrictions on information provision to the media and the public. Since 2002, when a raft of new provisions related to terrorism was introduced into Australia's Criminal Code and the Australian Secret Intelligence Organisation (ASIO) Act, journalists have faced, and sometimes fallen foul of, a complex legal environment when reporting terrorism-related events and court cases. Some of these provisions were exclusively related to media and public access to court hearings and information about terrorism cases, while others specifically covered what the media could publish about terrorism suspects.

In next section of this chapter we examine the experiences of Australian journalists in relation to three terrorism-related cases. These examples provide salutary lessons about the impact of anti-terror laws on the ability of the media to report these types of stories and fulfill their fourth estate role. The experiences of journalists in Australia provide insights into some of the problems that anti-terror legislation can cause for a free media and the resultant impacts on democratic process, including the public's right to information about terrorism cases. While some might consider these experiences to be particular to Western democracies, the aforementioned examples from Ethiopia, Turkey and Russia reveal that the problems anti-terror legislation cause for the media are not confined to Western democracies. Indeed, the experiences of journalists in relation to the restrictive nature of laws ostensibly passed to deal with terrorism appear to be remarkably similar regardless of the nature of the political environment.

The Australian experience

Australian journalists have had relatively few experiences with the anti-terrorism laws compared with their colleagues in other countries, but, when their attempts to report on terrorism-related cases have fallen foul of these laws, they have attracted significant public and media attention. One of the first experiences Australian journalists had of these laws and their impact on journalism was in 2005 during a police operation codenamed Pendennis. Suppression orders were issued under the anti-terror provisions to prevent publication of some details of the court case associated with this operation, which gave rise to questions about the media's and public's right to access information in these types of cases. Two years later, in 2007, the case of Dr Mohammed Haneef, arrested and charged with providing material support to a terrorist organization, presented serious challenges for journalists, who were forced to interpret and work within legislation that very few, if any, were knowledgeable about (Ewart, 2009; McNamara, 2009). In 2009, public tensions erupted between policing agencies and *The Australian* newspaper over the timing of the publication of a story about police raids to arrest terror suspects in the Holsworthy Army Barracks case. In the following section of this chapter we provide background details of each of these cases and their associated events, followed by a discussion of their implications for journalists and the public. We also discuss the findings of research that has been undertaken internationally and nationally into Muslims' responses to media coverage of terrorism and the resultant implications for social inclusion.

Australia has, to date, remained relatively isolated from the kinds of terrorism events that have occurred elsewhere in the world. Although several terrorism plots have been uncovered on Australian shores and Australians have been caught up in terrorism events in other countries, none of the terrorism plots in Australia post-2001 have been successful. At the time of writing, 38 people have been charged with terrorism offenses in Australia, and, since 2007, 21 people have been convicted of terrorism offenses (McClelland, 2011). The Australian media, like many of their international counterparts, have an important role in informing their audiences about terrorism and the court proceedings associated with those charged with terrorism offenses. The examples we examine highlight the importance of the media in relation to their fourth estate role and the challenge of balancing the public's right to know with national security interests.

The response of Australia's Muslim communities to media coverage of terrorism has had significant impacts on social inclusion opportunities for Muslims. The cases we examine presented opportunities for Australian Muslims to engage with the media and broader Australian publics, in order to reframe public conversations that frequently link Muslims to terrorism. However, for a variety of reasons, either Australia's Muslim communities have decided not to engage with the media during specific terrorism cases or, when they have attempted to voice their opposition to terrorism, they have not been sufficiently heard (Ewart, 2009). The absence of the Muslim voice is a lost opportunity to reframe national discussions about Muslims and terrorism. Adding to this problem is a tendency on the part of certain media organizations to feature the views of radical Muslims, or at least those with views that are hostile to Western society (Rane, Ewart and Abdalla, 2010).

Terrorism laws and their impact on the media

While Australian journalists and media organizations feel that Australia's anti-terror laws have been over-judiciously applied to suppress reportage of terrorism trials and cases (Herman, 2005; Australia's Right to Know, 2007; The Media, Entertainment and Arts Alliance, 2007; Warren, 2009), members of the former Federal Government, which introduced these laws, believe these restrictions are justified (Ewart, 2009). Johnson and Pearson examine some of these laws and the ways they restrict media reportage, including 'laws relating to freedom of information, camera access to courts, shield laws and whistleblower protection and finally, revamped anti-terrorism laws' (2008, p. 72). They suggest that the restrictive nature of these laws means public access to information about particular cases is limited. When anti-terror legislation was introduced post-9/11, Nash (2005) was one of the few journalism researchers to examine the various pieces of new legislation in an effort to identify their impacts on journalists. He suggests the anti-terror laws make journalists and editors 'think long and hard before publication' (Nash, 2005, p. 3). Nash also points out that some journalists supported these laws, including Patrick Walters, national security editor for the national newspaper *The Australian*. Many media outlets were supportive of the introduction of the anti-terror legislation. Pearson and Busst (2006) considered Australia and New Zealand's anti-terror laws and their impacts on journalism and journalists, and came to the same conclusions as Nash.

Although the anti-terror legislation attracted criticism from civil and human rights organizations, as well as the Media, Entertainment and Arts Alliance, which represents some of Australia's journalists, there remains a paucity of research in this area. One of the few studies to have explored this issue is McNamara's examination of the 'actual and potential effects' of Australia's counter-terrorism laws on journalists, public debate and circulation of information (2009, p. 27). In his article he makes the point that 'an investigation of how Australian counter-terrorism laws affect the media is important because it provides the occasion for a critical study of how (both putative and real) liberal democratic commitments to press freedom are operationalized in the context of national security' (McNamara, 2009, p. 31). McNamara reveals, through interviews with journalists and in-house media lawyers, how some of these commitments to press freedom are affected by Australia's anti-terror laws. He suggests both groups have limited understanding of the anti-terror laws and their operation. He identifies that the coercive powers given to ASIO which force journalists to reveal sources or face five years in jail 'have the potential to affect the way journalists, editors and media lawyers make judgments and decisions about news gathering and publication' (McNamara, 2009, p. 33). Although McNamara finds that the laws appear to have 'only limited direct effects on the media', he raises the important question of what impacts they might have on media freedom (2009, p. 36). He identifies that journalists and media organizations 'have many concerns about their freedom and that anti-terrorism laws are relevant to those concerns, even if not in a direct or causal way' (McNamara, 2009, p. 36).

Perhaps one of McNamara's most significant findings is that journalists had 'a strong commitment to not undermining policing and investigation of matters involving terrorism' (2009, p. 41). However, the journalists McNamara spoke with also revealed they had problems with security and policing agencies' selective and non-disclosure of information. He made a crucial point in the following quote:

> The interviews reveal the need for a much greater degree of openness by the authorities: where something can be made public, then it should be made public. The security authorities will almost inevitably tend to err on the side of caution when it comes to openness, but there is a difference between erring on the side of caution and keeping information hidden unnecessarily. It is difficult to know whether the latter is in fact happening, but media practitioners seem fairly convinced that it is. At the very least, that perception needs to be addressed because it fosters a culture of distrust.
>
> (McNamara, 2009, p. 42)

The Benbrika case

Operation Pendennis, which began in July 2004 and ended on 9 November 2005, involved key national security and policing agencies, including Australian Federal Police (AFP), ASIO and the Victoria Police (Hughes, 2008). It culminated in the arrest in November 2005 of nine men in Sydney and eight men in Melbourne on terrorism charges, including possession of bomb-making materials and instructions, firearms and ammunition. It was thought that several high-profile Australian venues were the target of the bombing plot, but it was never conclusively proven what sites were targeted. Shortly prior to the arrests, the Australian Federal Parliament passed an amendment to the anti-terror legislation changing the reference from 'the' terrorist act to 'a' terrorist act, thus broadening the legislation's application. This amendment was attributed directly to Operation Pendennis.

After the arrests of the 17 suspects, the then AFP Commissioner Mick Keelty stated that the Department of Public Prosecution (DPP) would apply for suppression orders to prevent details of the allegations against those arrested being published, arguing the AFP wanted to 'give these people a fair opportunity to prepare their defense before the court rather than run the trial in the media' (Australian Broadcasting Corporation, 2005, para. 6). Eventually 12 of the men faced trial, which began in February 2008 and ended with the handing down of verdicts in September 2008. Seven of the men were found guilty of one or more of the charges.

This case was unusual because the AFP's actions in seeking suppression orders had two impacts – the allegations against the men were withheld from the public domain prior to the trial, and, during the associated court cases, the media were prevented from publishing the names of the men on trial. For the duration of the trials the men were referred to by names other than their real names. Victoria's Supreme Court made a total of 21 suppression orders, which impacted on the information journalists were able to provide to the public before, during and after the court hearings. In an unusual precedent, the day before the trial began Justice Bongiorno organized a pre-trial briefing for journalists and media lawyers (Australia's Right to Know, 2008). He told those at the briefing that he had some concerns about media coverage of the forthcoming trial and explained a range of processes the court had established to assist journalists covering the trial. Some of these processes were aimed at ensuring the accuracy of media coverage of the trial. He explained that some suppression orders had been made in pre-trial proceedings, but he emphasized that the media would be able to report the proceedings of the open court, notwithstanding the suppression orders (Australia's Right to Know, 2008).

Following an application from a media organization to access court exhibits from the trial, Justice Bongiorno allowed journalists to access the exhibits on the proviso that they should not refer to the information in them until after the verdicts were handed down (Australia's Right to Know, 2008). The media strictly observed this agreement. A report by Australia's Right to Know (2008) found that for the most part journalists reporting on the trials appreciated the pre-court briefings, provision of court documents and information arranged by Justice Bongiorno. The report also identified that the media were prepared to cooperate with the court's requests about reportage of the trial. Victoria's Supreme Court only recently lifted the 21 suppression orders (Caldwell, 2011).

This case was significant in that Justice Bongiorno established pre-court briefings for the media and facilitated access to documents and information in an effort to ensure the accuracy of reportage. It revealed that cooperative relationships can be established between the media and the courts during terrorism cases, although the incentive for the media to abide by conditions imposed may be related to journalists' reluctance to face a contempt of court order. However, the imposition of suppression orders concerning information that may have been in the public interest gives rise to some concerns. While the AFP asked for the names and allegations against the men to be withheld from the public, no such requests were made in either the Dr Haneef case or the Holsworthy Army Barracks terror plot. The inconsistencies in approaches relating to suppression orders in terrorism cases require further examination.

The Dr Haneef case

Dr Haneef, an Indian citizen, was working as a registrar at the Gold Coast Hospital in Southport, Queensland, Australia, in July 2007 when he was arrested on suspicion of a connection with terrorists who attempted to bomb a nightclub in London and Glasgow airport. Dr Haneef was held for 12 days without charge under the extended detention provisions incorporated into Australia's Crimes Act in 2004 and 2005. These provisions enable police to apply to a judicial officer for extensions of the downtime between interviews with suspects in terrorism cases. Dr Haneef was eventually charged with recklessly providing material support to a terrorist organization in the form of a mobile phone SIM card. Although Haneef was granted bail by a magistrate, his visa was withdrawn by the then Immigration Minister, Kevin Andrews, and he was transferred to immigration detention. The DPP eventually dropped the charge due to a lack of evidence, and Haneef elected to return to India on 29 July 2007, rather than remain in community-based immigration detention while legal proceedings continued. The full bench of the Australian Federal Court reinstated Haneef's visa in August 2007. The Federal Government ordered an inquiry into the matter, which revealed flaws in the AFP's management of the case (Ewart, 2009). Haneef's lawyers continued to pursue the Commonwealth Government for compensation for their client and he was awarded an undisclosed figure in December 2010.

The case gave rise to several issues for journalists. There was considerable confusion among journalists in the first few days of the case as to whether Dr Haneef had been arrested under provisions in the Crimes Act or the ASIO Act. The differences between these Acts have considerable ramifications for journalists' ability to report terrorism cases. For instance, if Dr Haneef had been arrested under the ASIO Act the media would not have been able to report the case, whereas under the Crimes Act journalists could cover the story. Journalists' lack of understanding of Australia's security laws led to misunderstandings about what they could and could not report (Ewart, 2009; McNamara, 2009). This had a critical impact on journalists' ability to report the story accurately, as did their initial forced reliance on spin (Ewart, 2009; McNamara, 2009). The story unfolded at an extremely fast pace, leading to some media publishing stories containing serious factual errors (Ewart, 2010). Dreher (2007) states that, during the first ten days of the case, the media framed the story through the lens of 'global threat and urgency', and she suggested that there was an initial attempt by the media to paint Haneef as 'guilty until proven innocent' (p. 211). This perception of guilt was fostered by leaks of information about the case from government and other organizations.

The government and policing agencies initially controlled the release of information about the case, and journalists were left with little option but to report selectively provided and leaked information. The demands of the 24/7 news cycle saw reporters from rival media organizations jostling for leads and breaks in the story, and many said that they fell for the government spin about the case, which positioned Haneef as a threat to national security (Thomas, 2007; Ewart, 2009). International human rights lawyer and barrister Geoffrey Robertson QC describes this process: 'Through smears and leaks, police and politicians had sent the media into a feeding frenzy of hostility against the defendant' (Ewart, 2009, p. 7).

Despite the control of information and placement of misinformation, Dr Haneef's barrister, Stephen Keim, was able to effectively address the misinformation flow. By giving a journalist a copy of his client's police interview transcript, Keim revealed the apparent weakness of the police case. He became an alternative source for journalists, which was important for changing the media angle from promoting Haneef's apparent guilt to professing his innocence until proven guilty. As the police case publicly unraveled, another journalist was able to reveal a key flaw in the case using investigative practices. This was in relation to the actual location of Dr Haneef's SIM card, which was in Liverpool, not in Glasgow as police had initially alleged.

Australia's anti-terror legislation initially restricted journalists' ability to report the case fairly and accurately, as did the strategic leaks of information in the case, which led to key mistakes and misinformation being published by some media outlets (Ewart, 2010). However, the investigative efforts of two journalists led to the collapse of the police case against Dr Haneef. The Haneef case highlighted that it is essential that journalists have a good working knowledge of the anti-terrorism laws before a terrorism case breaks. The 24-hour news cycle and Australia's very competitive media environment did not allow time for journalists to come to grips with a complex set of laws while reporting complicated terrorism-related cases. It also drew attention to the fractured nature of relationships between policing agencies, the media and government agencies. Ultimately it revealed the problems that occur when journalists are forced to rely on information from sources who have an agenda that is not in the interests of the public or democracy. It also highlighted that journalists can play an important role in shining a light on inadequacies in police investigations of terror-related cases, in the process contributing to fulfilling the media's fourth estate role.

The Holsworthy Army Barracks plot

Our third example reveals a number of additional issues for journalists not highlighted by the aforementioned cases. In 2009 tensions erupted between policing organizations and *The Australian* newspaper over the timing of publication of a story about police raids on the homes of individuals suspected of involvement in a plot to shoot army members at the Holsworthy Army Barracks in Sydney. On 4 August 2009, Operation Neath was launched in Melbourne, resulting in the arrests. Several days before the raids, Cameron Stewart, a journalist from *The Australian* newspaper, was allegedly contacted by an officer of the Victoria Police and given information about the plot. Stewart called the AFP media center on 30 July 2009 and said that 'he had sensitive information relating to a joint counter terrorism investigation in Victoria'. The AFP Commissioner Tony Negus phoned the newspaper's editor Paul Whittaker to request that the newspaper delay publication of the story until after the suspects' arrests. Whittaker and Negus agreed to the timing of publication of the story; however, copies of the newspaper were published as early as 1.30 am, which was before the arrest raids took place (Australian Broadcasting Corporation, 2011a). The then Commissioner of Victoria Police, Simon Overland, publicly criticized the newspaper because he believed the early publication of the story could have tipped off the suspects prior to their arrest. He was concerned about the potential for the terror suspects to change strategy and attack another target.

As the story gathered momentum, journalists from other media outlets wanted to visit the Holsworthy Army Barracks, and a *Daily Telegraph* journalist and photographer entered and photographed the barracks as part of a story about security at the barracks. The pair were charged with illegally photographing a military installation, and both were given nine-month good behavior bonds by a court (Kontominas, 2009). After a prolonged public argument between *The Australian* and Overland, the then Attorney General Robert McClelland spoke out about the need for protocols to cover media reportage of terrorism. His call met with fiery opposition from major media organizations, including *The Australian*. Australia's Office of Police Integrity investigated the alleged leaking of information to *The Australian* by an officer of the Victoria Police (Dorling, 2011). Reporter Cameron Stewart was asked by a magistrate to reveal the name of the source who had provided him with information about the police operation. Stewart gained permission from his source to reveal his identity to the court, raising potential issues in relation to how enduring and binding journalists' ethical commitments are to their sources (Simons, 2010). The discussions about the case between the AFP and *The Australian* newspaper's editor were made public during the committal hearing of the police officer charged with leaking information to *The Australian*, revealing in stark detail the interchanges, negotiations and agreements reached between the two groups. During the committal hearing, AFP Commissioner Tony Negus alleged in an affidavit that Whittaker had 'bargained with lives' during the discussion he had about the timing of publication.

> 'Negus: Look, I am formally requesting you...not to go ahead with this story. People's lives are at risk if you publish this story tomorrow.
> Whittaker: Well, how many lives are at risk?
> Negus: Well, if these people are aware of police interest they...may actually go to the nearest shopping center and decide to take action because they won't have time to prepare properly.
> Whittaker: Well, what are we talking about, one person being killed, or are we talking about a number of people being killed?' (Australian Broadcasting Corporation, 2011b, paras 15–19)

The case attracted further attention when Crikey reporter Margaret Simons posted reports on Twitter from the committal hearing. She was ordered by a magistrate to cease tweeting because of national security issues. The magistrate was concerned that any suppression orders made during the committal hearing would be meaningless if there was live reporting of the case.

The Holsworthy Barracks plot highlighted the conflict and tensions that can occur when a terrorism plot comes to the attention of the media. It also highlighted, in the instance of the *Daily Telegraph* staff, that some journalists are still not familiar with the national security laws. *The Australian* newspaper's desire to forge ahead with publishing the story, while involving some elements of public interest, also had the potential, according to Overland, to go awry. The case also revealed the behind-the-scenes discussions about the decision to publish the story, which could have had significant consequences, including potential loss of lives. Other ethical issues raised during the case include the extent to which commitments made to confidential sources are binding. This case showed the significant tensions that exist between the media, national security and the public's right to information about these cases. It was also unusual because this was the first time that an Australian terrorism-related case had been reported by a journalist using Twitter. It highlighted the inconsistent approach of Australia's courts to journalists' live reporting using Twitter and other social media tools.

Impacts of media reportage on Muslim communities

There has been very little research internationally into Muslim responses to media coverage of terrorism cases. This is surprising, because it would seem to be fertile ground for research, particularly because other research shows that the media consistently conflate Muslims with terrorism. The research that has been done suggests that Muslims have largely perceived media coverage of terrorism cases as associating Islam with terrorism, and this has had direct ramifications for them. Ahmad (2006) explores the responses of British Muslims to the media reportage of the events of 9/11. He interviewed 17 people and found that they perceived there was a 'Eurocentric and US bias in the Western media' and they had 'a profound belief that negative stereotyping, derogatory use of language and sensationalism in the early stages after the attacks contributed significantly to the noted increase in anti-Muslim attacks and resulted in infringements upon civil liberties' (Ahmad, 2006, p. 961).

Wicks (2006) showed video clips of television news stories about terrorism in the Middle East and Africa to groups of people from the Islamic, Jewish and Christian faiths in an effort to determine their emotional responses to the news frames in those stories. He found that, while participants in each of the groups showed similar emotional responses to the news stories, the emotional responses of the Muslims in the study 'appeared to be stimulated by narratives and images that may foster the stereotype that Islam is backward and Muslims are prone to violence' (Wicks, 2006, p. 261). Muedini (2009) interviewed 25 young Muslims living in the United States about a range of issues related to security after 9/11. In relation to their attitudes towards the media, his study reveals that the 'majority of Muslim students interviewed who were asked about the media said that it negatively portrayed Muslims and Islam' and they identified that the media conflated Islam with terrorism (Muedini, 2009, p. 51).

Australia's Muslim communities have responded in very different ways to the media coverage of terrorism cases (Aly, Balnaves and Chalon, 2007). After the terror attacks in the United States in 2001, Australia's Muslim communities reported 'high levels of fear of the possible repercussions of a terrorist attack and the impact on themselves, their families and the Muslim communities in Australia' (Aly, Balnaves and Chalon, 2007, pp. 251–252). Aly and colleagues asked participants in their research project whether they felt that they 'belong to a community that is viewed negatively by others' and 59 per cent of respondents responded in the affirmative (Aly, Balnaves and Chalon, 2007, pp. 251–252). Elsewhere Aly writes that 'the media discourse on terrorism has escalated into a voracious discourse that subsumes a range of issues involving Australian Muslims from the Cronulla riots in 2005 to controversial comments made by some Muslim religious figures' (2007, p. 28).

Aly identifies that Australian Muslims perceived the media 'as a defiantly anti-Muslim purveyor of social attitudes' and she finds this has resulted 'in Australian Muslims responding in ways which impact on their identity constructions' (2007, p. 35). She reveals that, among those Muslims who engaged with 'negative media messages that are perceived as anti-Muslim', there was a trend towards using these messages to position Muslim identity within a discourse of a 'shared sense of injustice' (Aly, 2007, p. 35). She identifies that they used a narrative of victimhood, which emphasized victimization because of their religion. However, Aly ascertains another response by some Muslims which was the opposite of the aforementioned one:

> On the other end of the spectrum are those Muslims who actively disengage with the media discourse, either out of necessity or choice. This type of response results in the creation of alternative narratives of belonging and the construction of alternative identities that are not framed by a shared sense of injustice but by a shared sense of citizenship.
>
> (2007, p. 35)

Participants in Aly's study also reveal that 'Arab media, the internet and conspiracy theories provided alternative discourses and afforded them opportunities to engage in alternative communicative spaces that did not perpetuate negative stereotypes of Muslims' (2007, pp. 35–36). They believe *Al Jazeera* and *Al Manar* provide a more balanced perspective of the Middle East than mainstream media.

Another study of Muslim communities in Australia finds that Muslims are overwhelmingly opposed to terrorism and highly likely to report suspicious activity to police, but are very mistrustful of the mass media (Rane et al., 2011). Rane and colleagues asked Muslim survey respondents whether 'the targeting of innocent civilians is never allowed in

Islam' (Rane et al., 2011). An overwhelming majority of 90 per cent agreed with the statement. Respondents were also asked how they would respond if they 'knew of a Muslim planning a terrorist attack in Australia'. Ninety-seven per cent of respondents expressed opposition, stating that they would either 'advise the person against committing the act' (17 per cent), 'report the person to a leader of the Muslim community' (24 per cent), or 'report the person to the police' (56 per cent) (Rane et al., 2011, p. 134). While Rane and colleagues identify considerable trust in law enforcement agencies among Muslims, the authors also find that Muslims express a significant lack of trust in the mass media and perceive the media as being the main cause of negative attitudes towards Muslims in Australia (2011). During the Haneef case, Muslim communities in Australia chose to refrain from making public comment until the police case fell apart and Haneef's innocence became more certain (Ewart, 2009). What is clear is that the media's focus on terrorism cases has, for many Australian Muslims, resulted in social exclusion.

Conclusion

In the years since 9/11, journalists around the world have had to try to come to terms with the complexities and impacts of anti-terror legislation on their ability to report terrorism-related stories and trials. These laws have been particularly challenging for journalists wanting to fulfill their fourth estate role. The rapid unfolding of events has posed difficulties for journalists unfamiliar with national security legislation. It is encouraging that some journalists are willing to work with authorities to ensure national security interests are protected, while informing the public of terrorism plots or threats within the established constraints. This indicates that there is potential for journalists and courts to work together without compromising national security or the public interest.

While reporting on terrorism cases is certainly in the public interest, it does tend to reinforce the perceived connection between Islam and terrorism, as many of the high-profile terrorism cases involve Muslims. Unfortunately, that acts of terrorism have been planned or conducted by Muslims under the banner of Islam has resulted in journalists having to report events as such. It is a matter of professional ethics that in such cases journalists not only remain open to explanations beyond religion but also transcend stereotypes and political rhetoric to uncover information that exposes the truth, as in the case of Dr Haneef. The overwhelming majority of Muslims globally reject terrorism and do not consider the targeting of civilians a legitimate form of *jihad*. Moreover, the Muslim world is currently charting a new course away from repression, political violence and authoritarianism towards freedom and democracy. That this process, which has come to be known as the Arab Spring, began as peaceful, non-violent, non-*jihadist*, even non-Islamist uprisings needs to inform our understanding of the contemporary Muslim world. It is to the Arab Spring that we turn in the next chapter.

6
The Arab Spring

Since the end of 2010 and the beginning of 2011, the world has witnessed popular uprisings against long-standing regimes in the Middle East and North Africa (MENA) region. To date these uprisings have resulted in the toppling of the Tunisian president Ben Ali, the Egyptian president Hosni Mubarak and the Libyan president Muammar Gaddafi. Other regimes in the region have been forced to make socio-political concessions and reforms. However, the situation in Syria has evolved from peaceful protests to a civil war that is now in its third year. Elections in Tunisia and Egypt have resulted in Islamic-oriented governments coming to power. In the case of Tunisia, the En-Nahda Party won the election but has been unable to maintain control in the face of social unrest and political opposition. In more spectacular fashion, Egypt's democratically elected government, led by the Freedom and Justice Party of the Muslim Brotherhood, has since been overthrown in a military coup, essentially returning Egypt to the rule of a military regime as has been the case since 1952.

These uprisings and revolutions have generated significant and ongoing discussion about the potential of social media to impact upon political reform and regime change. The toppling of the Tunisian and Egyptian dictators, Ben Ali and Mubarak, was even referred to as 'Twitter' and 'Facebook revolutions'. The Arab Spring also provides an important case study of the evolving relationship between mass and social media and professional and citizen-journalists. This chapter explores the emerging relationship between social media and mass media in the context of the Muslim world. It examines the role of mass and social media in informing the Western and Muslim publics about the uprisings and other events in the Muslim world. In so doing, this chapter considers how partnerships between mass media journalists and citizen-journalists using social media have resulted in a shift in the coverage of the Muslim world. This coverage appears to benefit from a focus on the context of the MENA region and experiences of its people told from their perspective. This coverage also seems to transcend previously dominant paradigms based on a clash of civilizations, orientalist discourse and stereotypical representations. However, it seems that optimism in this regard is short-lived. Western media became increasingly critical of the situation under Islamic-oriented governments. Western publics also began to express unfavorable views suggesting that Islam remains a concern for the West and that Islamophobia may be an enduring factor for Islam–West relations further into the 21st century.

Uprisings and revolutions

Adverse social, economic and political conditions mobilized people across the MENA region to go out on to the streets. However, those who made the uprisings effective were a range of other actors. Political opposition groups and unions assisted in organizing and mobilizing protests. NGOs and human rights groups played an important role in disseminating information about human rights abuses and lobbying Western governments to express their support for the uprisings. The involvement of NGOs and human rights groups was also central in the framing of the uprisings as social movements for freedom and democracy (Rane and Salem, 2012).

One of the aspects of the uprisings many would find remarkable is that they were framed as movements for freedom and democracy and not Islamist revolutions; they were non-violent and were not *jihadist*. The prevailing wisdom concerning the region was that only political Islam could unite and mobilize sufficient numbers for such uprisings to occur. That the movements were not framed as Islamist, or led by those identifiable as Islamists, is testament to the changing discourse and emerging trends in political thought across the Muslim world since the turn of the century. In this context, concepts, principles and values concerning justice, dignity, freedom and democracy have come to be seen as part of Islam's higher objectives, while such slogans as 'Islamic state' and 'Islamic solutions' have been discredited as lacking in substance and viability (Rane, 2011). This shift in thinking has created space for the emergence of social movements that are consistent with Islamic values and principles but without the modern conventional Islamist label and slogans. Consequently, the uprisings were more inclusive, comprised of Muslims and Christians as well as Islamists and secularists.

It is also noteworthy that the uprisings were not overtly anti-Western or anti-American; nor were they pro-Western or pro-American. The actions of protesters in uploading information in English and ensuring that news and images of the uprisings reached mainstream media suggests an awareness of the importance of support from Western governments. However, a tweet on the day Mubarak stepped down proclaimed: 'dear Western governments, you've been silent for 30 years supporting the regime that was oppressing us. Please don't get involved now #Jan25'. This tweet reverberated in the Twittersphere and was retweeted by other Twitter users 3764 times. Such sentiments are indicative of a newfound self-sufficiency among a new generation of Arabs inclined towards transcending the slogans and labels of previous generations (Rane and Salem, 2012).

While many elements of the uprisings suggest a break with tradition, even with the advent of social media, traditional indirect channels, namely the mass media, are no less relevant. Mainstream media played a critical role in disseminating news and images about the uprisings, and in putting them at the top of the news agenda they raise their prominence in the eye of the international community. The media were also profoundly important in the framing of the protests as pro-democracy and freedom movements, which gave them credibility and translated into support from Western publics and governments. As *Guardian* journalist Peter Beaumont noted, 'where social media had a major impact was conveying news to the outside world, bloggers and twitter users were able to transmit news bytes that would otherwise never make it to mainstream news media' (Beaumont, 2011, para. 48).

Since the turn of the century, those who study social movements have taken an increasing interest in the use of information and communication technologies or ICTs, including various forms of social media, and their implications for social movements (Van de Donk et al., 2004). The advent of such technologies raises important questions in respect to which channels will remain dominant in the diffusion of ideas, which in turn impacts on the operations, structure and identity of social movements (Van de Donk et al., 2004). Several years ago, when social media were still an emerging phenomenon, Rucht (2004) affirmed the critical role mass media continue to play in terms of how social movements are perceived and responded to. The Arab uprisings occurred at a time when social media were more prevalent. However, mass media were still the most dominant source of information about the uprisings, even for those in the MENA region. One notable study reveals that, among Egyptians, 81 per cent relied on Egyptian state television as their main source of information about the uprising, while another 63 per cent relied on *Al Jazeera*. Only 8 per cent relied on social media (Abu Dhabi Gallup Centre, 2011). Before proceeding to discuss the role of social media in detail, it is first necessary to discuss *Al Jazeera* and the critical role it played in laying the foundations for shared information and consciousness in the MENA region, which eventually led to the Arab Spring.

Al Jazeera

In the 21st century *Al Jazeera* offers an emerging global public sphere within which to discuss and debate political and social matters. Based in Qatar, *Al Jazeera* was founded in 1996 by Sheikh Hamad bin Thamer Al Thani (Zayani, 2008). Intended to replace the BBC Arabic language station, *Al Jazeera* provided an alternative to previously heavily censored and nation-based news organizations (Allied Media Corp., 2013). Sheikh Hamad's support of freedom of the press is demonstrated in his 1997 speech vowing to allow *Al Jazeera* to report at will and that 'some discomfort for government officials is a small price to pay for this new freedom' (Allied Media Corp., 2013, para. 1). Latching on to this new sense of media freedom in the Middle East, *Al Jazeera* began and continues to present strongly alternative views in the form of news programs, sports and documentaries. Being the first independent Arab news channel to report the news of the Arab world, the network was widely influential and revolutionary in its reporting of previously ignored human rights issues (Parks, 2007).

Though having been established five years prior, it was not until 2001 that the network was acknowledged on a global scale. It gained the world's attention when, after the 9/11 attacks, the network broadcast pre-recorded videos of Osama Bin Laden and Al-Qaeda. Despite the videos being rebroadcast on a number of American and international networks, *Al Jazeera* was slandered by the then current US President Bush as being the 'mouthpiece of Osama Bin Laden' (Parks, 2007, p. 227). With a permanent base in Kabul, the network continued to gain attention as the only network providing live coverage of the Afghan war. Likewise, it was quickly noted that the reporting style of such issues differed from that of its American counterparts, as a new level of cultural understanding of the MENA region was now being brought to the fore (Parks, 2007). Through the *Al Jazeera* coverage, a new and grisly look at the US invasion was now being made available internationally (Parks, 2007).

As of 2013, the network claims to broadcast to over 220 million households in over 100 countries (*Al Jazeera*, 2013). The network publicizes that the majority of its (over 65) bureaus are located in the Global South (*Al Jazeera*, 2013). *Al Jazeera* is comprised of more than 20 channels and is the most watched news channel on YouTube, with 2.5 million views monthly (*Al Jazeera*, 2013). *Al Jazeera* English was launched in 2006, providing another international news channel for the network which sought to bring global coverage and awareness of stories coming from underdeveloped regions (*Al Jazeera*, 2012). The popularity of this network in the West is reflected in that nearly 40 per cent of all its online viewing comes from the United States (*Al Jazeera* America, 2013). In response to such demand, in January 2013 the media network announced it would be launching yet another channel based within the United States; *Al Jazeera* America (*Al Jazeera* America, 2013).

Most scholars acknowledge the important revolutionary role of *Al Jazeera* in the media landscape of the Arab world. Essentially, *Al Jazeera* filled a previously vacant role, providing common information and a common consciousness for all people across the MENA region. Both Mellor (2012) and Parks (2007) highlight that *Al Jazeera* has rewritten a history which was previously only perceived from a Western viewpoint. The network has been credited with a fair reporting style and news-gathering techniques, particularly in regard to the Iraq war, and in particular the contentious battle of Fallujah (Mellor, 2012). This is said to have strengthened its credibility in respect to the network fulfilling a fourth estate or 'watchdog' role vis-à-vis other media and government institutions in the region (Mellor, 2012, p. 103). Likewise, *Al Jazeera*'s incorporation of the cultural and regional representation of the MENA is often discussed. Both Mellor (2012) and Parks (2007) note that the network's cultural knowledge and background establishes a sense of authority when covering stories from such regions. Similarly, *Al Jazeera*'s encouragement of a common cultural and regional pride is noted by Barkho (2011). Through his analysis of its design, discourse and social strategies, Barkho comments on *Al Jazeera*'s step away from the Anglo-Saxon mannerisms of its BBC counterpart. This attitude appears to be welcomed by the Arabic-speaking world, as, according to Miladi (2006), *Al Jazeera* is the most trusted network, more than CNN or BBC, especially following the events of 9/11.

Within scholarly discourse, however, there is also prominent criticism of the network and its operations. Concerning issues of political violence and terrorism, the network is criticized for focusing on and reiterating 'official positions' of the powers that be and thus overlooking the 'humanitarian sufferings' that have occurred (Zeng and Tahat, 2011, p. 433). Further questioning of the network's relationship with such powers and the independence of the network is likewise examined where Pintak and Ginges (2009) explore the perception of the Arab media from the viewpoint of Arab journalists. Since *Al Jazeera*'s launch, the Arab media landscape has undergone a great shift in respect to both the qualitative and quantitative coverage now accessible to audiences in the MENA region. Despite an initial determination to transcend state-controlled media, it is argued that *Al Jazeera* has succumbed to commercial and political interests, most notably in respect to the network's softer stance and commentary concerning Saudi Arabia from 2007 onwards (Pintak and Ginges, 2009). Just as political control of Arab state media enhanced the demand for *Al Jazeera*, the network's actual or perceived tempering by commercial and political forces has contributed to the rise in demand for social media in the MENA region.

Social media in the MENA region

Historically, government sponsorship and control of the mass media has ensured that ruling regimes in the MENA region had a monopoly over the information and ideas that define the region's states and societies. This was first challenged by the advent of satellite television networks like *Al Jazeera*, which not only presented alternate information that contradicted official government propaganda, but also acted as a fourth estate, provided citizens across the region with common content, and helped to construct a common consciousness. However, some observers suggest that Arab satellite channels 'may still pose a challenge, but it is not a major one, as everybody has made the necessary compromises' (Da Lage, 2010, para. 16). Now governments in the MENA region have come to recognize that their control over the masses is rapidly being undermined by the adoption of social media. Consequently, most are using a range of laws to justify arresting, fining and imprisoning online activists who challenge the status quo. As of 2013, the Arab world was estimated to have over 125 million internet users (Dubai School of Government, 2013). Already this has surpassed previous predictions that the MENA region would have over 100 million internet users by 2015 (Ghannam, 2011).

To suggest that social media were primarily responsible for the uprisings across the MENA region or the ensuing revolutions is an overstatement. Although undoubtedly increasing at a rapid rate, social media use in the region is still only emerging. As of May 2013 there were more than 54 million Facebook users in the Arab world, yet, at the time of many of the uprisings, this number was closer to 20 million (Arab Social Media Report, 2013). Alongside this, the national average for Facebook penetration was only 7 per cent for the region when the uprisings first began in 2010. As identified by the Arab Social Media Report (2012), in some countries Facebook penetration was relatively high, such as in UAE (45 per cent), Bahrain (34 per cent), Qatar (34 per cent), Lebanon (23 per cent) and Kuwait (20 per cent). In others, Facebook penetration was more modest: Tunisia (18 per cent), Jordan (17 per cent), Saudi Arabia (12 per cent) and Palestine (11 per cent). Lower Facebook penetration rates were found in Oman (8 per cent), Morocco (8 per cent), Egypt (5 per cent), Algeria (4 per cent), Libya (4 per cent), Iraq (1 per cent), Syria (1 per cent) and Yemen (1 per cent) (Arab Social Media Report, 2012). Egypt had the largest proportion of Facebook users in the region (22 per cent), followed by Saudi Arabia (15 per cent), Morocco (11 per cent), UAE (10 per cent), Tunisia (8 per cent) and Algeria (7 per cent) (Salem and Mourtada, 2011). These figures alone deny a positive correlation between social media use and the emergence of the Arab Spring. Indeed, more collective action has been witnessed in countries with lower Facebook penetration than in most of those with higher rates of Facebook penetration (Rane and Salem, 2012).

The uptake of social media such as Facebook is due largely to the MENA region's youthful population (Ghannam, 2011; Salem and Mourtada, 2011). The main demographic using Facebook was, and still is, those aged 30 and below (68 per cent) (Arab Social Media Report, 2013). This is significant as, according to the UN Population Database, the majority of the population in most countries in the region are aged under 25: Yemen (65 per cent), Iraq (60 per cent), Syria (55 per cent), Jordan (54 per cent), Egypt (52 per cent) and Saudi Arabia (51 per cent). In others, including Morocco, Algeria, Libya, Iran, Bahrain and Tunisia, between 40 and 49 per cent of the population are aged under 25. This will mean that more people in the region will become connected to the tools that are important for the facilitation of collective action.

Since the start of 2012, Facebook users in the MENA region have increased by 29 per cent, and the region is home to 44 million monthly active Facebook users (4 per cent of the world's total). Age is the main factor positively correlating with Facebook penetration, with no reliable correlation between Facebook penetration and either per capita income, digital access, internet freedom or even internet access (Salem and Mourtada, 2011). Social media penetration is not a predictor of whether an uprising will emerge, let alone whether it will evolve into a revolution. As put by one activist, it is not 'as if the social, economic and political problems the people are protesting against would disappear if only the media would stop talking about them' (Harb, 2011, para. 16). However, these figures do indicate that social media will become increasingly prominent in the MENA region. Moreover, the reputation that social media have acquired in the region since the uprisings began will also contribute to their further penetration. Social media use will continue to grow and expand, with the number of social network users in the Middle East and Africa as of 2013 surpassing totals in North America, Western Europe and Central and Eastern Europe (European Travel Commission, 2013).

Aside from Facebook, Twitter has proven increasingly important to the Arab region, with the total number of active Twitter users reaching almost 4 million as of March 2013. The Arab Social Media Report Series provides a useful overview of Twitter users in the region, and finds that the country with the current highest number of active Twitter users is Saudi Arabia, with 1.9 million users. This accounts for over half of all active Twitter users in the Arab region. At the beginning of the Arab Spring, while Twitter use was relatively low, it was accessed by many protesters and activists wishing to disseminate information. More than anything, Twitter provided a dynamic and powerful tool with which to spread information and discuss political matters. Although it is not the 'maker of political revolutions', Twitter does have the power to be at the vanguard of a media revolution in the Arab world (Blake, 2011, p. 20).

The uprisings that have occurred across the MENA region share a number of common elements. In all the countries involved, authoritarian regimes have ruled for decades over their citizens, who have been denied basic social and political rights and freedoms; they have also been humiliated and oppressed by corrupt institutions and brutal security forces. In most cases, there is widespread poverty as well as high unemployment and underemployment. Additionally, in most cases, the uprisings were triggered by a tragic event or injustice. It should also be noted, however, that one uprising provided inspiration for the next. Together, these factors were the catalyst for collective action. That a critical mass of citizens was mobilized in each of the countries where uprisings have been significant is indicative of widespread repression and grievances with the status quo.

Other critical factors involved in the successful mobilization of protesters included overcoming the fear factor concerning the brutality of police and security forces; being inspired by counterparts in the region and nationally placing their lives on the line, and being shocked by the loss of life; and government attempts to block access to the internet and other communication services (Musleh, 2011). One social media specialist contends that the Egyptian government's decision to block access to the internet actually resulted in more young Egyptians going out into the streets to actively protest rather than passively protesting online from their bedrooms (Musleh, 2011).

Overall, social media's key role in the uprisings was in the facilitation of communication and the transfer of information. This included communication between protesters concerning the mobilization of communities, as well as assistance and advice in relation to non-violent tactics, medical treatment and overcoming internet restrictions and blocks. Social media also enabled protesters to function as citizen-journalists by disseminating information about the protests and the responses of police and security forces and transmitting news, photos and videos to mainstream media for wider distribution (Rane and Salem, 2012). The following section of this chapter examines the socio-political conditions in selected Arab nations where uprisings have occurred and the use of social media among protesters.

Revolutions: Tunisia and Egypt

Events in Tunisia evolved in response to the self-immolation of a young Tunisian vendor named Mohammad Bouazizi. His desperate act symbolized Tunisian frustration with the corruption, injustice and brutality of the ruling regime. Over one-third of the Tunisian population are connected to the internet and almost one-fifth use Facebook (Salem and Mourtada, 2011). Like Facebook, Twitter also played a prominent role in the revolution. The Twitter hashtag #SidiBouzid was used by Tunisian activists and tweeted over 200,000 times in the first few weeks of protests.

While some have referred to the revolution in Tunisia as the first 'Twitter revolution', others have pointed out that prior to the revolution Tunisia had only 200 active tweeters and only 2000 registered accounts (Beaumont, 2011). The moniker of 'Facebook revolution' has also been raised, which is more fitting in the case of Tunisia, as even before the uprising there were two million users of Facebook (Khondker, 2011). However, despite doubts that these were social media revolutions, the role of social media in informing and mobilizing Tunisians cannot be denied. Mohammad Bouazizi's self-immolation is said to have been the spark that ignited the Tunisian revolution, but he was not the first Tunisian to self-immolate. Three months earlier another Tunisian from Monastir performed the same act, but it was not filmed, not on Facebook, not widely disseminated and, therefore, did not inspire collective action (Khondker, 2011). Likewise, as cited by Khondker (2011), Tufekci explains that the protest movements of 2008 – when Facebook user penetration was at only 28,000 individuals – failed to gain momentum and were ultimately crushed. In the case of Tunisia, a greater level of social media use occurred in response to the self-immolation of Bouazizi, which coincided with an expansion of collective action (Tufekci cited in Khondker, 2011).

Turning to Egypt, about 36 per cent of the population are connected to the internet, and the country represents more than one-quarter of all Facebook users in the region (Freedom House, 2012a; Arab Social Media Report, 2013). However, proportionally, social media penetration is still relatively low. Egypt is classified as an 'emerging country', with only 13.1 per cent of Egypt's total population using Facebook and approximately 300,000 active Twitter users (Arab Social Media Report, 2012, p. 10). At the beginning of the uprising in Egypt, these numbers were even lower, and overall internet penetration was at only one-quarter of the country's population. In spite of a relatively low level of social media penetration, the social movement for freedom and democracy in Egypt evolved into a revolution that forced Mubarak from power.

Egyptians were inspired and encouraged by the events in Tunisia. Facebook pages such as 'Egyptian supporting the Tunisian revolution' are indicative of this phenomenon. Tunisians and Egyptians shared similar grievances with their respective governments concerning social, economic and political conditions. The uprising in Egypt also had its own trigger, the brutal killing of a young man named Khalid Said by Egyptian police. Activists in Egypt used the Twitter hashtag #Jan25 as well as Facebook pages 'We are all Khalid Said' in Arabic and English to mobilize collective action. Said was a blogger and the attack occurred after he was dragged from an internet cafe, which makes the slogan all the more poignant. As of the time of Mubarak's fall from power, the Arabic version of this Facebook page had over 1,200,000 fans and the English version had over 100,000 fans. At the same point in time, the Twitter hashtag #Jan25 had almost two million tweets (Rane and Salem, 2012).

In Egypt, activists were able to build on earlier social movements such as the April 6 Movement. Social media were also used for spreading practical and tactical information from Tunisian to Egyptian activists, such as tips on medical treatment for exposure to tear gas and making homemade tear gas masks. Geographical locations such as Tahrir Square were not only important as gathering points for protests and the symbolic value that the image of such large numbers of people provided; they were also were critical in practical terms, as they functioned as online hubs from which information was filmed and uploaded to the internet and disseminated to mainstream media. One activist summarizes the use of new media in the popularly reposted tweet: 'we use Facebook to schedule the protests, Twitter to coordinate, and YouTube to tell the world' (Chebib and Sohail, 2011, p. 139).

The authorities in both Egypt and Tunisia responded to the protests by blocking access to social media, disrupting text messaging services and even attempting to prevent *Al Jazeera* from covering the events. Social media became even more relevant and were used by online activists as a means of transferring codes and information to assist others to overcome internet blocks and access proxy servers. Google also assisted with the provision of its Voice2Tweet service. Attempts by the ruling regime to discredit the movement as rogue trouble-makers, Islamists, criminals or even terrorists failed to gain traction in the mainstream media and certainly failed to disrupt the tide of social media activity. In fact, the status of social media as the conveyer of the accurate and honest picture of unfolding events was strengthened in the face of such government propaganda campaigns (Zuckerman, 2011).

In the case of both Tunisia and Egypt, it took only a few weeks of collective action to force Ben Ali and Mubarak to step down. Why did regime change occur by way of non-violent protests in these cases but not in Libya or Syria or Iran in 2009? The answer has little to do with social media. Part of the explanation is the pro-Western orientation of Tunisia and especially Egypt. Television screens of Western audiences were filled with scenes of non-violent mass protests initiated by young non-sectarian, non-Islamists calling for freedom, democracy and basic human rights. This framing of the uprisings left the United States with little option but to be supportive, or at least not openly oppose the democratization of the MENA region. Moreover, the international media spotlight on these revolutions restrained the governments of Tunisia and Egypt in terms of the level of force the United States could permit them to employ against unarmed peaceful protesters. However, in the case of Libya, Syria, Iran and other regimes in the region, the United States does not have the leverage to encourage restraint against protesters or to persuade leaders that their time is up (Rane and Salem, 2012).

Western support for democracy in the MENA region remains questionable following the fall of Ben Ali and Mubarak. Following the toppling of these long-standing dictators in Tunisia and Egypt, democratic elections have been held which have resulted in Islamic-oriented parties coming to power in both countries. In Tunisia the largest plurality of votes was won by the En-Nahda Party, while in Egypt the political party of the Muslim Brotherhood, the Freedom and Justice Party, won a majority of votes. The leaders of both emphasized their respective party's commitment to the principles of democracy and their respect for the will of their people, which were widely reported in the Western media. The euphoria for the Arab Spring was not immediately replaced with the old orientalist reporting about the potential fate set to befall the Arab countries led by Islamist parties. Rather, there was, for a time, some acknowledgement from the mainstream Western media that the Islamic parties that have come to power are moderate and genuinely committed to democracy – at least up until the recent tensions that have arisen once more in both countries, especially Egypt. Since the election of the Muslim Brotherhood candidate, Mohammad Morsi, as Egypt's president in June 2012, Western media coverage has focused on the ongoing tensions and intermittent conflict between Egypt's Coptic Christian and Muslim communities, Islamic and secular parties, and the old and new regimes. When Morsi was overthrown in what was ostensibly a military coup in July 2013, the Western media generally followed the lead of Western governments in raising little objection and even avoiding the term 'military coup' to describe the events.

For the most part, Western perceptions of Egypt have been largely favorable, with positive ratings of the country at about 60 per cent for the last few decades. With the election of a Muslim Brotherhood-led government, however, Egypt's ratings fell dramatically, with Americans expressing only around 36 per cent favorable views of Egypt. This reflects the current renewed tension in Egypt, where religion, democracy and liberalism are contested within the state. While many Americans initially felt 'hopeful' that the Arab Spring would 'bring about some positive change in societies and governances across the Arab World', in 2013 only 14 per cent of Americans continued to feel hopeful, with 42 per cent saying they were 'disappointed' (Zogby, 2013, p. 2). Views on the Muslim Brotherhood differ, with only 4 per cent of Americans in 2013 saying that the Muslim Brotherhood victory was a positive development. Rather than the conflict and tension previously being framed within the concepts of democracy and freedom, religion has been brought more heavily into the discourse surrounding Egypt. Consequently, when asked about the 'first thought that comes to mind when you think of the Muslim Brotherhood', the most popular responses were those such as 'anti-American', 'dangerous', 'terrorists', 'fanatics' and 'extremists' (Zogby, 2013, p. 4).

Finding what accounts for this swift change in attitude from the start of the Arab Spring to the present situation is difficult and embedded in a number of different factors. Regarding the Muslim Brotherhood and its role in Egypt's governance, the most negative views from Americans are noted when they are asked whether the group is democratic or not. A majority of respondents say that the group is not committed to democracy. Another key finding of Zogby's (2013) study is that almost 90 per cent believe that US support should be conditional on the requirement that governments protect the rights of all their citizens, whether that government was democratically elected or not. This demonstrates that at the core of the current negative views of Egypt are humanitarian concerns and perceptions that the rights and liberties of Egyptian citizens would not be fully protected under an Islamic-oriented government. Although the media seem to have focused on the politics, protests and attacks, polls such as Zogby's (2013) imply that audience concern is firmly rooted in a concern with Islam in politics, which suggests the enduring relevance of orientalism and Islamophobia.

The relevance of geopolitics: Libya and Bahrain

Libya is another example where limited internet connectivity and social media penetration have not inhibited the emergence of social movements demanding political reform and regime change. Only 6 per cent of Libyans were connected to the internet and fewer than 5 per cent of the population used Facebook in 2011. However, some sources indicate that internet penetration could now be as high as 17 per cent (Salem and Mourtada, 2011; Freedom House, 2012b). For Libya, the past several years have seen a dramatic shift in regard to internet access, and the government only recently relinquished the monopoly on providing internet services. Despite heavy restrictions, Libyan protesters using the Twitter hashtag #Feb17 called for protests to begin on that date. As an indication that the uprisings in Tunisia and Egypt inspired others, such as in Libya, the following tweet was popularly retweeted to the extent that it was even broadcast on mainstream television news: 'My name is freedom. Born in Tunisia, raised in Egypt, studies in Yemen, fought in Libya and I'll grow up in the Arab world' (@AliTweel, Twitter). Libyans not only drew inspiration and ideas from the Egyptians, but they also assisted through the provision of SIM cards, passed across the border so that the Libyan protesters could maintain lines of communication in spite of government blocks, disruptions and interference (Beaumont, 2011).

Libya's social movement for freedom and democracy maintained corresponding pages on Facebook, which within a week of the first protests had attracted 82,000 followers. Additionally, within the same period, the Facebook news page for the Libyan uprisings, RNN Libya, had over 22,000 followers. This number doubled within weeks. Libyan activists also utilized dedicated websites such as www.libyafeb17.com, onto which were uploaded images and news in English that could be accessed by a global audience, including Western media. Interviews conducted with Libyan activists suggest that they were inspired by the events in Tunisia and Egypt, as well as images and information which were widely circulated among Libyans through social media (Channel 4 News, 2011). Libyan activists also relied on Libyan diaspora networks, such as the Libyan Youth Movement based in the United Kingdom, to present to the Western world not only the brutality of the Gaddafi regime but also the humanity of Libya's people (Rane and Salem, 2012).

It is noteworthy, however, that Libya's non-violent social movement for freedom and democracy was relatively quickly overtaken by armed resistance fighters, which increased the uncertainty of the uprising. The outcome in Libya was significant for all in the region. Had Gaddafi prevailed, a strong signal would have been sent to other regimes in the region that the lethal suppression of the uprisings would be tolerated by the international community and would result in regime preservation.

Following the international community's recognition of the anti-Gaddafi rebel group, the National Transitional Council (NTC), NATO initiated military operations in support of the NTC's bid to overthrow the Gaddafi regime. Gaddafi having been a leader who had long attracted the ire of Western powers and had also languished out of favor with most Arab regimes, the opportunity to replace his regime was met with little opposition in the MENA region and was welcomed by Western governments, particularly the United States. In this respect, the case of Libya contrasts sharply with that of Bahrain, where geopolitical considerations were strongly in favor of maintaining the status quo.

The case of Bahrain is significant not only in terms of the potential impact and limitations of social media but also in terms of the critical role of international politics in determining those uprisings that might evolve into revolutions and those that will not. The Bahrain uprising used the Twitter hashtag #Feb14 to mark the date when protests there began. Twitter, as well as blog sites such as Global Voices, was used to collate information and images and disseminate them to the diaspora community and the international media. It is noteworthy that, although over half of Bahrain's population were connected to the internet and over one-third of Bahrainis were Facebook users (the second highest proportion in the Arab world), their uprising did not attract international attention to the same extent as others in the region (Salem and Mourtada, 2011; Arab Social Media Report, 2013).

A large part of the explanation is the relatively limited support and less prominent coverage from satellite television networks, namely *Al Jazeera*. There is a political dimension in this case, as Qatari foreign policy is committed to Gulf Cooperation Council security agreements. Observers have also noted the muted voice of the United States in respect to Bahrain. Given that Bahrain has a majority Shiite population ruled by a Sunni minority, there was some concern in the United States, and especially Saudi Arabia, that a transfer to democracy would result in another state in the region over which Iran would be influential. As Bahrain has not had the same degree of international media attention or support as Egypt, for instance, the United States is arguably less pressured in terms of supporting regime change. Another factor is that the Gulf Cooperation Council countries, particularly Saudi Arabia, are strongly opposed to a precedent of regime change, and especially a Gulf monarchy being replaced with a democratic government. Consequently, US relations with Saudi Arabia, based on a commitment to the political security of the ruling regime in return for a secure and stable supply of oil, preclude US support for regime change in Bahrain (Rane and Salem, 2012).

Civil war: Syria

While one-fifth of Syria's population were connected to the internet, only 1 per cent used Facebook in the heat of the uprising (Salem and Mourtada, 2011). This should not suggest, however, that a lack of social media penetration is necessarily a factor in Syria's initially stalled uprising. In early February 2011, Facebook pages calling for protests to be held in Syria on 4 and 5 February attracted about 15,000 fans, and not only did they fail to mobilize demonstrators for the 'day of anger', but pages opposed to the protests and in support of the government attracted comparable support. However, the social movement for freedom and democracy in Syria gained serious momentum from late April 2011. By mid-2011, the Facebook page 'Syria Revolution 2011' had almost 200,000 fans, and protests continued for months across the country.

Like other regimes in the region, the government in Syria insists that the unrest was the work of armed terrorist gangs backed by Islamists and foreign agitators (Rane and Salem, 2012). While such propaganda was not widely believed even in Syria, there are a number of important factors that initially inhibited collective action and a speedy revolution. First, poverty and unemployment levels are not as high in Syria as in other countries such as Egypt. Second, unlike Egypt, Syria's foreign policy, particularly in relation to Israel, is largely consistent with the will of the people. Third, in contrast to the aging dictators who had ruled Tunisia and Egypt for decades in almost complete disregard for the needs and aspirations of their people, Syria has a younger leader who has made economic and infrastructural reforms since taking over from his father. Fourth, Syria's population is over 70 per cent Sunni, while Shiites, including Alawites, comprise almost 15 per cent, and another 10 per cent are Christian. Syria also has a significant Kurdish population, among other ethnic minority groups. Syrians are intimately familiar with the civil unrest that has previously plagued Lebanon and now Iraq since the fall of Saddam Hussein; they are acutely aware of the dangers of sectarian divisions that can become enflamed in the midst of a power vacuum. These factors caused Syrians to hesitate in supporting a social movement for freedom and democracy (Rane and Salem, 2012).

Syrians were initially hesitant to put peace and stability at risk for ideals that are still yet to be fully realized in either Tunisia or Egypt. However, by mid-2011, the protest movement in Syria gained significant support among the population. The government and military responded with brutal force, which ultimately undermined the legitimacy of the Assad regime at home and abroad. Regional powers, such as Turkey, with which Syria had positive relations, also called on Assad to step aside. Turkey has also sheltered hundreds of thousands of Syrian refugees and actively supports the Syrian opposition. While Assad was never portrayed positively in the Western media, an important shift in the coverage of Syria has been a focus on the humanity of its people and the support for their struggle for democracy. However, the widespread concern that Al-Qaeda fighters are among the ranks of those fighting the Assad regime has weakened Western media and public support and prevented Western governments from providing more substantial support, including the provision of weapons, to the Free Syrian Army.

This is particularly poignant as, at the time of writing, the news media have been filled with stories and images of the most recent events in the conflict – the deadly gas bombing of over 1000 people near Damascus. Syria's main opposition group has accused the government of the massacre, yet full details are still emerging. Commenting on Western reactions to this, Halla Diyab, a spokesperson for the Organization of Freedom and Democracy in Syria, stated:

> What is the objective of the intervention of the West? Is it to get rid to Bashar al-Assad? Or is it to help Syrians to achieve democracy and freedom? Or is just because Bashar al-Assad has used chemical weapons? There should be [an] investigation and tangible evidence that the regime has used chemical weapons; [they should] not base their claims on YouTube videos that have not been verified.
>
> (*Al Jazeera*, 2013, para. 1)

More than anything, his comments highlight the fact that, while much information and perceptions can be garnered from social media's reporting of Syria, it is hard to sift facts from fiction. Footage leaked through social media platforms is being questioned, and where Syria's government and Western governments move from here will be important. Social media are again likely to provide an important platform for information dissemination, yet mass media will be pivotal in authenticating, legitimizing and promoting such claims and information and, in turn, influencing the international community's response to the situation in Syria. However, the situation in Syria has increasingly become a propaganda war for both sides, which has led professional journalists to question the wisdom of relying on opposition activists on the ground. *The Global Mail* journalist Jess Hill observes that 'amid the growing fog of war, it's becoming harder to tell the difference between truth, rumor and spin' (Hill, 2012, para. 1). This chapter now turns to the issue of professional and citizen journalism in the Arab Spring.

Professional and citizen journalism

The Arab uprisings of 2011 were remarkable from the perspective of Western media coverage for a number of reasons. For most of the current generation of Western correspondents in the region, this was their first experience in covering a major story in which neither the United States nor Israel was the protagonist. These correspondents had mostly spent the last decade covering the Iraq war, and they and their organizations had viewed the MENA through the prism of the 'war on terror' and the US-led conflict in Iraq. Demand for coverage of the war in Iraq meant that many of the correspondents based in the region covered very little else for the duration of that conflict. The conditions for

Western reporters in Iraq through much of the war meant that most lived in guarded compounds and either worked with private security contractors or were only allowed by their organizations to be embedded with the American military when in the field. With a few very notable exceptions, most Western media coverage in Iraq, particularly through the worst years of the sectarian bloodletting from 2005 until 2007, was exclusively from the perspective of the United States and what it was trying to achieve in Iraq. Many news organizations employed local Iraqi reporters to basically cover the war for them, going out to bombsites and seeking witnesses to quote. By late 2004, the level of hate directed at foreigners in Iraq because of opposition to the US occupation, the tactics of the insurgency, particularly kidnapping, and the splintered non-hierarchical and sectarian divide among those fighting the Americans meant that covering the violence in Iraq and covering Iraqi society was very difficult for even the best-intentioned reporter. It was the era of what seasoned British correspondent Robert Fisk in 2005 called 'mouse journalism', when reporters had to virtually hide themselves in Baghdad to be able to stay there (Fisk, 2006).

If you fast-forward to 2011 and read the same journalists covering the Arab uprisings, you can get a sense of how the changed dynamic between the reporters and those they were reporting on affected perceptions and coverage. Russian photographer Yuri Kozyrev worked for *Time* magazine through the entirety of the Iraq war. He was also the only photographer to cover all of the uprisings in 2011. He told *Euronews* about being one of the first Westerners to arrive in Benghazi after Gaddafi's overthrow in that town: 'they didn't know there was going to be a civil war yet. It was just an enormous celebration and we were part of it. It was incredible. From one celebration to another from Tahrir square to another square' (*Euronews*, 2011). Kozyrev made this statement during an interview in Perpignan at the International Festival of Photojournalism, where he was awarded the Gold Visa award in 2011 for his work covering the uprisings. Foreign journalists were welcomed by the rebels in Benghazi, as they were in Egypt, Bahrain, Yemen and, later, Syria. The uprisings were the first time since 2001 and the so-called 'war on terror' that the Western media were not perceived as being in support of US policies in the region. Talking about the photos that secured him the award, Kozyrev said: 'each man has their own history and that is what I would love to see and hear again' (*Euronews*, 2011). Such personal reporting and connection with the subjects was possible for Western reporters covering the Arab Spring simply because they were welcomed by those protesting. This quickly marginalized the conservative commentators in the Western media, who continued to warn of the dangers of Islamic rule emerging in the region even as the regimes of Mubarak and Gaddafi used that same reason to justify their respective security crackdowns. A reporter like Yuri Kozyrev, employed by a well-known US magazine such as *Time*, was no longer seen by the protesters as representing an aggressive foreign intervention, as had been the case in Iraq, where since 2004 he had been forced to live and work with armed guards for his safety.

Cairo-based senior CNN international correspondent Ben Wedeman described these scenes when he was one of the Western correspondents to drive into the rebel-held areas of Libya in February 2011:

> Every step along the way, through the various towns and cities we passed through, was a mind-bending scene because as the first jour-nalists to arrive we were treated as if we were actually liberating the country. In some areas, even in the middle of the night, our car was just mobbed by hundreds of people throwing dates and cheering us and thanking us.
>
> (Marshall, 2011, para. 4)

He also found that, even though foreign journalists were demonized in the state media by the Gaddafi regime, it was still possible to talk to people who did not support the rebels:

> When we would go to towns that were 'liberated by the rebels' I always tried to seek out people who weren't cheering, who weren't celebrating the arrival of the new regime, just to get their opinion and I was always impressed by the civility of these people in speaking with us because the media under Muammar Gaddafi, certainly dur-ing the uprising, would often describe foreign journalists as spies, as collaborating with Al-Qaeda, but these people who were sympathetic to Gaddafi were polite and willing and able to explain the reasoning for their support for him. Whatever story you cover it's important to try to listen to the other side, you don't have to agree with it.
>
> (Marshall, 2011, para. 10)

The fact that Wedeman is an Arabic speaker with ten years' experience living in Cairo allowed his reporting to be far more intimate with the people on the ground than many other commentators. CNN, *Al Jazeera* and NPR all won prestigious Peabody awards for their coverage of the Arab Spring in 2011.

The access enjoyed by Western media crews in the rebel-held areas of Libya at the start of the conflict was unprecedented. As visas were unnecessary for the correspondents traveling overland from Egypt, the decision to travel to the rebel-held areas was based on that access. However, at that time correspondents who had entered with no visa were subject to arrest by Gaddafi's forces if they fell into their hands, further increasing their dependence and reliance on the rebel forces and thus their identification with them in their coverage. It was during this initial phase of tight control over the news media by Gaddafi that the availability of footage from those posting videos on YouTube provided the visual material to allow mainstream news services to continue to cover the story. The utilization of mobile phone footage of demonstrations, and in some cases shooting by pro-Gaddafi forces, simply gave the international networks such as CNN, BBC and *Al Jazeera* something to talk over as they analyzed the latest developments with their usually hotel-bound correspondents in Tripoli, who were subject to tight government control and restrictions on what they could film and where they could go.

The significance of social media in the coverage of the Arab Spring has been overplayed in some media and academic analyses in terms of the dynamic between the local population and the international media. Each uprising presented different logistical challenges to the media endeavoring to report on events such as visa restrictions, intimidation by government forces and, in some countries, even incarceration and death. The figures for 2011 alone speak for themselves. In Tunisia: one journalist killed, 11 assaulted and six imprisoned. In Egypt: one journalist killed, 84 assaulted and 85 journalists and bloggers questioned. In Libya: five journalists killed, 32 imprisoned, 15 kidnapped and 30 forced to leave the country. In Bahrain: one blogger killed, one newspaper founder killed, 36 journalists imprisoned or interrogated, 40 forced resignations and six expelled. In Syria: 84 journalists imprisoned and seven expelled in 2011 and two journalists killed in 2012 (Reporters Without Borders, 2011). In all these countries it has been the media that have been subject to restrictions and obstructions as unsubtle as the targeted rocket attack on the makeshift press office in February 2012 in the Syrian city of Homs that killed US reporter Marie Colvin and French cameraman Remi Ochlik. Social media and the use of media uploaded by those involved in protests is simply the new version of the smuggled footage that journalists used to chase when trying to report on regimes that denied them access.

In all these countries the role of social networks and the uploading of camera phone footage have provided a way for the international media to gain an insight and specifically to obtain images of events and places they are excluded from. This simple technological development allows mainstream media to access the raw footage they need to tell the story of events that are trying to be hidden by the governments imposing restrictions on the media for that same reason. The change which has been of greater significance in terms of Western media coverage of the uprisings of 2011 is the identification with and reporting of those who are demonstrating for change. The simple security realities for the reporters on the ground in places like Libya in 2011 and Syria in 2012 mean that they are faced by hostile regimes trying to prevent them from doing their jobs, and the only individuals they can rely on to assist them to get the story are from the opposition. In places like Syria they are relying on the opposition to help them save their own lives, and it is natural that they will be reporting from their perspective.

Foreign journalists trying to report on the uprising are seen by those protesting for change as essential for their demands to be publicized. It is a 180-degree change from the perception of foreign journalists held by, for example, a protesting Iraqi in 2004. Back then many Western journalists responded to the anger expressed against them as representatives of foreign occupation in Iraq by having to hide in fortified compounds and travel with armed guards, making it very hard to identify with the society they were supposed to be reporting on. The same journalists now find themselves reporting on and relying on the protesting populations in the face of hostile regimes, and this identification with their aims and their perspective has meant a shift in the coverage away from the old regimes' rhetoric of a fear of regime change due to the threat of Islamism. When the Western media finally went out to find out what the people of these countries wanted, it was not Islamism but a replacement of the regimes that had long used that threat as a way to retain Western backing for their regimes.

However, one lesson we are learning from the Arab Spring is that, as the uprisings descend into civil war and become more dangerous and intractable, it becomes increasingly difficult for journalists to report the reality in terms of the complete picture, including competing perspectives, images and information. It is illegal for reporters to enter Syria's conflict zones, and those who do so are targeted as 'terrorists' by the Syrian government (Hill, 2012). Middle East correspondent for *The Guardian*, Martin Chulov, reported that the situation in Syria is more dangerous for journalists than that previously experienced in Iraq or Libya (Hill, 2012, para. 6). Consequently, journalists reporting on Syria have come to rely on Syrian activists for information and footage of the conflict zone. Hill observes that 'about 75 per cent of news from inside Syria comes directly from activists, 10 to 15 per cent from Syrian state media, and a small percentage from "normal people" when, on the rare occasion the news team can find someone willing to speak' (2012, para. 7).

Not dissimilarly to the plight of journalists who were embedded with US military forces during the Iraq war, journalists in Syria have effectively embedded themselves with Syrian activists. The result is that journalists are completely reliant on their Syrian hosts for their safety, security, food, shelter, information and footage. They become impressed by their struggle and able to report only a specific perspective of the conflict. Hill asserts:

> the longer journalists are kept out of Syria, the more elusive that truth will become. In the short term at least, journalists have little choice but to continue to rely on activists for much of their information. The challenge for the media, however, is to go beyond the heroes versus villains narrative that's developed over the past year, and to interrogate some harder truths.
>
> Why, after a year of horrific violence, do significant number[s] of Syrians still support the regime, or at least the status quo? Why, after so long, have there still been no major defections from the government? And who are the armed opposition groups known as the Free Syrian Army?
>
> (2012, paras 51–52)

Conclusion

There is no positive correlation between levels of social media penetration and the emergence of social movements calling for political reform and regime change. Rather, the uprisings occurred in response to adverse social, economic and political conditions endured by people across the region, including decades of authoritarian rule, corruption, socio-economic injustices and a lack of rights, freedoms and opportunities. Social media enabled direct and relatively constant channels of communication for the diffusion of ideas to occur. They facilitated communication that helped mobilize and sustain collective action as well as the dissemination of information and images of the protests (and government responses) to the global community via international mass media.

The successes of the Arab Spring hinged on a rare alignment of a few key factors and provided hope that, in respect of Islam–West relations, a future based on mutual identification and understanding could be achieved. Arabs were courageously protesting against repressive regimes not under any religious banners but for freedom and democracy, goals with which Westerners could identify. Western journalists, who were welcomed by activists and protesters, were able to report the events from the perspective of the Arab people and frame them in ways that pressured Western governments to provide at least rhetorical support for the uprisings. This support simultaneously strengthened the uprisings and weakened the regimes.

However, the Arab Spring also demonstrates the limits of Islam–West relations, particularly in respect to their ability to identify with and understand the other. With the election of Islamic-oriented governments in the aftermath of the revolutions, the Western media became uncertain, and support for the new regimes declined amid a growing chaos of new protests; while in Syria the civil war left journalists in a situation similar to that in Iraq a decade earlier, where they became tools trapped amid a propaganda war.

In general, the Western media coverage of the Arab Spring demonstrates that a level of understanding has been achieved through a focus on context and reporting that is informed by the experiences of the people involved. When the media fail to reach this level of empathy and understanding, however, the coverage often looks quite different; orientalist perspectives can displace responsible journalism. At this point, we should consider the prospect of a clash of civilizations. It is to this issue that we turn in the next chapter.

7
A Clash of Civilizations?

Is there a clash of civilizations? Is conflict between Islam and the West inevitable? A quick scan of history would suggest that this is the case. Since the advent of Islam in the 7th century, Christian writers in the Near East and Europe have regarded the conquering Muslim empires as an enemy, a civilizational rival sent by God as punishment. In the 11th century Crusaders from Europe were able to briefly reverse the tide of Muslim expansion by capturing Palestine for almost a century. By the end of the 15th century Christian forces had reconquered Spain and ended Muslim rule in the Iberian Peninsula. In the 17th century the advancing Turks were turned back from the gates of Vienna, and soon afterwards the ascending European powers brought much of the Muslim world under their colonial rule. As most Muslim lands emerged as independent nation-states by the middle of the 20th century, they were confronted with a world of Western economic, political, military, technological and cultural domination. For Muslims committed to ensuring the preservation of Islamic identity, culture and order in the face of this modernity, the challenge has been formidable.

A dominant perspective since the turn of the century contends that the future of Islam–West relations will be characterized by a clash of civilizations. An obvious approach to examining the veracity of this theory might be to examine wars and conflicts, or even foreign policies and diplomatic relations, between Muslim and Western nations. More profound, however, are issues and events that concern the ideas, identity and values of the masses on both sides. This chapter examines the theory of the clash of civilizations as articulated by its major proponents, Bernard Lewis and Samuel Huntington. It then discusses a number of cases concerning representations of the other, freedom of expression and religious sensitivities, including the *Satanic Verses* book, Danish newspaper cartoons and the *Innocence of Muslims* film controversies, as these cases have reinforced a perception that Islam and the West are destined to clash. We conclude this chapter with an examination of the principle of freedom of expression in the Islamic tradition in order to assess the extent to which Islam and the West differ in this regard as well as the prospects for reconciliation.

The clash of civilizations

The idea of a clash of Islamic and Western civilizations is said to be heightened by media imagery (Powell, 2011). The Western media's orientalist framework is said to both advocate and reinforce a clash of civilizations (Morey and Yaqin, 2011). While the notion of a clash of civilizations was made famous by the work of Samuel Huntington (1993), the concept originated in a paper by Bernard Lewis (1990). In an attempt to explain Muslim resentment of the West, Lewis stated:

> we are facing a mood and a movement far transcending the level of issues and policies and the governments that pursue them. This is no less than a clash of civilizations – the perhaps irrational but surely historic reaction of an ancient rival against our Judeo-Christian heritage, our secular present, and the worldwide expansion of both.
>
> (1990, para. 46)

Lewis casts Islam as the 'other' vis-à-vis Western civilization. The key points of difference are religion (Judeo-Christian versus Islam) and political order (secularism versus theocracy). He argues that the modern Muslim world is going through a mood of violence and hatred, which is directed against the West. Muslims resent the West for its technological, military and political success and blame the West for their own failings. Lewis, however, acknowledges that such Muslims constitute significant numbers, but probably not a majority. With most Muslims, he contends, 'we share certain basic cultural and moral, social and political, beliefs and aspirations' (Lewis, 1990, para. 5). The most problematic parts of the Muslim world for Lewis are those that assert an Islamist identity and oppose Western values and interests, regarding the West as 'enemies of God' (1990, para. 6). His logic is that Muhammad was not just a prophet and teacher; he was also a political leader and a warrior. Thus, those who fought for Islam fought for God, and those who opposed them opposed God (Lewis, 1990).

Lewis (1990) reads historic relations between the Muslim world and Christendom to be a 1400-year rivalry, a view denied by other historians such as Tolan, Veinstein and Laurens (2013), whose reading is of a much richer and complex history based on conflict but also cooperation and coexistence. For Lewis, however, the contemporary clash has its origins in the Turks' failed siege of Vienna in 1683 and successive defeats at the hands of the Christian West ever since. Not only did Muslims suffer the loss of their world dominance, followed by a loss of sovereignty over their own lands, but their sense of humiliation was compounded by the undermining of Islamic values, norms and identity by Western culture. Lewis reduces the clash to 'a rising tide of rebellion against the Western paramountcy, and a desire to reassert Muslim values and restore Muslim greatness' (1990, para. 14). In specific reference to America, Lewis recalls that the Muslim world initially paid little attention, and that relations began only after World War II, when the prosperity and power of the United States came to be admired. The anti-Americanism that has become characteristic of many Islamist groups and publics is only partially explained by US support for Israel and corrupt, authoritarian Muslim regimes, according to Lewis. For Lewis, the central factor explaining Muslim rage towards the West is imperialism, narrowly defined as 'the invasion and domination of Muslim countries by non-Muslims' (1990, para. 34). This invasion and domination need not necessarily be in physical or military terms; a more threatening form of imperialism comes from the transformational power of ideas. Lewis explains that from the Muslim perspective 'the great social and intellectual and economic changes that have transformed most of the Islamic world, and given rise to such commonly denounced Western evils as consumerism and secularism, emerged from the West' (1990, para. 37). It is precisely because 'Western capitalism and democracy... provide an authentic and attractive alternative to traditional ways of thought and life' (Lewis, 1990, para. 38) that the West, and the United States in particular, has become the enemy of Islamists. In essence, the battle of Islamists is against secularism, as it undermines the traditional role of Islam in the socio-political order, and modernism, which is physically manifested in the social, cultural, political and economic structures of the modern Muslim states.

Perhaps Lewis has missed his own point, however. The frustration from the Muslim perspective is less about 'the West' and more about 'Islam', specifically the relevance of Islam and the security of Islamic identity. Taking Lewis' argument to its logical conclusion, one might add that the Muslim sense of humiliation is due to the success of the West in exceeding that previously achieved by Islamic civilization. Islamists' reading of history is that the greatness of Islamic civilization was achieved by the grace of God and was proof of Islam's truth. This belief is shattered by the dominance of the West in the modern world. The West has developed systems and institutions that are more responsive to Islam's higher objectives in terms of social justice, prosperity and human well-being than those which Islamic civilization ever achieved. Through secular systems and liberal democracies, modern Western states grant all their citizens the equal rights, freedoms, protections and opportunities that historically religion did not. That the accomplishments of Western civilization have been produced without religion, or at least by mitigating the role of religion in politics, presents a formidable challenge to the Islamic conception of God and theology.

Lewis cites two examples to support his theory of a clash of civilizations. The first is the attack on the US embassy in Islamabad, Pakistan, in 1979 in response to the seizure of the grand mosque in Mecca by a group of Muslim dissidents. The second is the attack on the United States Information Service (USIS) center in Islamabad in response to the publication of Salman Rushdie's book *Satanic Verses*. Neither the seizure of the mosque nor the publication of the book was the work of the US government, yet the US government was the target of both attacks. Similar incidents occurred in 2006, when Muslims worldwide protested the publication in a Danish newspaper of cartoons insulting the Prophet Muhammad, and in 2012, when Muslims across the globe protested against a film, *Innocence of Muslims*, deemed to be insulting to Islam.

The theory of a clash of civilizations gained prominence in the field of international relations due to the work of Samuel Huntington (1993). Huntington's central argument is that in the post-Cold War world conflicts will be based on culture and religion rather than along ideological and economic lines. Within this context, the United States' allies will be those with whom it shares culture and values as civilizational alliances are formed. Huntington defines civilization as 'the highest cultural grouping of people and the broadest level of cultural identity people have short of that which distinguishes humans from other species' (1993, para. 6). The principal characteristics of civilization include language, history, religion, customs, institutions and the self-identification of people, according to Huntington. He argues that, while Western civilization has two main subdivisions, European and North American, Islamic civilization is comprised of Arab, Turkic and Malay subdivisions. One might argue, however, that Turks and Europeans have more in common than Turks and Malays. The only explanation is that religion is an overriding factor in Huntington's categorization. Indeed, for Huntington, religion is the most fundamental marker of identity and the primary reason for the emergence of the civilizational groupings and their inevitable clash.

These fault lines will also emerge as a consequence of increased interaction between people of different civilizations. As religion replaces the nation-state as the dominant source of national identity and thereby provides the cement for civilizational identity, there will be growth of civilizational consciousness and the immutability of cultural characteristics compared with political and economic ones. In respect to this last point, Huntington explains that Soviet communists can become democrats and rich can become poor, but 'Russians cannot become Estonians and Azeris cannot become Armenians' (1993, para. 15). He is less clear in respect to religion, explaining that one can be 'half-French and half-Arab and simultaneously even a citizen of two countries [but] it is more difficult to be half-Catholic and half-Muslim' (Huntington, 1993, para. 15).

However, one may wonder why for Huntington one cannot be a Muslim Australian or a Catholic Chinese. And, if such combinations are possible, where does that leave the boundaries of civilizations? To the extent that Muslims do not self-identify as Australian, American or European or are not recognized as such by the Western society in which they live, perhaps Huntington is correct. Huntington (1993) does not specifically address the question of Muslim integration in the West, but does note that political and economic groupings are increasingly being formed along cultural and religious lines in the international community. Different cultural/religious groupings will create different policy responses to various fundamental issues, including human rights, immigration, trade and the environment, which will lead to the deepening of civilizational divides.

In his brief account of Islam–West relations, Huntington narrates a history marked by conflict from the advent of Islam to the present. From the early expansion of Arab armies into the Near East and Spain, the Crusades and Turkish conquests in Europe to the era of European colonization of the Muslim world, wars of independence and modern conflicts in the Middle East, Islam and the West have always been at war. Huntington contends that 'this centuries-old military interaction between the West and Islam is unlikely to decline' (1993, para. 25).

According to Huntington (1993), continued conflict between Islam and the West is inevitable, but it is possible for certain countries to redefine their civilizational identity. To do so, a country's political and economic elite as well as its public must support the shift, and their counterparts in the receptive civilization must embrace the move.

Turkey is an interesting case, as it satisfies the former but not the latter in respect to membership of the European Union. Huntington acknowledges that Europe is not sufficiently receptive to Turkey on account of its Muslim identity. He also notes that 'a world of clashing civilizations, however, is inevitably a world of double standards: people apply one standard to their kin-countries and a different standard to others' (Huntington, 1993, para 38).

Application of Huntington's criteria for change of civilizational identity is also relevant in the context of Western Muslims. The decision to migrate may represent a desire to make a geographical shift but not a cultural one. Similarly, a country's decision to grant a visa or even citizenship may represent a desire to fulfill humanitarian, economic or even social imperatives, but not necessarily a willingness to accommodate overt manifestations of a foreign religion, such as places of worship, schools, laws and dress codes. The fact that many Western countries have taken exception to physical markers of Islamic identity within their borders affirms Huntington's argument. While Huntington's clash of civilizations theory is often seen as right-wing, even racist or Islamophobic, it does make an appeal for positive inter-civilizational engagement. Huntington encourages the West to 'develop a more profound understanding of the basic religious and philosophical assumptions underlying other civilizations and the way in which people in those civilizations see their interests [and] ... identify elements of commonality between Western and other civilizations' (1993, para. 62).

Controversies and their implications for Islam–West relations

Depictions of the Prophet

As Islam arose out of a polytheistic context, idols, statues and even images were generally proscribed. Many Muslims consider it blasphemous to visually depict Muhammad, regardless of whether the depiction is in a positive or a negative light (Christensen, 2006). According to Islamic tradition, when Muhammad conquered Mecca in the year 630, he issued the Meccan people a general amnesty but destroyed their idols, which were housed in the *ka'ba*, the main shrine in the center of the city. There are also a number of prophetic traditions attributed to Muhammad in which he is said to have proclaimed: 'Whoever makes a picture will be punished by Allah till he puts life in it, and he will never be able to put life in it' (Hadith: Bukhari, 3:428, Narrated by Said bin Abu Al-Hasan). According to another narration, Aisha, the second wife of Muhammad, relates an occasion when she made a pillow for the Prophet, decorating it with pictures of animals:

> He [Muhammad] came and stood among the people with excitement apparent on his face. I said, 'O Allah's Apostle! What is wrong?' He said, 'What is this pillow?' I said, 'I have prepared this pillow for you, so that you may recline on it.' He said, 'Don't you know that angels do not enter a house wherein there are pictures; and whoever makes a picture will be punished on the Day of Resurrection and will be asked to give life to (what he has created)?'
> (Hadith: Bukhari, 4:47, Narrated by Aisha)

Although there are narrations that describe the physical appearance of Muhammad, images of him were discouraged for fear that they might become objects of worship. However, there are classical stories from the early years of Islam in which the Prophet was portrayed in images without negative backlash from Muslims of the time (Grabar, 2003). In the mid-11th century, two identical stories, *Dala'il al-Nubuwwah* by Abu Bakr Ahmad b. al-husayn al-Bayhaqi and *Dala'il al-Nubuwwah* by Abu Nu'aym al-Isfahani, tell of a Meccan merchant, Hishan b. al-As al-Umawi, who traveled for trade and to spread the message of the Prophet. In Constantinople he is said to have met with Heraclius, intending to convert him to Islam. Both tales involve the presentation of images of various prophets, including Muhammad, demonstrating that there was not always a negative reaction to the physical portrayal of the Prophet Muhammad (Grabar, 2003). Indeed, while representations of the Prophet Muhammad were rare, particularly in the Sunni tradition, they did appear infrequently in books which retold stories from the life of the Prophet (Bloom and Blair, 2002).

In the modern era, however, the context is very different. The depictions of the Prophet that have caused offense to Muslims have been produced not by other Muslims but by non-Muslims from non-Muslim countries. Such images seem not to have been produced for educational purposes, such as telling the life story of the Prophet or history of Islam. Rather, they have been perceived by Muslims as insults and provocations.

Hostile reactions by groups of fanatical Muslims in response to what they perceive as unacceptable depictions of the Prophet date back almost a century. In 1927, Islamic scholars from al-Azhar University in Egypt erupted in protests over the announcement of a movie about Muhammad, in which he would have been played by actor Yusof Wahba

(Bakker, 2006). After unrest again in 1930, the physical portrayal of Muhammad was prohibited, and so the film was not produced. Following the 1973 release of *Jesus Christ Superstar*, there was again a rumor of a movie about Muhammad. This time it was to be Charlton Heston who would play the Prophet. The producer and director, Moustapha Akkad, was a Syrian who resided in the United States. Akkad had asked the Shiite Council of Lebanon as well as the scholars of al-Azhar to approve the script for the new film. As Muhammad would not be physically portrayed – only his cane and his camel would be featured – both parties approved the script. However, after production of the film had begun in 1974, the scholars of al-Azhar changed their decision and condemned the production. This, as well as pressure from Syrian leaders, resulted in the expulsion of the cast and crew from Morocco, where the film was being made. Although filming was completed in Libya, it was not graciously accepted around the world. The day that the film was set to premiere in Washington DC, Muslim militants stormed the Jewish B'nai B'rith building, holding all of the employees hostage. The militants threatened to kill everyone if the film premiere went ahead (Bakker, 2006).

Another such incident occurred over a decade later. Written in 1988, Salman Rushdie's *The Satanic Verses* was regarded as blasphemous by Muslims globally. The book is a fictional story about two Muslim Indians who fall from a plane explosion during a terrorist attack and develop inhuman characteristics. The offense against Muslims comes from the characters in Rushdie's book that closely resemble prominent figures in Islamic history and tradition. The main characters are Saladin Chamcha, who represents the historical Saladin, the first Sultan of Egypt and Syria, and Gibreel Farishta, who represents Archangel Gabriel. Gibreel lacks faith, despite being an archangel. The third and most notable 'Islamic' character in Rushdie's story is Mahound, who represents the Prophet Muhammad. Mahound accepts three other deities when converting the Meccan merchants to monotheism, but retracts the proclamation, saying that the devil was putting words in his mouth rather than God. Like Muhammad, Mahound is burdened and pained by God speaking through him. The novel was also offensive to Muslims due to its depiction of Mahound's wives as whores (Rushdie, 2000).

Muslims were so offended by Rushdie's novel that mass riots ignited around the world. On 5 October 1988, within a week of the book's release, India became the first country to ban the novel. Seven people were killed during violent protests in Pakistan and India. At the beginning of 1989, Muslims burned the novel in the streets of Bradford in Northern England. On 14 February 1989, Iran's supreme leader Ayatollah Khomeini issued a *fatwa* (religious edict) calling for the death of Salman Rushdie (Strother, 1989). Tehran offered a five million dollar reward for the person who killed Rushdie, and relations between the United Kingdom and Iran became particularly tense (Mazrui, 1990). Rushdie and his wife went into hiding, but he continued writing. Hitoshi Igarashi, the Japanese translator of Rushdie's work, was stabbed to death in 1991 (Helm, 1991) and William Nygaard, the Norwegian publisher of the book, was shot in 1993 (*New York Times*, 1993). That same year, 35 people were killed in a hotel in eastern Turkey as hundreds of rioting Muslims burned down the hotel (Gurdilek, 1993).

The Danish cartoon controversy

Traditional mass media such as newspapers, radio and television have always had a power and potential to reach large audiences and inform about people, places and events that these audiences have not directly experienced. However, with the advent of global satellite news networks, the internet and social media, the reach and instantaneity of the mass media are even more apparent. The issue of *Jyllands-Posten*, a Danish newspaper that published cartoons of the Prophet Muhammad in 2005, is a case in point. The 12 cartoons depicting the Prophet Muhammad were reportedly in response to ongoing demands for political correctness and a prevailing fear of insulting or even depicting the prophet (Yilmaz, 2011). This fear emerged in the aftermath of the brutal murder of Dutch filmmaker Theo Van Gogh, whose film *Submission* caused offense to groups of Muslims in Europe (Dalgaard, 2006).The *Jyllands-Posten* cartoons were published alongside an article on the problem with political correctness in the context of self-censorship and free speech (Harkness et al., 2007).

Hostility ensued between Muslim protesters who claimed the cartoons were blasphemous and those who cited the exercise of the right to free speech, determined not to be intimidated by Islamist threats and violence, as their motivation for publishing the cartoons. A number of newspapers in various Western countries reprinted the cartoons, and, in response, groups of Muslims in these countries protested in the streets. While various governments in Muslim-majority countries suspended diplomatic relations with Denmark, Danish products were boycotted and the embassies of various Western countries were attacked. The fallout from the publication of the cartoons was referred to as 'Denmark's worst foreign affairs crisis since the Second World War' (Bødker, 2009, p. 81).

Ambassadors from embassies of 11 Muslim countries petitioned for a response from the Danish government (Harkness et al., 2007). Danish Prime Minister Ander Fogh Rasmussen refused to meet with the representatives, saying that the publication was fair use of the media's freedom of speech (Yilmaz, 2011). In an attempt to get an official apology from *Jyllands-Posten*, Muslim activists raised a 17,000-signature petition and held a 3000-person demonstration in Copenhagen. The petition was unsuccessful, and as a result the Muslim activists, along with the 11 ambassadors, arranged for small groups of representatives to travel to Muslim countries to gain support and provoke responses towards the situation in Denmark. Egypt's Grand Mufti, Muhammad Said Tantawy, and Lebanon's Minister of Foreign Affairs, Fawzi Salloukh, were both engaged and the matter was taken to the Organization of Islamic Cooperation (OIC), which is the largest transnational Muslim organization, consisting of 57 countries, and the world's largest international body after the UN. Having reviewed the images and the situation in Denmark, all 57 members of the OIC agreed that the case represented a growing Islamophobia and expressed alarm that Denmark's media was evidently using freedom of expression to vilify Islam (Jensen, 2008).

By late January 2006, the majority of Muslim countries had condemned the publication of the cartoons and a significant number of them, led by Saudi Arabia and Kuwait, boycotted the use of Danish products (Jensen, 2008). From there, tensions elevated even further, with worldwide protests. On 30 January, armed forces stormed the European Union office in Gaza, threatening to take the workers hostage if the EU did not issue an apology for Denmark publishing the cartoons (Hansen, 2006). The media imagery of such incidents suggested that the greater Muslim world held the whole of Europe, and the West in general, accountable for the actions of one newspaper in Denmark.

On 1 February 2006, *Jyllands-Posten* representatives apologized for the offense that they had caused but not for publishing the cartoons. A few days later, the Danish embassy in Syria was burned down, the Danish embassy in Beirut was set on fire and the Danish embassy in Iran was violently attacked (Jensen, 2008). By February 2006, certain newspapers in Norway, France, Australia, Britain and the United States had republished the cartoons. Subsequently, Norwegian NATO soldiers in Afghanistan were attacked and Norwegian products in the Middle East were boycotted (Stephens, 2006). While violent protests continued around the world, many prominent Muslim leaders and Islamic organizations spoke against the violence and also against the calls for the death of the cartoonists, condemning such responses as un-Islamic (BBC News, 2006).

In part, the issue of the Danish cartoons represents different conceptions of press freedom and responsibility (Nacos and Torres-Reyna, 2007). Nacos and Torres-Reyna explain that

> in the case of the Danish cartoons, news organisations were forced to decide whether it was more important to demonstrate their commitment to press freedom in the face of violence or to refrain from re-publicizing offensive images that were hardly in the public interest apart from the violence they had caused already and were likely to refuel.
>
> (2007, p. 123)

That the publishing of the cartoons would spark offense was recognized by the Danish newspaper, and perhaps the prospect of a hostile response from Muslims was the motivation. It is noteworthy that the same newspaper rejected an earlier request to publish cartoons of Christ on the grounds that, according to the Sunday editor, 'they would provoke an outcry' (Nacos and Torres-Reyna, 2007, p. 124). Indeed, many newspapers in the West decided not to publish the cartoons in order to avoid hostile reactions (Nacos and Torres-Reyna, 2007). However, an inescapable fact is that, had Muslim reactions been peaceful and civilized, Western newspapers would have been even less inclined to publish the cartoons, as they would not have felt compelled to assert their right of press freedom (Nacos and Torres-Reyna, 2007).

The Danish cartoon controversy reignited debate over whether there should be limits to freedom of expression or free speech. As the backlash from publishing the cartoons was erupting, *Jyllands-Posten* published a response, stating:

> The modern secular society is dismissed by some Muslims. They demand special treatment when they insist on special consideration of their religious feelings. This is incompatible with secular democracy and freedom of speech, where one should be ready to stand scorn, mockery and ridicule. This is certainly not always very sympathetic or nice to look at, but this is irrelevant in the context (2005).

Similar defenses of secularism and freedom of speech were presented by others. Essentially, the argument is based on the principle that freedom of expression should not be suppressed for moral or ethical implications and that there can be no progression in society if there is not freedom of expression in an absolutist form (Mill, 2011). Christopher Hitchens (2007) argued that the right to publish the cartoons is a right of the free world, a demonstration of freedom of speech, but many publishers around the world did not publish the cartoons out of fear. Hitchens contends that this stems from fear of retaliation by the religion's followers or fear of offending them, two reasons which he believes to be as bad as each other. Randell Hansen (2006) offered a different argument in defense of the publication of the cartoons. He contends that, while cartoons are misconstrued as racism, there is a significant difference between racism and discrimination against a religion. Hansen (2006) claims that, while there is no rational reasoning for racism, there are plenty of logical reasons to object to a religion.

Opposing views tend to focus on the civil rights of minorities and the need for media responsibility in the exercise of free speech. Ambalavaner Sivanandan (2006) argued that *Jyllands-Posten* and newspapers that republished the cartoons around the world manipulated freedom of speech to incite hatred and increase Islamophobia. This view is supported by a number of scholars worldwide, including Tariq Modood (2006), Christian Rostboll (2009, 2010) and Miklós Haraszti (2006).

Western publics around the world shared the view that, while the press might have a right to publish the cartoons, to do so would be irresponsible and a pointless provocation. In early 2006 a poll conducted in seven Western countries on the publishing of the cartoons found this to be the case. In Norway, the first country to reprint the cartoons, 57 per cent of Norwegians thought that it was wrong to publish the cartoons, with only 30 per cent arguing that it was right. Similarly, in France, 54 per cent considered the publication of the cartoons to be 'pointless provocation' (Stephens, 2006, para. 4). The majority of Australians agreed with this sentiment; 62 per cent of respondents said that the cartoons should not have been published. Britain was one of the Western countries that had decided not to publish the images, a decision supported by 72 per cent of British people, who believed that, while the media had the right to publish the cartoons, this was not necessarily the right thing to do, while 52 per cent went even further, agreeing that the images should be banned, as they caused great offense to Muslims. In the United States, 61 per cent stated that the European newspapers that published and reprinted the cartoons had acted irresponsibly. However, 61 per cent attributed the angry Muslim response to Muslim intolerance of difference of opinions, with only 21 per cent agreeing that the Muslim response was predominantly due to Western nations' lack of respect for Islam (Stephens, 2006). In Denmark, where the cartoons originated, opinion on the topic was divided, with 49 per cent responding that *Jyllands-Posten* was wrong to have published, yet 57 per cent believing that upholding freedom of expression was more important than 'consideration of religious sentiment' (Stephens, 2006, para. 28).

'Innocence of Muslims' film

On 1 July 2012, Nakoula Besseley Nakoula, also known as Sam Bacile, uploaded a 14-minute trailer for his film *The Real Life of Muhammad*, which became known as *Innocence of Muslims*. The trailer is a crude representation of Islam, Muslims and Arabs in general. It shows Muhammad as an insane man who believes that he can hear animals talking to him and Muhammad's first wife Khadija appealing to her uncle for help with Muhammad's condition. The film suggests that, within this context, the Quran was fabricated based on pre-Islamic monotheistic sources. At one point, the characters even state that Muhammad and his companion Umar were homosexual. From there on, the trailer shows Muhammad seducing many women and inventing verses of the Quran to justify his behavior and advance his aspirations. The film repeats familiar stereotypes and clichés depicting Muhammad as untrustworthy, unfair and violent, and Muslims as criminals who abuse women and are intolerant of other religions (Basile, 2012).

The United States as a whole was blamed for the film and was accused of using it as a weapon in its attack on Islam and Arabs (Ismael, 2012). During protests in Iran, amid the burning of the American flag, demonstrators shouted anti-US slogans and demanded that the film's makers be brought to justice (BBC Worldwide Limited, 2012). Similar protests were held outside US embassies in Syria and other capitals around the Muslim world (Parker, 2012; Said, 2012).

Australia was one of the many countries that saw mass riots, now referred to as the '2012 Sydney Riots'. After police dispersed a crowd of about 100 Muslims who were protesting in front of the US consulate, the number of protesters swelled to about 300 as they demonstrated through the streets of Sydney. The protests resulted in damage to civilian and public property, including police vehicles. Six police and 19 protesters were injured and nine people were arrested. Although the number of protesters was relatively small, given that approximately half of Australia's almost 500,000 Muslim population live in the state of New South Wales (of which Sydney is the capital), the media portrayal of the incident suggested that a mass uprising of Australia's Muslims was occurring as 'Muslims stormed the city' (Channel Ten News, 2012). Despite the fact that leaders of the Australian Muslim community's 25 most prominent organizations condemned the protests as 'unacceptable and un-Islamic', such statements were significantly underreported compared with the protests themselves (Olding, 2012). It is indicative of how entrenched news values are in respect to prioritizing negativity, controversy and conflict that the article in the *Sydney Morning Herald* concerning the Muslim leaders' denouncement of the protests carried the headline 'Muslims inundated with messages of hate' (Olding, 2012) rather than a more positive headline such as, perhaps, 'Muslim leaders condemn protests'.

It is noteworthy that the film had nothing to do with the United States, but still protests were directed at US embassies and consulates around the world. The gravest of these was the attack on the US diplomatic mission in Benghazi, Libya, which resulted in four deaths, including that of the US ambassador. On 25 September 2012, President Barack Obama condemned the *Innocence of Muslims* film, referring to it as a 'crude and disgusting video' (Obama, 2012, para. 20). He went on to say that the best way to fight derogatory speech, is not to suppress freedom of speech, but to instead speak against the attack and show tolerance. Obama, like many world leaders, also condemned the use of violence in response to the film, stating that 'on this we must agree: there is no speech that justifies mindless violence' (Obama, 2012, para. 23). Then Secretary of State, Hillary Clinton, addressed the 19th ASEAN Regional Forum Foreign Ministers Retreat, stating that the American Government had no association with the film and that she personally considered it 'disgusting and reprehensible' (Ghosh, 2012, para. 5). In spite of the absence of US involvement in the production or distribution of the film, not to mention the condemnation of it by US leaders, the fact that Muslim anger over the film was directed at US symbols and territory indicates that, at least for some Muslims, there is a clash of civilizations.

Freedom of expression in Islam

Almost since political Islam captured Western media headlines in the late 1970s and until today, there has been an ongoing debate about the compatibility and incompatibility of Islam and such democratic principles as freedom of expression. An initial question is necessary: what does society expect of its media? Denis McQuail (2005) identifies four main goals or expectations of society for the media. First, the media are expected to maintain a constant surveillance of events, ideas and key people important to public life. The purpose is to facilitate a flow of information to the public and also for the media to act as a check on violations of moral and social order. Second, the media are expected to provide an independent critique of society and social institutions such as the family, government, church [mosque] and schools. Third, the media are expected to encourage and provide the means for access, expression and participation by as many different people, voices and opinions in society as necessary for constructive social discourse and debate as appropriate for maintaining social order and progress. Fourth, the media is expected are contribute to shared consciousness and identity and the cohesion of diverse social groups (McQuail, 2005). These objectives do not just apply to the Western context but universally, including in the Islamic social context (Rane, 2010b).

It is pertinent at this point to define normative social order in the Islamic context. Islam is a monotheistic religion with a very clear vision for a particular type of social order. The overriding principle in this order is social justice. Rahman (2002) explains the relationship between the concept of monotheism and social justice in Islam in the following words:

> Muhammad's monotheism was, from the beginning, linked up with a humanism and a sense of social and economic justice whose intensity is no less than the intensity of the monotheistic idea, so that whoever carefully reads the early Revelations of the Prophet cannot escape the conclusion that the two must be regarded as expressions of the same experience.
>
> (Rahman, 2002, p. 12)

It would be useful to examine how the Prophet Muhammad dealt with the issue of free expression, media content, media effects and the role of media in society. Obviously, there were no mass media at that time in the forms we have today; however, comparison is still possible. Arabian society, even prior to the advent of Islam, relied on the transmission of oral traditions. Poetry was central to the culture and poets were highly esteemed. Through their oratory, poets shaped the culture, conveyed the greatness of their tribe, told their history and denounced their enemies. Contests were held to crown the best poet of the land; their poems were written in gold and hung in sacred places. It could be said that poetry was the mass medium of the time. Thus, it is useful to examine how the Prophet Muhammad dealt with this medium (Rane, 2010a).

There are certain verses of the Quran, such as 26:225, that appear critical of poets and poetry of the time, and some scholars have suggested that such verses amount to restrictions on free expression. In turn, this could certainly be used by Muslims oriented towards authoritarianism to support strict media controls and censorship laws. The consensus of Islamic scholars is that such criticism was directed at the content of the poetry, specifically due to its encouragement of alcoholism, sexual promiscuity and polytheism, which were all deemed to be detrimental to the well-being of Arabian society and hence forbidden by Islam. The Prophet had a balanced view of such Quranic verses; essentially, his position regarding poetry was that 'the good of it is good, and the bad of it is bad' (Karim in Rane, 2010a, p. 162). Indeed, the Prophet himself employed a poet as a means of conveying certain messages to certain groups of people, and is quoted as having said that 'there is wisdom in poetry' (Karim in Rane, 2010a, p. 162).

A reading of the relevant prophetic traditions shows that, first, there is a belief in a causal relationship between the recitation of poetry and the thoughts and behavior of their audiences. Such media are seen to have the potential to persuade, mislead and disseminate falsehoods, but are also seen as a source of wisdom. On this basis, it could be concluded that an Islamic theory of media accepts the view that the media do have effects on audiences and that there must be consistency between one's moral or ethical code and media content.

There is a general view, particularly among Western scholars of Islam, that Islamic law places almost exclusive emphasis on duties and that the concept of rights and freedom are alien to Islam. Some regard Islamic law as 'a system of duties, of ritual, legal and moral obligations', while others have stated more explicitly that 'individual rights could not have existed in Islam' and that in the Islamic system 'the individual cannot have rights and liberties' but only obligations (Kamali, 1999, p. 17). However, Mohammad Hashim Kamali, a world-renowned professor of *sharia* law, explains that 'although the nature of these communications [Quranic verses and Prophetic traditions] . . . may tend toward obligation rather than right, a closer examination of *hukm* [Quranic legal rulings] reveals that a mere propensity in the style of communication does not negatively affect the substance and validity of rights in the *shariah*' (1999, p. 17).

In the Western context, rights developed out of constitutionalism as part of an ongoing struggle between the power of the state and individual rights and liberties. However, the relationship between the state and individual rights is fundamentally different in Islam, as fundamental rights precede state formation. Such rights as the safety and sanctity of life and property as well as human equality and dignity were enshrined in the Quran from the outset. Moreover, those in authority were made responsible for ensuring the promotion of public benefits and prevention of harms to people. This entails such fundamental rights as the right to life, justice, equality before the law, protection of property, privacy, freedom of movement, protection of dignity, and so forth. Another important point in this context is that, in the West, by way of constitution or bill of rights, fundamental rights are presented in a single document, whereas in the Islamic context such rights are scattered across various writings of scholars and jurists. However, there are certain broad categories in these writings under which the fundamental rights can be found. We will come to this shortly.

First, it is pertinent to address the concept of freedom. Freedom is a term that has become central to Western civilization. It could be said to characterize Western liberal democracies. There are multiple meanings of freedom. Quoting from Islamic sources, Kamali defines freedom as 'the ability of the individual to say or do what he or she wishes, or to avoid doing so, without violating the rights of other, or the limits that are set by the law' (1999, p. 7). This definition does not see freedom as absolute but as conditioned by the rights of others. Freedom of expression, Kamali explains, is the 'absence of restraints upon the ability of individuals or groups to communicate their ideas to others, subject to the understanding that they do not in turn coerce others into paying attention or that they do not invade other rights essential to the dignity of the individual' (1999, p. 7).

On the issue of balance between free speech and what might be considered offensive, hate speech or even sedition, the Quran seems to support restrictions on speech. Only in the case of injustice or wrongdoing does the Quran permit speech that might be hurtful to individuals or groups. It states: 'God does not love the public utterance of evil speech except by one who has been wronged' (Quran, 4:148). Kamali explains that 'the Quran ... tolerates utterances of hurtful speech in pursuit of a higher objective, which is to establish justice' (1999, p. 9). Even in the pursuit of justice, however, there are limitations based on individual rights to privacy. In such verses as 49:12 and 2:189, the Quran specifically prohibits people spying on one another and establishes the right to privacy in one's home. Islamic law affirms freedom of expression through its endorsement of such provisions as enjoining right and proscribing wrong (*hisbah*), sincere advice (*nasihah*), consultation (*shura*), personal reasoning (*ijtihad*) and legitimate criticism of authority (*hurriyyat al-mu'aradah*) (Kamali, 1999, pp. 28–72).

The last of these provisions, *hurriyyat al-mu'aradah* or legitimate criticism of authority, is central to an effective media and a functioning
democracy. It is a means by which authority can be monitored and
kept in check, akin to the concept of the 'fourth estate'. As originally
expressed by Edmund Burke in the late 18th century, the fourth estate
refers to 'the political power possessed by the press, on par with the
other three "estates" of power in the British realm: Lords, Church and
Commons' (McQuail, 2005, p. 169). The term is used widely in media
studies in reference to the media's responsibility to act as a watchdog on
leaders, governments and judiciary in the interest of the people.

Islam also imposes certain restrictions that impact upon free
speech. An overriding objective of Islamic law is the prevention of harm.
Both the legal and moral restraints on free speech in Islam arise from this
objective. Islam places certain restraints on free speech in circumstances
where that speech would unfairly and negatively impact on the rights
and dignity of another person or people. Some of these restraints are
legal and carry specified penalties in Islamic law, while others are moral
and carry no specific sanctions. All are intended to ensure the integrity
of society's moral and ethical standards. Generally speaking, the public
utterance of hateful or hurtful speech is prohibited, and only permitted
in the face of injustice or in pursuit of truth and right (Quran, 4:148).

Among the legal restraints placed on free speech are slander (Quran,
24:1–5), libel, defamation and malicious insults, including insulting the
religious beliefs of others (Quran, 6:108). Another restriction on free
speech arises when that speech is deemed to be blasphemous or when it
constitutes 'a contemptuous and hostile attack on the fundamentals of
religion, which offends the sensibilities of its adherents' (Kamali, 1999,
p. 213). There is a view among some Muslim jurists that blasphemy
carries a death penalty. However, it is Kamali's (1999) view that blasphemous speech would also have to constitute sedition in order to carry
such a penalty; in the absence of a threat to national security, blasphemous speech may be insulting and offensive but not a capital offense
(Kamali, 1999, pp. 213–214).

Among the main moral restraints to free speech are lying, defamation, ridicule and hate speech (Quran, 49:11; 49:12). There is a general
moral code in Islam which discourages revealing the faults and short-
comings of others. Among the circumstances when the faults of others
may be divulged, however, is when one is a victim of a crime, giving
testimony in court; giving sincere advice to someone concerning the
character of another; deterring someone from further wrongdoing; and
in the interest of protecting the safety and security of the state, society

or individual. There is also a general moral restraint imposed by Islam on acrimony or the intentional humiliation of others, known in Arabic as *mira'* (Kamali, 1999, p. 147). In sum, while the Islamic tradition never developed the democratic systems and institutions characteristic of Western countries, freedom of expression does have a place in Islamic scripture, albeit within an Islamic moral and ethical framework.

Conclusion

For Muslims, such representations of Muhammad as the cartoons published in 2005 failed to meet Islamic standards of rightful expression and also failed in respect to social expectations of media. More importantly, as intended, they were provocative, insulting and offensive. However, most Western publics also disagreed with the publication of the cartoons. A majority of Americans, Australians, British, French and Dutch as well as 49 per cent of Danes agreed that, while the media have a right to publish the material, they generally regarded the decision to do so as unnecessarily provocative and irresponsible (Stephens, 2006). These statistics deny a clash of civilizations. Similarly, it should be appreciated that in the West, although the media coverage tends to construct an image that overwhelming numbers of Muslims are engaged in protests and enraged with the West, in reality the numbers of such Muslims are small. Most Muslims, including the leaders of prominent Muslim organizations, are opposed to such actions as those displayed by protesting Muslims. Moreover, Islamic and Western conceptions of freedom of expression are not necessarily incompatible, especially when considered from the perspective of social and media responsibility, which both sides value. So is there a clash of civilizations? There is, for significant minorities on both sides, because of their failure or inability to be more discerning in their view of the other and a preoccupation with blaming this monolithic other. For those who are able to understand and recognize that the other is comprised of various groups, interests and identities, and that common ground exists with at least some of these groups, the theory of a clash of civilizations is far less convincing. In the next chapter, we test this hypothesis in relation to media coverage of, and audience responses to, the 9/11 terrorist attacks.

8
Moving on from 9/11?

As discussed throughout this book, the events of 9/11 have had a profound impact on Islam–West relations in terms of both intercommunity relations in Western countries and international relations in the global context. In the international realm, we have witnessed war and conflict between Muslim and largely Western forces. Within Western countries, Muslims have been subject to Islamophobic attacks and found themselves at the center of debates on immigration and asylum seekers, Western versus Islamic values, integration and the failure of multiculturalism. While such issues have been around for a number of decades, it is only since 9/11 and subsequent acts of terrorism that Islamic and Muslim issues have dominated political, media and public discourse.

In this chapter we use television news coverage from Australia and Australian public opinion as a case study to examine the extent to which, first, the news media have moved on from 9/11 and, second, whether audiences have recognized this shift and have also moved on from 9/11. This chapter consists of two parts. The first analyzes Australian television news programs' framing of the tenth anniversary coverage of 9/11. The second part of the chapter discusses the findings of focus groups conducted with Muslim and non-Muslim participants, including their reactions to the 9/11 coverage over the past decade and the evolution of their perceptions and understanding of Islam and Muslims over time.

Media framing of Islam and Muslims post-9/11

A number of studies have demonstrated that, post-9/11, the media frames used in the coverage of Islam and Muslims have been based on orientalist depictions of a religion and people as a different, strange, inferior and threatening 'other' (Poole, 2002; Manning, 2006; Steuter and Wills, 2009; Kumar, 2010; Powell, 2011). Since 9/11, media and political discourse has tended to associate Islam with violence and values inimical to those of Western societies (Martin and Phelan, 2002; Celermajer, 2007; Steuter and Wills, 2009; Powell, 2011). These studies have consistently found that terrorism, violence and the threat of Islam tend to be the dominant media frames used in the coverage of Muslims. Since the events of 9/11, numerous studies have identified that Western news media conflate Islam and terrorism through portrayals of Muslims as terrorists and Islam as a religion that condones terrorist acts (Norris, Kern and Just, 2003; Ryan, 2004; Papacharissi and de Fatima Oliveira, 2008). It has also been suggested that 9/11 profoundly changed the nature of journalism (Zelizer and Allen, 2002).

Much of the research concerning the representation of Muslims in relation to coverage of terrorism has focused on the use of language. In an analysis of editorials about the 'war on terror' in the ten largest newspapers in the United States, Ryan found that terms such as 'patriotic', 'heroic', 'tolerant' and 'generous' were frequently used to describe Americans and their allies (and later 'good' Arabs), whereas 'cowardly', 'vicious', 'jealous' and 'extremist' were terms used to describe everyone else (2004). This study also noted a heavy reliance by editorial writers on official government sources as they constructed their frames (Ryan, 2004).

The representation of terrorism and terrorists has also been a focus of this area of research. Numerous studies of the media's representation or portrayal of Islam and Muslims invoke Said's notion of orientalism as an explanatory framework. The term 'Islamophobia' has been used to describe the contemporary manifestation of orientalist discourse. Like orientalism, this discourse 'does not allow for diversity; contradictions and semiotic tensions are ignored as the homogenizing ethnocentric template of otherness assumes that there is only one interpretation of Islam' (Saeed, 2007a, p. 457). Saeed (2007a) argues that this discourse manifests in direct links being made between Muslims and support for terrorism and fundamentalism and with British Muslims being implored by voices in the media and politicians to make a more concerted effort to integrate into British society. These findings are not peculiar to the British context but are relevant to the experiences of Muslims in other Western countries.

In his study of coverage of Muslims in the American media, Karim (2006) identifies some of the visual signifiers that have developed in the transnational media's imaginaries of 'Islamic fundamentalism', including the hijab, the cloak and turban worn by Muslim *ulama*, the Arab headdress and cloak, the face of Ayatollah Khomeini, people performing the pilgrimage at Mecca and domes of mosques, among others. He says that these images are deployed in the media and communicate a vast amount of information without the need for words. He also notes that the frames used to portray Muslims are deeply entrenched and draw from cultural assumptions about Islam that have developed over many generations. According to Karim (2006), the media coverage focused on the incidents themselves, rather than the broader issues, and alternative voices, when heard, were brushed aside as interviewers sought confirmation for their pre-existing stereotypes of Islam. He suggests that the persistent representation of violent Muslims serves a propaganda function as well as being highly profitable for media businesses.

Within the cognitive framing paradigm, some scholars have advocated the idea of associative framing, which focuses on the co-occurrence of news frames and their potential to influence strong mental associations of issues in the audience's minds (van Atteveldt, Ruigrok and Kleinnijenhuis, 2010 cited in Ewart and Rane, 2011). While this paradigm is not without its weaknesses, researchers within it have produced some tentative findings in regard to media coverage of immigrants, Islam and terrorism. In the Dutch press between 2000 and 2005, van Atteveldt, Ruigrok and Kleinnijenhuis (2010) found that after the 9/11 attacks strong associations were made between Islam, migrants and terror relative to coverage prior to the attacks. However, as these authors acknowledge, the existence of an association between concepts or issues tells us little about the direction of the association or the types of associations and the extent to which they are translated from the media to the audience (cited in Ewart and Rane, 2011). Caution must, therefore, be exercised when interpreting findings such as these. What the above-mentioned studies do confirm, however, is that post-9/11 the reporting of Islam and Muslims has been routinely presented with the frame of terrorism and hostility towards the Western world.

Television news analysis

Our focus is on the television news items broadcast on free-to-air television stations in Australia on 11 and 12 September 2011. Our sample includes these two days because of the time difference between Australia and America, and we note that the bulk of coverage on Australian television news broadcasts was on 11 September 2011, with follow-up stories about the commemorations across the United States broadcast on Australian television news programs on 12 September 2011. We identified stories broadcast on their main evening news bulletins to determine the answer to questions concerning the framing of events, trends in reporting, and the representation of Islam and Muslims.

The five main free-to-air television channels in Australia include the Australian Broadcasting Corporation (ABC), Special Broadcasting Service (SBS), Seven Network, Nine Network and Network Ten. ABC and SBS are both public broadcasting services, while Seven, Nine and Ten are commercial entities. All provide an evening news service. While ABC and SBS provide a national evening news service, Seven, Nine and Ten offer a state-based news service that is broadcast out of Australia's main capital cities. Seven evening news is Australia's highest-rating news service, followed by Nine's evening news, Ten's evening news, ABC's evening news and SBS's World News Australia. In terms of audience share for 2010, Seven News gained 30 per cent; Nine News, 28 per cent; Ten News, 26 per cent; ABC News, 19 per cent; and SBS's World News Australia, 4 per cent (Figures provided by OzTAM, February 2011. OzTAM is Australia's official source of television audience measurement).

Across the five free-to-air television channels included in this study, a total of 32 stories concerning the tenth anniversary of 9/11 were broadcast. Of these, 18 were broadcast on 11 September 2011 and 14 on 12 September 2011. The latter were included to correspond with marking of the occasion in the United States (east coast), which is 15 hours behind Australia's east coast. The 32 stories amounted to over 97 minutes of coverage, almost one hour on 11 September and over 38 minutes on 12 September. However, it should be noted that on 12 September SBS' stories on the anniversary alone amounted to almost 23 minutes, accounting for over half the broadcast time of all channels on that date. The tenth anniversary of the 9/11 terrorist attacks occupied a significant place on the Australian news media agenda, particularly on 11 September 2011.

11 September 2011

The tenth anniversary of the attacks broadcast on 11 September 2011 was the lead story of all five free-to-air channels. The dominant frame across all channels on 11 September was remembrance of the victims. The central theme of the coverage revolved around the memorials that had been constructed in New York, in Pennsylvania and at the Pentagon and the ceremonies at these three sites in honor of the victims of the attacks. All channels ran stories that specifically focused on both the memorials and the ceremonies. News values of proximity and local relevance also shaped the construction of the stories across the various channels. All five channels included features on Australians who had lost a family member in the attacks as well as memorial services taking place in Australia.

Some specific differences in the coverage of the various channels were notable, however. ABC ran four stories totaling 12:23 minutes, all framed in terms of the Australia–United States alliance. The main story of the broadcast not only featured highlights from the memorials and ceremonies in New York, Pennsylvania and the Pentagon, including Australians attending the events, but also constructed strong links between Australia and the United States through coverage of the war in Afghanistan and a retrospective account of *jihadist* terrorism in Indonesia, which culminated in the Bali bombings and a wave of terrorist attacks in Jakarta. The other, shorter stories featured the prime minister speaking at a memorial service in Canberra, at which the close relations shared by Australia and the United States were reiterated; a memorial service in Sydney; and also South Australian fire fighters commemorating the sacrifices of their US counterparts.

Channel Seven framed its coverage of the anniversary in terms of moving forward beyond the negative relations that had characterized Islam and the West over the past decade. Its coverage consisted of three stories totaling almost seven minutes. The first featured the memorials and ceremonies in New York, Pennsylvania and the Pentagon. The second story began with a feature on Australians who had lost family members in the attacks, but focused on Simon Kennedy's (an Australian whose mother, Yvonne Kennedy, was killed in the attack on the Pentagon) condemnation of revenge attacks against Muslim people. The story then featured an interview with a Muslim person who had lost an eye in a revenge attack, followed by an interview with Zaid Shakir, a leading African-American Islamic scholar. The focus of this interview was the need for a 'way forward' in terms of relations with America's Muslim communities. Channel Seven's third story covered memorial services in Victoria for two local victims of the attacks. The US consul general was interviewed as part of this story, and he was featured expressing the need to move beyond the grief and towards reconciliation.

Channel Nine ran four stories totaling almost seven minutes, which, as with ABC, were framed in terms of Australia's close connection with the United States. The first story focused on the memorial sites and ceremonies in New York, in Pennsylvania and at the Pentagon. The second story featured an Australian who had lost a relative in the attacks, while the third and fourth stories focused on memorial services in Melbourne and Canberra. The US consul general was featured acknowledging the strong connections between the United States and Australia, while at the service in Canberra the prime minister spoke of Australia's strong bond with the United States.

Channel Ten ran one lengthy story on the anniversary that lasted for almost 15 minutes, more than double the time allocated by Channels Seven and Nine and also significantly longer than the stories run by the ABC and SBS. This was followed by a number of shorter stories, which ran for a further six minutes and focused on tributes and commemorations around Australia for the victims and heroes of the attacks. Channel Ten's coverage was framed in terms of a comprehensive retrospective which featured the memorial sites and ceremonies in the United States and Australia, as well as the Australians whose family members had been victims of the attacks. Unlike the other channels, however, Ten also featured its own coverage of the original events and included interviews with its presenters and reporters who had covered them.

SBS framed its coverage in terms of Australia feeling the United States' pain on the occasion. It ran two stories totaling over 12 minutes. The first story detailed the memorial sites and services in New York, in Pennsylvania and at the Pentagon, while the second focused on memorial services conducted in Australia. With both stories, an overriding theme was how the anniversary was bringing people together.

All five channels framed their coverage with the parameters of the official version of the events of 11 September 2001. There was no questioning of the official version and no reference to dissenting voices, in spite of the plethora of opinions that challenge various details of the events. Overall, the coverage was framed in terms of honoring the victims. In this respect, the ten Australians who were killed were central to the framing of the anniversary in terms of Australia's shared experiences with and connection to the United States. Within this context, the ABC and Channel Ten also included Australia's involvement in Afghanistan.

In spite of a focus during the earlier years of the post-9/11 decade on the threat of Islamist terrorism, the tenth anniversary coverage made very few references to Islam or Muslims. We will expand on this point later. For now, it is important to observe that the infrequency of reference to Islam and Muslims might be best explained in terms of the news frames employed. Coverage of the Islamist threat does not fit within frames based on honoring victims and moving beyond the pain of the original event. References to Islam and Muslims are telling in this regard. Only one story, broadcast by the ABC, made reference to Islam-inspired violence, which was presented in the context of pre-9/11 violence between Muslim and Christian communities in Indonesia. This formed the 'background' of the story's feature on Islamist terrorism carried out in Bali and Jakarta post-9/11. By contrast, Channel Seven and SBS both positioned their references to Islam and Muslims with the dominant frame of shared loss and moving on from 9/11. The former focused on hate crimes against Muslims post-9/11 and the initiatives of American Muslim leaders to build bridges of understanding with the wider society, while the latter focused on a memorial service that addressed the importance of interfaith dialogue post-9/11.

12 September 2011

Overall, 12 September 2011 offered less coverage of the tenth anniversary then the previous day. Channels Seven and Nine, as well as the ABC, broadcast only one story on the event, for 2:45, 1:50 and 2:42 minutes respectively. Channel 10 presented four stories with a total time of 8:31 minutes. SBS broadcast five stories, which amounted to 22:56 minutes. These stories presented a comprehensive recap of the original attacks, the memorial sites and services in the United States, the responses of people attending the ceremonies, memorials taking place in Europe and a retrospective of the war on terror.

It is noteworthy that the coverage on 12 September was not at the top of the news agenda, as had been the case on the previous day. With the exception of SBS, on which the tenth anniversary coverage was the lead story, on all the other channels the event occupied third or even fourth place behind such stories as a car chase, an Australian tennis player's (Sam Stosur) victory at the US Open, the escapades of an Australian football player (Brendan Fevola), and investigations into the death of a convicted Australian criminal (Carl Williams).

Across all five channels, the coverage focused entirely on the memorial services held in New York, in Pennsylvania and at the Pentagon, as well as featuring the Australian relatives of the victims killed in the attacks. The dominant frame across all channels was the remembrance of the victims, that they should not be forgotten. As with the coverage of the previous day, the frame of honoring the victims did not involve blame or animosity towards people of the Islamic faith. Amid the tributes to the victims, sentiments of moving on from 9/11 were repeated, which had also been a feature of the ninth anniversary coverage (Ewart and Rane, 2011).

Islam and Muslims in the tenth anniversary coverage

It is remarkable that the tenth anniversary coverage of 9/11 by the Australian television news media made only limited reference to Islam or Muslims. The two groups most closely associated with the 9/11 attacks, Al-Qaeda and the Taliban, were mentioned by a number of channels. Channel Ten, for instance, reported on the ongoing threat from the Taliban to disrupt the memorial services with a terrorist attack. This report, however, made no reference to Islam as an inspiration or ideological driver of either group. The ABC also mentioned Al-Qaeda and the Taliban, but in reference to the war in Afghanistan. The focus of this story was the cost of the war in terms of human lives and dollars, as well as the plight of the Afghan people, who will be 'left to fight the Taliban' once coalition forces withdraw. The ABC also reported on Al-Qaeda 'continuing the fight' with the West and continuing to 'spread its message around the globe'. The impression these reports convey is that Al-Qaeda and the Taliban are groups that reside outside the mainstream of Muslims, and that they are isolated and rejected. SBS, for instance, reported on a press conference held by the NATO secretary-general, who stated that Al-Qaeda have been sidelined by the Arab uprisings as the people demand freedom.

Where Muslims were mentioned in the coverage, the focus was on mainstream Muslims. Channel Seven featured a Muslim man who had been assaulted in a 9/11 revenge attack 'because of [his] Islamic faith'. The Muslim man stated that 'my Islamic faith taught me not to take his life'. The story then featured an American Imam, Zaid Shakir, who stated that 'It's easy to hate, it's easy to demonize, but we have hard work before us to build bridges'. Similarly, SBS also positioned its references to Islam and Muslims with the frame of reconciliation and working together. SBS featured a 9/11 memorial service held at Saint Mary's Church in Sydney, which was attended by Jewish, Christian and Muslim leaders. The theme of the service was the importance of interfaith dialogue, and the Muslim leader was shown addressing the audience. SBS also focused on the difficulties faced by Muslim communities in the United States as a consequence of 9/11. The correspondent in New York, Brian Thomson, started the segment with the words:

> Well the tenth anniversary of the attacks marks a particularly difficult time for Muslims here in the United States. Attacks on the community continue and a recent report has revealed that thousands have been subjected to extensive surveillance by the New York

Police Department. Even moderate Muslim leaders are questioning the direction in which the country is moving.

The story went on to present the perspective of a number of Muslim leaders, including the Imam of the New York mosque, about whom the correspondent stated: 'Imam Shamsi Ali, originally from Indonesia, is a renowned moderate. His message is one of tolerance, understanding and engagement. And it is not just directed at his own community. He says he has viewed with dismay, the recent political discourse here – in particular the US Presidential debates'. Following comments from the Imam, the correspondent then added:

Many Muslims see the situation as now worse than it was in the immediate aftermath of the attacks. They say the hostility to the election of President Obama, and the divisive debate last year over the so called ground zero mosque – which is in fact some distance from where the twin towers once stood – has made a bad situation worse.

The story was likely to elicit some degree of identification, as well as sympathy and understanding, from audiences. In this regard, the Muslim Mayor of Teaneck, New Jersey, Mohammed Hameeduddin, was featured stating:

We're Muslim Americans, we're neighbors, we're politicians, we're doctors, we're lawyers. You know we're teachers. We're part of the American fabric. And to single us out and to put out these bills that are unconstitutional saying you can't practice your religion and anti-*sharia* bills and things like that. These pavlovian triggers that the Islamophobes are very good at putting out there. That's something that our community really, I'd say we are hurt by.

Such references to Islam and Muslims were not made as part of a narrative about an Islamic threat or Islam versus the West. Rather, they were presented by the Australian television news media as part of a reconciliation process that has been identified in previous research (Ewart and Rane, 2011). This finding is highly significant, given the plethora of scholarly research over the past decade that has identified a close association between Islam and terrorism in news reporting since 11 September 2001 (Poole and Richardson, 2006; Aly, 2007; Abou-El-Fadl and Öktem, 2009; Rane, Ewart and Abdalla, 2010; Morey and Yaqin, 2011). Our study suggests that the mass media have not remained static in their representation of Islam and Muslims and that there has been an evolution in journalistic practice in respect to the reporting of issues concerning Muslims and Islam, at least in respect to 9/11. Absent from the coverage of the tenth anniversary were the types of stereotypical images of Islam and Muslims that numerous other studies have identified as being commonly used in the media. The dominant frames used in the coverage of the tenth anniversary were not associated with terrorism, threat, enmity or even blame. Rather, they were based on remembrance of the victims and reconciliation. Within these frames, the Taliban and Al-Qaeda were mentioned, but presented as being outside the Islamic mainstream. The focus was on Muslims engaged in initiatives to promote mutual understanding, bridge-building and reconciliation.

The findings of this study also have important implications for Muslim minorities in the West. As previously cited, studies have found that media reporting of Islam and Muslims has been identified by Muslims in the West as a key factor in their perceptions of social exclusion. Moreover, Muslims in the West tend to blame the mass media for the negativity they perceive towards Islam and their communities (Rane et al., 2011). Over the past two anniversaries of 9/11 we have observed more responsible reporting of Islam and Muslims by the Australian television news media. While several years of pejorative reporting may well have contributed to negative attitudes towards Muslims in the West, the 9/11 anniversary coverage may indicate a turning of the tide as far as news reporting is concerned. We do not suggest that negative attitudes towards Muslims will change immediately as a consequence; however, we would expect that Muslims will feel a stronger sense of contentment in the absence of media reports that they find offensive. We suggest that further research needs to be conducted in order to test this hypothesis.

Audiences' responses to 9/11

Our study was inspired by Adams and Burke's (2006) research into individuals' responses to media coverage of 9/11. Their study involved participants from three English villages and also focused on the participants' perceptions of Islam and Muslims. Their participants were all from 'white' ethnic backgrounds and the interviews took place four to six months after 9/11. The authors explore how the participants engaged emotionally with the victims of 9/11 and found 'competing discourses of belonging and difference demonstrated the complex and active processes of identifications present in recollections of responses to the media coverage of those tragic events' (Adams and Burke, 2006, p. 1001). Adams and Burke identified study participants engaged in a very complex negotiation of identification with the victims of 9/11, which, while centering on 'white ethnicity and/or national belonging', involved processes of ambiguity, qualification, contradictions and criticism (2006, p. 1001). They suggest that 'audiences actively engage with media narrations, such as news coverage of 11 September, in a broader context of domestic and social relationships' (Adams and Burke, 2006, p. 1002). Adams and Burke also find a high correlation between 'the strong perception among our informants that the British media and the Labour government are tightly constrained by discourses of political correctness' and the study participants' own accounts of 9/11 (2006, p. 983).

Other research involving news media audiences has focused on media audience members' perceptions of bias in television news programs during and after 9/11 (Banaji and Al-Ghabban, 2006). Banaji and Al-Ghabban interviewed Indian television viewers in Bombay and British-Asian television viewers in South-East England between December 2001 and March 2002, and discovered that international news coverage, which focused on the key themes of 'blame, evidence and retribution with regard to the Twin Tower and Pentagon attacks', had a significant impact on their study participants' levels of dislike for Muslims, while also cementing animosities towards Muslim communities internationally (2006, p. 1005). In exploring how participants in their study responded to the events of 9/11, Banaji and Al-Ghabban found that their study participants expressed concern for relatives and friends abroad. Additionally, they found that their participants were critical of some aspects of the television news coverage of 9/11, particularly what some believed was the misuse of images of Palestinians that purported to show them cheering at the news of the attacks, but which were actually associated with events in 1992. Their study participants expressed frustration at the news media's presentation of Western events such as 9/11 as 'more tragic and significant than troubles in non-Western nations' (Banaji and Al-Ghabban, 2006, p. 1014).

Matar examined how the reportage of 9/11 in the United Kingdom and Arab/Muslim news media impacted on the ways Palestinians living in Britain engaged with issues around 'identity and difference, exclusion and inclusion, memory and belonging' (2006, p. 1027). She used individual interviews and focus groups to investigate these issues between November 2001 and March 2002. Muslim participants in her study reported feeling closer to their religion and defensive about their identity. Some of her study participants felt vindicated when they heard the news, while others felt sympathy for the Americans killed in the attacks.

We were surprised to find that there were relatively few identifiable studies of news media audiences and their responses to 9/11, and even fewer longitudinal studies of this kind. However, a number of studies have examined the longer-term impact of 9/11, both in terms of perceptions of Western societies about Islam and Muslims and in terms of Muslims' perceptions of prejudice and Islamophobia attributed to the media coverage of 9/11 and the war on terror. For instance, Tayob (2006) documents an accelerated call for the integration of Muslims in the Netherlands, coupled with arguments that Islamic values are incompatible with those of Dutch society. Yousif (2005), however, identified both negative and positive impacts of post-9/11 media coverage on the Canadian Muslim community, including an association of Islam with terrorism, discrimination and hate crimes against Muslims and increased levels of fear and anxiety. Positive impacts included a greater interest in Islam among Canadians, increased interreligious dialogue, and a shift in journalistic practice aimed at increasing objectivity and reducing bias (Yousif, 2005). In another study, Panagopoulos (2006) used a survey method to track American attitudes towards Arabs and Muslims post-9/11, and found that anxiety about Islam and its compatibility with Western values of tolerance, acceptance and civility reached a peak in the years following 9/11 but had stabilized by the middle of the decade.

Based on qualitative data gathered through focus group sessions with Muslim students in New York in October 2001, Peek (2003) found that the participants were shocked by the attacks and feared a backlash against their community if Muslims were responsible for the attacks. The students reported being more cautious than usual and fearful in respect to their personal safety. Peek also found that her participants overwhelmingly blamed the discrimination they experienced on the media reporting on Islam, Muslims and Arabs following the 9/11 attacks (Peek, 2003). As a consequence of the media coverage, most participants reported feeling pressure to prove they were American and not disloyal to the nation. In a study based on interviews with Muslim university students conducted five years after 9/11, Muedini (2009) found that the impact of 9/11 continued to be experienced in the form of feelings of being less safe in an atmosphere of fear attributed to the discourse around the PATRIOT Act. In terms of integration and acceptance, the same study found that, while the interviewees expressed a desire to be Americans, they felt excluded (Muedini, 2009).

Overwhelmingly, the interviewees attributed the negativity towards Arabs and Muslims to the media, which they considered responsible for their social exclusion. Indeed, there has been a plethora of studies concerning media representations of Muslims and Islam since 9/11 which have found that portrayals of Muslims as terrorists and Islam as a religion that condones terrorism continue to be commonplace (Martin and Phelan, 2002; Tayob, 2006; Aly, 2007).

Audience analysis

We held four focus groups with news media audiences, two for non-Muslims and two for Muslims, in May 2012. We held separate focus groups for these cohorts so that non-Muslims and Muslims would feel free to express their feelings without fear of having to censor their opinions or language. Although we were keen to ensure the participants represented a range of ages and included a relatively even mix of women and men, our aim was to ensure we had a sample of participants who had followed the events of 11 September 2001 in various media and who were willing to discuss their recollection of that coverage and the media coverage of the tenth anniversary of 9/11.

The focus groups allowed an exploration of participants' experiences in relation to the research theme, and they could also 'generate their own questions, frames and concepts, and pursue their own priorities on their own terms, in their own vocabulary' (Kitzinger and Barbour, 1999, pp. 4–5). We primarily aimed to bring together a theoretical sample with the purpose of creating conversations that would allow the building of thought on an issue (Glasser and Strauss, 1967; Macnaughten and Myers, 2006). While we recognize that self-nomination to focus groups can be problematic, it can also be useful in that participants tend to be more actively engaged with and interested in the research topic.

Initial reactions

We began our focus group sessions by asking our participants to recall their initial reactions to the coverage of the attacks on 11 September 2001. Remarkably, the responses given by Muslims and non-Muslims differed significantly. Overwhelmingly, non-Muslims were shocked by the events of 9/11. Many of our participants expressed that they were in a state of distress and bewilderment. Some even conveyed that as the news was initially breaking they were in a state of disbelief and thought they were watching a movie or a 21st-century version of *War of the Worlds*. As expressed by one non-Muslim participant:

I said 'well this is an interesting movie'. Then I realized that it's, hang on, this is happening now....Think I went bed for a while. Just an initial sort of worry and then it's all 'do we know anybody over there?' Um, aw, hang on a minute; we've got some friends over there who are actually working in New York...As we sort of, woke up in the morning...the other plane hit. And it was (mimes chewing fingers of both hands), sort of, (mimes chewing fingers of both hands) you know. And sort of, so, holy cow!...It was surreal.

This response was typical of our non-Muslim participants, whose recollections combined initial disbelief, concern for friends or relatives in the United States, and a general impression of the event as 'surreal'. Notably absent from their stories were any immediate thoughts about who or what was responsible, namely the terrorists, Muslims or Islam. Very few of our non-Muslim or Muslim participants had even heard of Al-Qaeda or Osama bin Laden prior to 9/11. However, in the days following the attacks, as the media coverage began to report that Muslim terrorists were responsible, perceptions of Islam and Muslims began to form. Many of our non-Muslim participants stated that they had had little or no familiarity with Islam or Muslims prior to 9/11, but the news coverage of the event brought Islam and its adherents into sharp focus for them. The media coverage of those responsible for the attacks evoked mixed responses from our non-Muslim participants. Some responded with pragmatism or even skepticism. For instance, one non-Muslim participant expressed: 'You know, they blamed the Muslims but really it was American fault too. They shouldn't have gone into Iraq, pushed them around you know. This was a big mistake'.

Contrasting experiences were expressed by some of the younger non-Muslim participants who were in school in 2001. For example, one participant commented that 'all of the boys in my grade were ready to go to war straight away. That day they were ready to pack up and leave and go to war'. This participant later explained that the response of her classmates was not driven by hostility towards Muslims per se, but whoever happened to be held responsible for attacking America: 'at the time the feeling was it doesn't matter so much who has done this, what matters is that it's happened and that America is intending to do something about it and we will support America'.

In contrast to the non-Muslim participants, whose initial reactions to the coverage of 9/11 were marked by shock and disbelief, our Muslim participants responded to the news with fear and anxiety. This is consistent with the findings of other studies of Muslim responses to 9/11

(Peek, 2003; Muedini, 2009). Overwhelmingly, the participants of both Muslim focus groups all conveyed that when they became aware of the terrorist attacks on 9/11 their immediate response was one of concern for their own personal safety and that of their family and friends. This response was a consequence of the abuse and prejudice Muslim communities in Australia had experienced in the aftermath of such events as the Gulf War in 1991 (Poynting and Noble, 2004). The news of the 9/11 terrorist attacks was accompanied by a collective sense of dread and hope that Muslims were not responsible. As one Muslim participant explained:

> I watched the second plane go in but my first thought was I hope they are not Muslims. That was my first thought and that is usually my first thought with anything that goes on around the world – God I hope they don't have a Muslim name.

Another Muslim participant elaborated, conveying the concern of Muslims for their personal safety:

> I remember getting dressed to go to uni [university] that day, that morning and my dad said to me, 'do you know what has just happened' and I said 'no' and so he told me. My heart just dropped and I thought how could this happen. He said 'do you know who has done it?' and I said 'obviously not', and he said 'Muslims, have claimed responsibility'. And my heart dropped again and I thought okay right I am going to uni and I got scared . . . because I was wearing hijab at that time and I thought safety, fear, what's going to happen. My friend came to pick me up . . . on the way to uni [we] kept silent, didn't say anything, we were in shock.

This particular participant informed us that, while she did not experience any physical abuse, she and other Muslim university students experienced taunts from other university students targeting their sense of belonging in Australia. Younger Muslim participants reported being fearful to go to school after 9/11 and concern for their own social acceptance: 'I was hesitant and I was hyper-vigilant about what might happen afterwards . . . not for my personal, physical safety, more my social safety at school, my acceptance'. Other Muslim participants who were also school-age at the time of 9/11 also reported being under similar pressure as a consequence of the media coverage and the fear prevalent in the Muslim community. One participant, who had just begun high school at the time of 9/11, explained that, in an attempt to protect her from social exclusion or ridicule, her relatives coached her on how to respond to questions about the attacks. This defensive response was more pronounced among Muslim participants who were young men at the time. One Muslim participant, who was 20 years of age when the attacks occurred, described his emotional turmoil in terms of confusion about the attacks, defensiveness in respect to his identity, and offensiveness towards segments of the wider Australian society.

The fears of Muslims intensified in the weeks after 9/11 when a school bus carrying Muslim children was pelted with bottles and stones and the Kuraby Mosque in Brisbane, Australia was burned down in an arson attack. It resulted in a strong sense of vulnerability among the Muslim community and a perceived need to physically defend the mosques. As one participant explained:

> And it got worse when the Mosque got burned... everyone was running to the mosque and it was like 'if they can burn the mosque and are they going to get away with it?' The young men were really outraged, how could this happen, and what's next are they going to take our sisters, and with the bus, the Islamic school bus got stoned... and my girls were going to the school and I was thinking, 'what they are going to barge into the school and burn it down, how far are they going to go?' I felt my brothers were like okay, they had guards at the mosque the boys had shifts who is going to guard the mosque, so there was a lot of emotion and it took a lot of the leaders of the community to say 'calm down. Let's not do what they do'.

The Muslim participants' reading of the media coverage of the events of 9/11 was that it targeted all Muslims and Islam as being responsible for the terrorist attacks. This made many Muslims feel very defensive. As put by one participant:

> With the media, I remember always feeling demonized, it made you feel horrible, sad, brought up so many emotions, and defensive as well and there were some programs I can't believe I sat through an hour watching it, just crying my eyes out thinking, how could people think this and believe this, how is this popular?

The general consensus among our Muslim participants was that the media coverage of 9/11 was responsible for the prejudice they experienced and the tension they felt from the wider society.

Muslims also responded to the coverage of 9/11 with a combination of anger and disappointment arising from what they perceived to be an absence of Muslim voices and a failure to report the Muslim perspective. While our Muslim participants did express sadness for the deaths of Americans on 9/11, they also conveyed a deep sense of frustration with what many of them described as a double standard, inequality or unfairness in the media coverage of victims. For instance, one Muslim participant recalled her thoughts and feelings as she watched the coverage of 9/11 during the first day following the attack as follows:

> I feel for these people [victims of 9/11], my heart goes out to them, regardless of whether they were Muslim or non-Muslim and I am thinking about this projection of these non-Muslims who had died. Nothing was mentioned about Muslims who had died, or you know any other faith or culture, it was just these white American people, that was all that was projected and that you kept on getting. And I am thinking you know, everything that has happened around the world, especially in Palestine, it was nothing like this, we never were bombarded constantly, bombarded by images, women screaming. And I started thinking I feel for these people but why is it that some races are seen as superior and are able to be all around the world, sympathy towards them, but another race gets dismissed and is seen as less equal.

In this respect, our Muslim participants saw the media as biased and unfair to the extent that they do not provide audiences with the necessary context to have an informed opinion about issues concerning Islam or Muslims.

Ten years on

Research on the ninth and tenth anniversary coverage of 9/11 found that the media have moved on from a focus on those responsible to a focus on the victims and reconciliation with Muslim communities (Ewart and Rane, 2011; Rane and Ewart, 2012). We conducted the focus groups for this study in order to identify whether our study participants shared this view. Overall, our non-Muslim participants did recognize a significant change in the 9/11 anniversary coverage over the past ten years. The general sentiment among the non-Muslim participants was that, compared with the early years, the media coverage of the tenth anniversary was 'less sensational and less intense'. Almost all participants noted a shift in focus away from terrorists to a focus on the victims of the attacks. Many participants specifically recalled the main features of the tenth anniversary coverage, including the memorial services and stories of the victims' families. The following statement by one participant encapsulates the views expressed by most of our non-Muslim participants:

> As the years went by the focus of the coverage was more on honoring the people who have died, honoring, I mean celebrating their lives and there's more acceptance I think, there's more acceptance of the fact that it happened because we cannot change it any more. We cannot change it, so we just have to accept and celebrate the lives of those people who were involved in it. There's not too much hype anymore because emotions died down, emotions of the people have died down, although there are still some who are maybe extremists.

Similarly, many of our non-Muslim participants not only reported being far less emotionally involved ten years on but also reported being disengaged, desensitized and fatigued by the coverage of 9/11. Some, however, expressed frustration with the fact that the questions they had about the original event and how it was carried out have still not been answered a decade later. They regard this as a failure of the media in terms of investigative reporting and what media studies scholars would refer to as the media's role as the fourth estate (Rane, Ewart and Abdalla, 2010).

The responses we received from our Muslim participants contrasted sharply with those of the non-Muslims. Among the Muslim participants, recognition of a shift in media coverage over the decade was more modest. A number of Muslims commented on the absence of the image of the planes hitting the towers in the tenth anniversary coverage and the focus on memorial services for the victims. A number of participants commented that ten years on from 9/11 there are fewer negative stories and more positive reporting about Muslims. However, there was a general sentiment that the coverage continues to 'find an angle' to portray Muslims negatively. Others also criticized the media for what they perceived to be a continued practice of denying Muslims a voice. Many reported criticism from non-Muslim friends, colleagues and family members in respect to the Muslim community not 'standing up to' or making definitive statements condemning the terrorists. They complained that numerous and repeated statements have been made by leaders of the Muslim community but that these are not reported in the media.

It is noteworthy that, towards the end of each of our focus groups, there were more acknowledgements from our Muslim participants that the media had evolved and had become more balanced in their representations of Muslims. It was also acknowledged that this shift in media coverage correlated with more positive public sentiments. As explained by one Muslim participant:

> I think Australian media is growing up quite a bit. I don't think David Hicks or Dr Haneef would have had the same sympathetic coverage back in say 2002 or 2003 that they had. The Federal Police certainly wouldn't have gotten the same lambasting that they got in the media, publicly for such a sustained period over Dr Haneef that they [would] have ten years ago.

Perceptions of Islam and Muslims

It is widely acknowledged that the 9/11 terrorist attacks had a major impact on relations between Muslims and non-Muslims in Western countries (Rane, Ewart and Abdalla, 2010). We were specifically interested in our focus group participants' views on the impact of the media coverage of 9/11 on their understanding, attitudes and opinions regarding Muslims and the extent to which those views have changed over the past decade. The general sentiment of our non-Muslim participants is that the coverage of 9/11 made them more aware of Islam and Muslims. Most reported that their recollection of the initial coverage was that the media focus on Islam and Muslims was not immediate but developed in the weeks, months and years following the terrorist attacks. For a number of non-Muslim participants, their negative perceptions of Muslims formed in response to footage of Muslims allegedly cheering in response to the attacks. As one participant stated: 'I got angry when I saw the Islamic nations cheering. Like the footage of them out in the streets burning the American flag going yeah' (waved his fist in the air). Another participant was able to put this coverage in perspective, rightly noting that the footage pre-dated 9/11, and also expressing:

> I think September 11 that was before *Al Jazeera*, so I guess we weren't really getting balanced media coverage from the Middle East and things like that, and you've got rent a crowds anywhere, potentially ill-informed, ill-educated poor peasants, that's a side-effect. Nonetheless it is damaging, yeah it's offensive.

While our non-Muslim participants acknowledged they knew little, if anything, about Islam in 2001, they acknowledged that the media coverage of 9/11 had had a major impact on public perceptions of Muslims. Conveying the general sentiments of both non-Muslim focus groups, one participant expressed: 'I think that the two [Muslims and terrorism] are so inextricably linked that people's perceptions of Muslims now are totally, not totally but to a large extent informed by those events, by 9/11. Yeah and by the media coverage of that'. For some, their perceptions of Muslims were shaped gradually by media coverage and came to inform their negative views of Muslims in the context of the war on terror and Australia's asylum seeker debate. Some participants also reported that the media coverage of 9/11 had made them aware of their own naivety in respect to Muslims, and subsequently they began to identify a problem with Muslim integration. The following statement exemplifies such views:

> My feelings are that I did change after that [9/11]; I was less naive I think, a little bit concerned when people stick in their own. Like they come to Australia or they go to America and they want to integrate but they don't. They send their children to a Muslim school; well they're not going to integrate are they?

Other participants responded to such statements by giving context to the Muslim integration debate, noting that the media do not respond in the same way to the clustering of Chinese and Vietnamese in particular suburbs.

There was, however, general agreement among our non-Muslim participants that the media representation of Muslims in the aftermath of 9/11 made them suspicious of Muslim people. Examples of such responses include:

> You know where I work we will get a whole heap of Arab people all coming in and I think hmm they could be plotting something, you know. It just puts things in your mind that weren't there before. You're just more aware and because it happened, it could probably happen again.

For some of our older non-Muslim participants, the 9/11 terrorist attacks confirmed their existing perceptions of Islam and Muslims. One participant, for instance, reported having grown up with Muslims in Sydney and believed fighting to be 'ingrained' in their culture, 'drummed into them from an early age'. Other participants countered this view with one stating that 'there's good and bad in every race'. However, conveying a sentiment shared by others in the group (acknowledged by nods of agreement), another participant retorted: 'Mine's more against the culture, like what sort of culture would allow to have people blow themselves up and blow other people up?' Many of our non-Muslim participants disagreed with such views that tend to see Islam or Muslims monolithically, and expressed opinions that demonstrated a differentiation between extremism and the mainstream in relation to Muslim people and their beliefs.

A number of non-Muslims made sense of the 9/11 attacks and of Muslims by making comparisons with the conflict in Northern Ireland. For instance:

> I know what you are saying about Muslims in general, that you can't tar them all with the same brush because they are individual people. Just like in Northern Ireland it is a very small, a very small part of that society. And it's, I don't think, I am just thinking of how to word this, to call them Muslims is like they are all the same but they are actually terrorists. They might be Muslims, it's a religion, it is not a race. They are using the religious, well people generalize I think to say that wherever there are Muslims there is trouble. That's the impression I get probably through media as well.

Concurring with this view, a participant from another focus group conveyed his frustration with the media coverage of 9/11 by describing the representation of Muslims as 'an over-simplification; it's almost an "us" and "them" mentality'.

Some participants were able to make a distinction between Islam and terrorism but maintained that Muslims in general potentially pose a risk: 'It's [terrorism] a human problem but are we putting ourselves at a greater risk by bringing some of that potential problem into the country in the first place?' Another participant retorted by making a similar distinction to the one above, explaining: 'they said the same thing about the Irish a hundred years ago and these Muslims are just people like everyone else. There is nothing about their culture in particular that pre-disposes them to terrorism. Look at Anders Breivik right now, he was a radical Christian'.

Our non-Muslim participants generally attributed a central role to the media in terms of the negative sentiments towards Muslims that developed in response to 9/11. In an exchange between three participants, the first participant commented that 'the media themselves is a lot to blame for a lot of blowing it up more than it needed to be because the focus of it was news'. A second participant then stated: 'that's what sells papers'.

A third participant added: 'that's what sells papers. That's what gets people onto the tele [television] and stuff like that. But I think now we are starting to see a lot more, I am feeling a lot more stability in what people think'. This exchange suggests that participants are aware of news values related to conflict and crises as well as the economic imperatives of media organizations to attract audiences. This awareness seems to correspond with caution in media consumption and consequently inhibits the extent to which the media coverage continues to influence these participants' perceptions of Islam and Muslims.

Reflecting on how the media coverage of Muslims has evolved over the past decade, our non-Muslim participants also agreed that the public perception of Muslims has also improved to the extent that they are more accepting of Muslims in general. As one non-Muslim participant explained:

> You read about a lot of negative things, but it just feels, my family is more accepting, we were aware for a while, but we are now more accepting. We live in Calamvale and there's a lot of Muslims around us, but we're just more accepting of them. We're just looking at them as people like you said (points to another participant) everybody's got a bad and good and we're just sort of more accepting; we're putting them in the melting pot now.

A comment that was also met with general agreement was that the Muslim community gained appreciation for the support it gave to the victims of the 2011 Brisbane flood. In one participant's words:

> Everyone was just coming together, it didn't matter what your race, color or creed, was ... but you hear the same stories in the media and everyone just coming together from different walks of life and I guess that's kind of helped, a bit of understanding, a bit of appreciation of people regardless of whether it's Christian or Islam.

Towards the conclusion of our focus group sessions, a number of non-Muslim participants expressed sympathy for the Muslim community. For example, one participant said:

> I sort of feel a bit sorry for the Islamic community because you know we focus on what they did to us, but all of those people they had nothing to do with it, they just happen to have been lumped into the same category, the cultural, religious background, what about

them? You've got to feel a bit sad about them. I remember in Sydney some of the girls would get heckled because she's definitely a Muslim because she's wearing the headdress, so they would get heckled, but again they didn't do anything. So you've got to feel a bit of sympathy for them.

Her words encapsulated the sentiments of many of our participants who, since the 9/11 terrorist attacks, had clearly become more aware of Muslims and were able to contextualize the attacks as an act of extremist individuals not endorsed by the majority of Muslims. There was an important point of convergence between the responses of our Muslim and non-Muslim participants in respect to the acceptance of Muslims in Australian society. While some still felt a degree of fear and suspicion of Muslims, in general our non-Muslim participants differentiated between the majority and the extremists who represent a small proportion of the Muslim community. Equally important is that our non-Muslim participants demonstrated a heightened awareness that the mass media do not necessarily portray the reality of Islam and Muslims and there is a tendency to focus on the negative and sensational in the reporting of Muslim and other issues.

On the other hand, while our Muslim participants seem to perceive media and public negativity towards them to be more prevalent than our research suggests, Muslims are engaged in self-criticism, and they acknowledged that media and public negativity regarding Islam and Muslims has subsided over the past decade. Many of our Muslim participants recognized that the media are not entirely responsible for the negative coverage of Muslims. For instance, in reference to the concept of *jihad* and its use in the media, one participant commented: 'although we blame the media for it, at the same time those fanatics will actually use that word in that context incorrectly and the media would copy that'.

Our final focus group with our Muslim participants concluded on a note of optimism that was positively acknowledged by all in the room:

I do see lots of stories coming out that are fairly positive... that provides the opportunity for us [Muslims], as long as the community here, no matter where you come from, if you are saying 'I am an Australian Muslim and I am here to stay, I'm not going anywhere else, I love this country, by me being a good Muslim I will be an excellent citizen'. Because it is possible to be a great citizen but a terrible Muslim, but it is impossible to be an excellent Muslim and a bad citizen, impossible. So as long as we have that concern, it will destroy the 'us' and 'them'.

Reconciliation

We identified a number of similarities between our findings and those studies that explored the responses of media audiences to 9/11 news coverage shortly after those events occurred. As with Peek's (2003) and Muedini's (2009) studies, we found that our Muslim participants were shocked by the attacks, feared a backlash against their community, and were concerned for their personal safety in the weeks following 9/11. Both Peek and Muedini also found that their participants over-whelmingly blamed the discrimination they experienced on the media reporting on Islam and Muslims following the 9/11 attacks, and our study showed that Muslims continue to blame the media ten years on. However, having conducted our focus group sessions ten years after 9/11, we found that Muslims are recognizing a positive shift in media coverage, including more positive stories about Muslims, as well as self-criticism among Muslims that has enabled them to understand that the media coverage is not necessarily biased against Islam but reflects what Muslims themselves do, rightly or wrongly, in the name of Islam.

For our study participants, the media were the central channel through which they found out about and subsequently remembered 9/11, and, just as Kitch (2002) identified, the media are central in collective memory-making. It is important to recognize that our research was undertaken more than a decade after 9/11, and participants may have constructed and reconstructed their recollections of those events in the intervening years. However, our findings indicate that, for these media audience members, the media, in particular television, have had a powerful influence on their collective memory-making in relation to 9/11, just as Kitch (2002) and Edy (1999) demonstrated in their work. Participants in our study engaged with, or chose not to engage with, 9/11 through the news media, and their recollections of those events were largely constructed and reconstructed through television news coverage, even for those who decided not to continue to engage with news media about these events. Edy identified that the process of collective memory-making via the media 'informs our understanding of past events and present relationships, and it contributes to our expectations about the future' (1999, p. 71). According to our study participants, both Muslim and non-Muslim, the media have been central to the way Muslims and Islam are understood, or misunderstood, and how these Australian media audiences have come to perceive them. For some of the non-Muslims in our study this largely revolved around suspicion of Muslims, which does not appear to have abated over time, while for Muslims it largely involved responding to criticisms about their faith or being on the receiving end of attacks motivated by these events.

Our results bear some similarities to those of Adams and Burke (2006). The non-Muslim participants in our study reacted to the news of 9/11 in comparable ways to participants in Adams and Burke's (2006) study. Participants in both studies used terms such as 'shock' and 'disbelief' to describe their responses to the events of 9/11; many described the events as surreal and reported that they initially thought it was a hoax. Our study participants were, with the exception of one individual, able to recall exactly where they were and who they were with when they first heard the news about 9/11. Adams and Burke (2006) found that this was also the case with the people they interviewed for their study. Their research found that engagement with media, for their participants, formed part of a process of attempting to understand and make sense of why the events of 9/11 had occurred, and this was also the case for our non-Muslim participants. Adams and Burke (2006) did not interview Muslims as part of their study, so we are unable to make comparisons between their study and our findings in relation to Muslim participants. The other note of caution here is that their study was undertaken within a relatively short time after the events of 9/11 (four to six months), whereas ours was undertaken ten years later.

Conclusion

Our study shows that the narratives about Muslims and Islam in connection with 9/11 have shifted. The dominant frame across the five free-to-air Australian television news broadcasts was commemoration through the memorials and ceremonies taking place in both the United States and Australia, for which the central focus was the remembrance of the victims. Notably absent from the coverage was any reference to Islam or Muslims in terms of responsibility for the 9/11 attacks. While a number of the news stories make reference to the Taliban and Al-Qaeda, Muslims in general were not conflated with such groups, nor is the ideology of such groups presented as a mainstream interpretation of Islam. The coverage of the tenth anniversary did not make reference to an Islamic threat. Rather, the few references to the religion and its adherents appeared in the context of bridge-building, moving on and reconciliation. These findings mark a departure from previous research on media representations of Islam and Muslims post-9/11 and indicate a trend away from the pejorative reportage that has been apparent for much of the past decade.

Just as the news media have 'moved on' from 9/11 and come to focus on reconciliation, particularly in terms of relations with Muslims, in general audiences have also moved on. Our non-Muslim participants generally expressed informed and discerning opinions about Muslims. However, the process of moving on from 9/11 is less pronounced among our Muslim participants, who continue to feel targeted by the media and perceive negative public sentiments to have decreased but still remain prevalent. While it is not possible to extrapolate our findings to media audiences internationally, or even nationally, due to the small size of our sample, our study has revealed that the television news media in Australia have in some ways contributed to a sense of reconciliation and mutual acceptance between Muslims and non-Muslims, and this is an area that requires more research. Further research is needed to determine whether the increasing acceptance of Muslims by non-Muslims that we identified in our findings will be sustained into the future.

Conclusion

From the Western media perspective, the Muslim world looks monolithic, static, different and oppositional. We wrote in Chapter 1 that Muslims will soon comprise one-quarter of the world's population, with approximately 60 per cent residing in the Asia-Pacific region, while only 20 per cent live in the Middle East. These figures contradict the popular image of Muslims as Arabs. The overwhelming majority of Muslims remain committed to Islam's central beliefs and practices, which originated almost 1500 years ago in the same geographical milieu as the other Abrahamic faiths, Judaism and Christianity. These three faiths have more in common than is widely acknowledged. In general, however, the views of Muslims about social issues are more conservative than those of Westerners, but this should not be perceived as a source of conflict. Muslims are far more culturally, religiously and ideologically diverse than they are portrayed to be in Western media coverage. Moreover, the development of democracy in Turkey and Indonesia, and more recently its emergence in Tunisia and Egypt, denies the orientalist perspective of the Muslim world as static and incapable of progress. A limited understanding of these facts among audiences leaves them susceptible to accepting narrow media coverage of specific Muslim individuals and groups as representative of Muslims in general. This results in flawed analysis and misconceptions concerning the evolving realities of the Muslim world.

This book set out to explain why pejorative representations of Islam and Muslims have become dominant. From a historical perspective, the Muslim world has been understood by Western thinkers through an orientalist framework, which emphasizes difference and positions Islam and Muslims as a strange 'other', which is antithetical to the West. In respect to the Muslim world, orientalism has influenced news values, which prioritize stories that are negative, controversial or unusual, including crime, violence, conflicts and crises. To the extent that a minority of Muslims continues to engage in actions that fit within these frames, they will continue to be part of the news agenda. Framing is a particularly useful approach to analyzing both media content and its potential impact on audiences. A sign of improvement in the West's view of Muslims will not be that Muslims become good news stories, as bad news rather than good news will continue to be the focus of the media in general. Rather, improvement in the situation will be apparent when Muslims cease to make the news as the fundamental teachings of Islam are not newsworthy. A deep-seated problem has been the overuse of religion (Islam) and religious affiliation (Muslim) to explain issues and events that are actually a consequence of political, economic, social, cultural, psychological or other factors. Journalists would do well to resist the temptation to use Islam as the basis for explaining all issues and events involving Muslims. Seeing Muslims as human beings first might allow a range of human factors, rather than exclusively religious ones, to inform public discourses and media analysis.

At the turn of the century, journalists were somewhat unprepared to provide the extensive and intense coverage of Islam that media organizations demanded in the aftermath of 9/11. Journalists at the time had limited, if any, knowledge of Islam and few, if any, contacts with Muslim communities. Initially, they were forced to rely on outspoken but unrepresentative Muslim clerics who had been sporadically featured in the news in the years prior to 9/11. Such representatives further marginalized Western Muslims by making them seem foreign and out of place in Western society. However, over time many journalists have acquired a sound knowledge of Islam and an extensive network of contacts with Muslim communities. Those who have more recently entered the profession may have benefited from the opportunity to take a course or two on Islam at university, as the field of Islamic Studies has grown at the tertiary level over the past decade. Journalists have also learned from colleagues who have spent time in the Muslim world as foreign correspondents. Meanwhile, Muslim communities have been proactive, appointing media spokespersons, establishing media liaison positions within their organizations, engaging with the media to get their voice heard, issuing press releases in an attempt to contribute to the news agenda, developing media kits and hosting workshops to provide journalists with information about Islam and Muslims.

However, Muslim individuals and groups continue to engage in acts of violence, terrorism, violations of human rights and the oppression of women. These are often done in the name of Islam, and journalists are correct to report them within this context. However, only an extreme minority of Muslims believe that terrorism or violence against innocent civilians can be justified by Islam, while human rights and gender issues are often a matter of Muslim culture, education, socio-economic factors and political conditions rather than religion. The context of the story is vital if audiences are to be meaningfully informed. This is not to deny that significant reform is needed in certain aspects of Islamic law and dogma. Chapter 2 identified that the hostility and negativity associated with Western media coverage of Islam and the Muslim world has been traced back to medieval Christian writings. These ideas influenced orientalist thought during the era of European colonial rule of the Muslim world and have continued into modern times. Western media portrayals of Islam and the Muslim world have been instrumental in evoking a fear of Islam and discrimination against Muslims. The phenomenon of Islamophobia is a major concern of the Organization for Islamic Cooperation (OIC), Muslim governments and Muslim organizations in Western countries. It is important to note that Muslim organizations that combat Islamophobia are not opposed to free expression, and these organizations recognize the right of others to question and engage in legitimate criticism of Islam and Muslims. We also identified a number of factors that mitigate the potential influence of the media's negative and stereotypical portrayal of Muslims, including higher levels of education, interaction with Muslims and perceptions of media credibility. However, the further removed audiences are from an issue or event, the more reliant they tend to be on the media.

In Chapter 3 we examined the image and reality of reporting war and conflict in the Muslim world. The war on terror resulted in massive death and destruction in Afghanistan and Iraq. Moreover, these invasions have resulted in the emergence of a range of new *jihadist* groups as well as grievances among Muslims that have on occasions manifested in terrorist attacks on the West. Given the controversial nature of the invasions of Afghanistan and Iraq, the Western governments that participated in them have been perplexed by media coverage of the devastating realities, which is vastly inconsistent with the image that these governments want to project. Consequently, journalists have not only faced grave security threats in reporting these wars but have also had to battle with political forces in order to uphold the principles of the fourth estate.

In Chapter 4 we examined the intersections between media coverage, public opinion and political responses to asylum seekers. Those who have fled their homeland as a consequence of these wars have not only found themselves as victims of conflict, but, in their search for refuge, have become the victims of prejudice, stereotypes and Islamophobia. Ironically, the regimes in Afghanistan and Iraq were so terrible that they warranted the forceful removal of their leadership, yet Western governments have dehumanized and mistreated those who fled these regimes in search of asylum. The policy of deterring asylum seekers responds to sentiments held by a segment of the public that these refugees pose a threat to the country, which is based on an unfounded fear that gained legitimacy post-9/11. Rather than acting as the fourth estate, some sections of the media have unquestioningly repeated political rhetoric and reinforced the public's negative sentiments towards asylum seekers. Government policies on asylum seekers that resonate with and reinforce misconceptions held by the general public become resilient and are further reinforced when the media fail to challenge them. We identified that there is potential for the news media to take more nuanced approaches to covering asylum seekers and that it is possible to change the way asylum seekers are portrayed.

The historic and contemporary discourses about Muslims as a threatening other have also impacted on security responses to the 9/11 and 7/7 terrorist attacks. Most Western countries have implemented robust anti-terror laws that have posed a challenge to journalists' ability to carry out their fourth estate responsibilities. Journalists have faced difficulties because of their lack of knowledge of national security legislation. In Chapter 5 we documented cases of journalists who have worked with authorities to ensure national security interests are protected, while informing the public of terrorism plots within the established constraints. This indicates that there is potential for journalists and courts to work together without compromising national security or the public interest. However, relationships between journalists and security agencies during terrorism cases are complicated by the strictures imposed by anti-terror laws. Moreover, the coverage of such issues, while in the public interest, significantly contributes to the pejorative image of Islam and perceptions of Muslims as a threat. However, there are important exceptions, such as the case of Dr Haneef, in which fourth estate journalism resulted in Haneef's release.

The Arab Spring was a rare good news story during 2011 on account of its framing as uprisings calling for freedom and democracy. In Chapter 6 we noted that Western journalists were welcomed by activists who used social media not only to organize protest activities but to transfer images and information for worldwide dissemination. The framing of the Arab

Spring in the Western media played a significant role in shaping the response of Western governments. The Western media were essential in telling the story of the people and showing their plight as they mobilized against brutal regimes. In Tunisia and Egypt, where these uprisings became revolutions, the Western media became less enthusiastic once Islamic-oriented parties were elected to government. Western publics' views of the uprisings also transformed from a sense of hope to concern, in spite of the fact that the elections were democratic, the parties elected were relatively moderate and they were committed to the democratic system as well as protecting civil rights and liberties. The shift in media and public discourse indicates the endurance of orientalist and Islamophobic sentiments. We also examined the relationship between citizen and professional journalists. Particularly in the context of the civil war in Syria, the danger faced by journalists has placed them in a similar situation to those who previously reported from Iraq. Being embedded with one side in the conflict has limited journalists' ability to obtain reliable information and report the reality. Again, journalists have found themselves on one side of a propaganda war.

Since the turn of the century, Islam–West relations have predominantly been viewed from the perspective of Huntington's clash of civilizations theory. According to this perspective, the Muslim world is destined to clash with the West on account of the former's resentment of the latter's power, success and dominance. Key issues that have been cited as evidence for this perspective include the 2006 Danish cartoon controversy and the 2012 riots in response to the *Innocence of Muslims* film. The fact that Muslims engaged in violent protests in response was seen by many as proof of their inability to accept such democratic principles as free speech and behave in a civilized manner. However, majorities among most Western publics agreed that the cartoons were provocative and offensive and that the decision to publish them was irresponsible. Additionally, the number of Muslims who engaged in violent protests against the film was relatively small and unrepresentative of the sentiments of the majority of Muslims, whose leadership opposed the protests as unacceptable and un-Islamic. We highlighted in Chapter 7 that Islamic and Western conceptions of freedom of expression are not necessarily incompatible, especially when considered from the perspective of social and media responsibility. There is a clash of civilizations where there is a monolithic view of the other informed by misconceptions and stereotypes. Those who are more discerning, able to find common ground and identify with the other are less convinced that a clash of civilizations is inevitable.

Chapter 8 identified not only a shift in media coverage in respect to the representation of Islam and Muslims but also a corresponding shift in audience perceptions and understanding of the religion and its adherents. Our findings show that the news media have moved away from conflating terrorism with Muslims and Islam in the context of 9/11. We found that the tenth anniversary coverage of 9/11 was presented within frames of 'reconciliation' and 'moving on'. The dominant news frames were based on a shared worldview, common experiences of lives lost in the attacks and a unified response in the context of the 'war on terror'. Notably absent from the coverage was the attribution of responsibility for the 9/11 attacks to Muslim communities. Rather, the news media tended to focus on bridge-building and reconciliation. These findings mark a departure from previous research on news media representations of Islam and Muslims post-9/11 and indicate a trend away from the pejorative reportage that has been apparent for much of the past decade. In respect to audiences, our findings show that, while Muslims and non-Muslims have different readings of the news media coverage, there are important points of convergence in respect to the process of reconciliation and mutual acceptance. While a number of the news stories made reference to the Taliban and Al-Qaeda, Muslims in general were not conflated with such groups, nor was the ideology of such groups perceived as a mainstream interpretation of Islam. In the main, news media audiences seem to be more discerning in respect of Islam and Muslims and better able to distinguish between extremists and the mainstream.

However, responses from segments of the Western media and publics to the 2013 Boston bombing and the murder of a British soldier in Woolwich, South-East London, raise doubts about the extent to which we have really moved on from 9/11. Based on current information, both attacks were committed by Muslim men with grievances about Western foreign policy concerning the Muslim world, specifically the involvement of Western forces in Iraq and Afghanistan. The Boston Marathon bombing on 15 April 2013 attracted broad public outrage, as did the execution-style murder in London on 22 May 2013. The issue of Islamist terrorism returned to the top of the news agenda. The Pew Research Center found that a majority of those surveyed followed the story of the bombing closely, while the media reporting could be construed as prejudicial towards Muslims (Pew Research Center, 2013b). Almost immediately after the initial reports of the bombing, *The New York Post* reported that a 'Saudi national was a suspect in the case' when, in fact, he was a witness and a victim; CNN reporter John King revealed that the suspect was a 'dark-skinned male' (Curry, 2013, pp. 25, 45). Neither report was accurate, yet these reports were among many examples of stories that reignited anti-Muslim sentiments. While the perpetrators were Muslims, as originally assumed by many Americans (Love, 2013), they were Caucasian Americans of Chechen descent. However, the pertinent point is the reported motivation of the perpetrators. When the perpetrator of such an act of violence and terrorism is one of ours, there is a tendency for the media to explain the attack as an act of insanity or some other factor that characterizes the perpetrator as not representative of our society (Love, 2013). However, it would seem that insanity is not a condition found among Muslims, as such an explanation is rarely, if ever, used in cases of violence or terrorism committed by Muslims. Rather, the media tend to explain the commission of such acts by Muslims as being motivated by Islam.

Muslims will soon comprise one-quarter of the world's population. Events in the Muslim world affect the entire international community. As such, the media are obliged to cover issues and events concerning Muslims, including crises and conflicts. However, context is essential and a more comprehensive picture is necessary. This includes consideration of the range of factors, beyond Islam, that accurately explain and will give audiences meaningful insights into the issues and events covered. Ultimately, the solution resides in greater awareness and understanding of the other through interaction and education, not only about the other but also about the workings and impacts of the news media. It is hoped that this book will contribute to both.

References

Abou-El-Fadl, R. and Öktem, K. (2009) *Mutual Misunderstandings? Muslims and Islam in the European Media. Europe in the Media of Muslim Majority Countries* (Oxford: University of Oxford Press).

Abu Dhabi Gallup Centre (2011) *Egypt: From Tahrir to Transition*, http://www.abudhabigallupcenter.com/147896/egypt-tahrir-transition.aspx, date accessed 15 September 2013.

Adams, M. and Burke, J. (2006) 'Recollections of September 11 in Three English Villages: Identifications and Self-Narrations', *Journal of Ethnic and Migration Studies*, 32(6), 983–1003.

The Age (2004a) *Australian Army Convoy Attacked in Baghdad*, http://www.theage.com.au/articles/2004/10/25/1098667681339.html?from=storylhs, date accessed 1 November 2013.

The Age (2004b) *Tip-Off Suspicion in Bomb Blast*, http://www.theage.com.au/articles/2004/10/26/1098667730872.html?from=storylhs, date accessed 1 November 2013.

Ahmad, F. (2006) 'British Muslim Perceptions and Opinions on News Coverage of September 11', *Journal of Ethnic and Migration Studies*, 32(6), 961–982.

AKP (2012) *Political Vision of the AK Parti 2023: Politics, Society and the World*, http://www.akparti.org.tr/upload/documents/akparti2023siyasiviz yonuingilizce.pdf, date accessed 21 September 2013.

Al Jazeera (2012) *Corporate Profile*, http://www.aljazeera.com/aboutus/2006/11/2008525185555444449.html, date accessed 2 August 2013.

Al Jazeera (2013) *Syria: The Drums of War?*, http://www.aljazeera.com/programmes/insidestory/2013/08/20138286039109569.html, date accessed 29 August 2013.

Al Jazeera America (2013) *About*, http://america.aljazeera.com/tools/about.html, date accessed 7 March 2014.

Ali, W., Clifton, E., Duss, M., Fang, L., Keyes, S. and Shakir, F. (2011) *Fear, Inc.: The Roots of the Islamophobia Network in America*, http://www.americanprogress.org/wp-content/uploads/issues/2011/08/pdf/islamophobia.pdf, date accessed 29 August 2013.

Alink, F., Boin, A. and t'Hart, P. (2001) 'Institutional Crises and Reforms in Policy Sectors: The Case of Asylum Policy in Europe', *Journal of European Public Policy*, 8(2), 286–306.

Allen, C. (2004) 'Justifying Islamophobia: A Post 9/11 Consideration of the European and British Contexts', *The American Journal of Islamic Social Sciences*, 21(3), 1–25.

Allen, C. (2007) 'Down with Multiculturalism, Book-Burning and Fatwas: The Discourse of the "Death" of Multiculturalism', *Culture and Religion*, 8(2), 125–138.

Allied Media Corp. (2013) *History of Al Jazeera Television*, http://allied-media.com/aljazeera/jazeera_history.html, date accessed 1 August 2013.

Altheide, D. L. (2006) 'Terrorism and the Politics of Fear', *Cultural Studies Critical Methodologies*, 6(4), 415–439.

Altheide, D. L. (2007) 'The Mass Media and Terrorism', *Discourse and Communication*, 1(3), 287–308.

Aly, A. (2007) 'Australian Muslim Responses to the Discourse on Terrorism in the Australian Popular Media', *Journal of Australian Social Issues*, 42(1), 27–40.

Aly, A., Balnaves, M. and Chanlon, C. (2007) 'Behavioral Responses to the Terrorism Threat: Applications of the Metric of Fear', in *Recent Advances in Security Technology*, Proceedings of the 2007 RNSA Security Technology Conference, 248–255, Melbourne.

Amin-Khan, T. (2012) 'New Orientalism, Securitization and the Western Media's Incendiary Racism', *Third World Quarterly*, 33(9), 1595–1610.

Arab Social Media Report (2012) *Social Media in the Arab World: Influencing Societal and Cultural Change?*, http://www.freedomhouse.org/report/freedom-net/2012/egypt, date accessed 23 August 2013.

Arab Social Media Report (2013) *Facebook in the Arab Region*, http://www.arabsocialmediareport.com/Facebook/LineChart.aspx?&PriMenuID=18&CatID=24&mnu=Cat, date accessed 10 August 2013.

Associated Press (2007) *AP: Russian Photojournalist in Iraq Died Doing What He Loved*, http://www.democraticunderground.com/discuss/duboard.php?az=view_all&address=102x2839176, date accessed 1 November 2013.

Australia's Right to Know (2007) *Report of the Independent Audit into the State of Free Speech in Australia*, http://www.australiasrighttoknow.com.au/files/docs/MR2007/31-Oct-07-Executive-Summary-2007.pdf, date accessed 31 October 2013.

Australia's Right to Know (2008) *Report of the Review of Suppression Orders and the Media's Access to Court Documents and Information*, http://www.australiasrighttoknow.com.au/files/docs/Reports2008/13-Nov-2008ARTK-Report.pdf, date accessed 13 November 2013.

Australian Broadcasting Corporation (2005) *Keelty Seeks Suppression of Terrorism Allegations*, http://www.abc.net.au/news/2005-11-08/keelty-seeks-suppression-of-terrorism-allegations/735670, date accessed 8 November 2013.

Australian Broadcasting Corporation (2011a) 'Ozleaks Update', *Media Watch*, 22 November, http://www.abc.net.au/mediawatch/transcripts/s3387906.htm, date accessed 10 November 2013.

Australian Broadcasting Corporation (2011b) 'The OZ Redefines Happiness', *Media Watch*, 7 November, http://www.abc.net.au/mediawatch/transcripts/s3358386.htm, date accessed 10 November 2013.

Australian Government (2013) 'Transnational Terrorism: The Threat to Australia', *Department of Foreign Affairs and Trade*, http://www.dfat.gov.au/publications/terrorism/chapter1.html, date accessed 10 November 2013.

Babacan, A. (2009) *Seeking Asylum in a Global World: A Comparative Analysis of Refugee and Asylum Seeker Citizenship Rights, Laws and Policies in Australia, Canada and New Zealand* (Saarbrucken: VDM Publishing).

Bakker, F. L. (2006) 'The Image of Muhammad in *The Message*, the First and Only Feature Film About the Prophet of Islam', *Islam and Christian-Muslim Relations*, 17(1), 77–92.

Banaji, S. and Al-Ghabban, A. (2006) 'Neutrality Comes from Inside Us: British-Asian and Indian Perspectives on Television News After 11 September', *Journal of Ethnic and Migration Studies*, 32(6), 1005–1026.

Banks, B. (2008) 'The Criminalization of Asylum Seekers and Asylum Policy', *Prison Service Journal*, 175, 43–49.

Barkho, L. (2011) 'The Discursive and Social Paradigm of Al-Jazeera English in Comparison and Parallel with the BBC', *Communication Studies*, 62(1), 23–40.

Basile, S. (2012) *The Real Life of Muhammad*, http://www.youtube.com/watch?v=LoBwR9KEGUc&bpctr=1379289075, date accessed 10 November 2013.

Bassiouni, M. C. (1981) 'Criminal Law: Terrorism, Law Enforcement, and the Mass Media', *Journal of Criminal Law and Criminology*, 72(1), 1–51.

Bassiouni, M. C. (1982) 'Media Coverage of Terrorism: The Law and the Public', *Journal of Communication*, Spring, 128–143.

BBC (2010) *Merkel Says German Multicultural Society Has Failed*, http://www.bbc.co.uk/news/world-europe-11559451, date accessed 8 November 2013.

BBC (2011) *State Multiculturalism Has Failed, Says David Cameron*, http://www.bbc.co.uk/news/uk-politics-12371994, date accessed 8 November 2013.

BBC News (2006) *OIC Denounces Cartoon Violence*, http://news.bbc.co.uk/go/pr/fr/-/2/hi/south_asia/4736854.stm, date accessed 10 November 2013.

BBC Worldwide Limited (2012) *Iran: Rally Held in Tehran to Protest Anti-Islam Film, Cartoons*, http://www.accessmylibrary.com/article-1G1-305060850/iran-rally-held-tehran.html, date accessed 10 November 2013.

Beaumont, P. (2011) 'The Truth About Twitter, Facebook and the Uprisings in the Arab World', http://www.guardian.co.uk/world/2011/feb/25/twitter-facebook-uprisings-arab-libya, date accessed 30 September 2013.

Bevelander, P. and Otterbeck, J. (2010) 'Young People's Attitudes Towards Muslims in Sweden', *Ethnic and Racial Studies*, 33(3), 404–425.

Blake, H. (2011) 'The Revolution Will Be Tweeted', *Foreign Policy*, 187, 20–21.

Bloom, J. and Blair, S. (2002) *Islam: A Thousand Years of Faith and Power* (New Haven: Yale University Press).

Bødker, H. (2009) 'Muslims in Print, or Media Events as Nodes of Cultural Conflict', in Marsden, L. and Savigny, H. (eds) *Media, Religion and Conflict* (Farnham: Ashgate Publishing).

Boomgaarden, H. and Vliegenthart, R. (2006) 'Explaining the Rise of Anti-Immigrant Parties: The Role of News Media Content', *Electoral Studies*, 26, 404–417.

Boswell, C. (2000) 'European Values and the Asylum Crisis', *International Affairs*, 76, 537–557.

Bouma, G. (2011) 'Islamophobia as a Constraint to World Peace: The Case of Australia', *Islam and Christian-Muslim Relations*, 22(4), 433–441.

Bradimore, A. and Bauer, H. (2011) 'Mystery Ships and Risky Boat People: Tamil Refugee Migration in the Newsprint Media', *Canadian Journal of Communication*, 36(4), 637–661.

Brennan, F. (2006) *Tampering with Asylum: A Universal Humanitarian Problem* (St Lucia: University of Queensland Press).

The Bulletin With Newsweek (2004) *I Was About to Die*, 27 October.

Burns, R. (2007) *US General, Diplomat: Give Bush's Iraq Strategy Time*, http://www.boston.com/news/world/middleeast/articles/2007/07/27/us_general_diplomat_give_bushs_iraq_strategy_time/, date accessed 1 November 2013.

Burstein, P. (1998) 'Bringing the Public Back In: Should Sociologists Consider the Impact of Public Opinion on Public Policy?', *Social Forces*, 77, 27–62.

Caldwell, A. (2011) *Terror Cells in Sydney and Melbourne Connected*, http://www.abc.net.au/news/2011-09-20/terror-cells-in-sydney-and-melbourne-connected/2908440, date accessed 8 November 2013.

CBS (2012) *Oral History of N. Ireland Strife Raises Dilemma*, http://www.cbsnews.com/8301-18563_162-57374314/oral-history-of-n-ireland-strife-raises-dilemma/, date accessed 8 November 2013.

Celermajer, D. (2007) 'If Islam Is Our Other, Who Are "We"?' *Australian Journal of Social Issues*, 42(1), 103–123.

Channel 4 News (2011) *Arab Revolt: Social Media and the People's Revolution*, http://www.channel4.com/news/arab-revolt-social-media-and-the-peoples-revolution, date accessed 30 September 2013.

Channel Ten News (2012) *EDL – Rioting Muslims Now Hit Sydney, Australia (15th September 2012)*, http://www.youtube.com/watch?NR=1&v=VqKRwU_DBNE&feature=endscreen, date accessed 10 November 2013.

Chebib, N. and Sohail, R. (2011) 'The Reasons Social Media Contributed to the 2011 Egyptian Revolution', *International Journal of Business Research and Management*, 2(3), 139–162.

Cherti, M. (2010) 'The Politics of Muslim Visibility in Europe: The Case of the Swiss Minaret Ban', *Public Policy Research*, 17(3), 157–161.

Christensen, C. (2006) 'Islam in the Media: Cartoons and Context', *Screen Education*, 43, 27–33.

Ciftci, S. (2012) 'Islamophobia and Threat Perceptions: Explaining Anti-Muslim Sentiment in the West', *Journal of Muslim Minority Affairs*, 32(3), 293–309.

CNN (2007) *Michael Ware on Baghdad 3–27–07*, http://www.youtube.com/watch?v=U7YPOaaTYfA, date accessed 1 November 2013.

Cohen, B. (1963) *The Press and Foreign Policy* (New Jersey: Princeton University Press).

Cohen, B. (1973) *The Public's Impact on Foreign Policy* (Boston: Little, Brown and Company).

Cohen, B. (1995) *Democracies and Foreign Policy: Public Participation in the United States and the Netherlands* (Madison: University of Wisconsin Press).

Committee to Protect Journalists (2007) *Roadside Bomb Kills Russian Photojournalist in Iraq*, http://cpj.org/2007/05/roadside-bomb-kills-russian-photojournalist-in-ira.php, date accessed 1 November 2013.

Coole, C. (2002) 'A Warm Welcome? Scottish and UK Media Reporting of an Asylum-Seeker Murder', *Media, Culture & Society*, 24, 839–852.

Council on American-Islamic Relations (CAIR) (2013) *Legislating Fear: Islamophobia and its Impact in the United States*, https://www.cair.com/islamophobia/legislating-fear-2013-report.html, date accessed 25 September 2013.

Crock, M. and Ghezelbash, D. (2010) 'Do Loose Lips Bring Ships? The Role of Policy, Politics and Human Rights in Managing Unauthorized Boat Arrivals', *Griffith Law Review*, 19(2), 238–287.

Curry, G. (2013) 'Boston Marathon's Media Frenzy', *Washington Informer*, 25 April, 25, 45.

Da Lage, O. (2010) *Politics and Media in the Middle East: The Post-Al-Jazeera Era*, http://odalage.wordpress.com/2010/08/13/politics-and-media-in-the-middle-east-the-post-al-jazeera-era/, date accessed 1 September 2013.

Dalgaard, S. (2006) 'The Right to Offend: The Causes and Consequences of the "Danish Cartoon Affair" ', *RUSI Journal*, 151(2), 28.

Damphousse, K. and Shields, C. (2007) 'The Morning After: Assessing the Effect of Major Terrorism Events on Prosecution Strategies and Outcomes', *Journal of Contemporary Criminal Justice*, 23(2), 174–194.

Dorling, P. (2011) *'Chilling' Bid by Government to Control the Media Rejected*, http://www.smh.com.au/national/chilling-bid-by-government-to-control-the-media-rejected-20111019-1m7wq.html, date accessed 8 November 2013.

Dreher, T. (2007) 'News Media Responsibilities', in Lynch, A., MacDonald, E. and Williams, G. (eds) *Reporting on Terrorism in Law and Liberty in the War on Terror* (Sydney: The Federation Press).

Dubai School of Government (2013) *The Arab World Online: Trends in Internet Usage in the Arab Region*, http://www.dsg.ae/en/Publication/Pdf_En/424201311017185100000.pdf, date accessed 22 August 2013.

Dunn, K. (2005) 'Australian Public Knowledge of Islam', *Studia Islamika*, 12(1), 1–32.

Edy, J. (1999) 'Journalistic Uses of Collective Memory', *Journal of Communication*, 49(2), 71–85.

Entman, R. (1991) 'Framing US Coverage of International News: Contrasts in Narratives of the KAL and Iran Air Incidents', *Journal of Communication*, 41(4), 6–27.

Entman, R. (1993) 'Framing: Towards Clarification of a Fractured Paradigm', *Journal of Communication*, 42(4), 51–58.

Erikson, R., MacKuen, M. and Stimson, J. (2002) *The Macro Polity* (New York: Cambridge University Press).

Esposito, J. and Mogahed, D. (2007) *Who Speaks for Islam? What a Billion Muslims Really Think* (New York: Gallup Press).

Esses, V., Medianu, S. and Lawson, A. (2013) 'Uncertainty, Threat, and the Role of the Media in Promoting the Dehumanization of Immigrants and Refugees', *Journal of Social Issues*, 69(3), 518–536.

Euronews (2011) 'Photojournalists Flood Into Perpignan', http://www.euronews.com/2011/09/06/photographers-flood-into-perpignan/, date accessed 23 August 2013.

European Travel Commission (2013) *Social Networking and UGC*, http://etc-digital.org/digital-trends/social-networking-and-ugc/, date accessed 23 August 2013.

Every, D. and Augoustinos, M. (2008) 'Constructions of Australia in Pro- and Anti-Asylum Seeker Political Discourse', *Nations and Nationalism*, 14(3), 562–580.

Ewart, J. (2009) *Haneef: A Question of Character* (Sydney: Halstead Press).

Ewart, J. (2010) 'Dr Haneef and the Media', in Rane, H., Ewart, J. and Abdalla, M. (eds) *Islam and the Australian News Media* (Melbourne: Melbourne University Press).

Ewart, J. and Rane, H. (2011) 'Moving on from September 11: How Australian Television Reported the Ninth Anniversary', *Journal of Media and Religion*, 20(2), 55–72.

Federal Bureau of Investigations (FBI) (2013) *Definitions of Terrorism in the U.S. Code*, http://www.fbi.gov/about-us/investigate/terrorism/terrorism-definition, date accessed 10 November 2013.

Fernando, M. (2010) 'Reconfiguring Freedom: Muslim Piety and the Limits of Secular Law and Public Discourse in France', *American Ethnologist*, 37(1), 19–35.

Finney, N. and Robinson, V. (2008) 'Local Press, Dispersal and Community in the Construction of Asylum Debates', *Social & Cultural Geography*, 9(4), 397–413.

Fisk, R. (2006) *The Great War for Civilization* (London: Harper Perennial).

Forest, J. and Dunn, K. (2007) 'Constructing Racism in Sydney, Australia's Largest Ethnicity', *Urban Studies*, 44(4), 699–721.

Freedom House (2012a) *Egypt: Freedom on the Net*, http://www.freedomhouse.org/report/freedom-net/2012/egypt, date accessed 23 August 2013.

Freedom House (2012b) *Libya: Freedom on the Net*, http://www.freedomhouse.org/report/freedom-net/2012/libya, date accessed 22 August 2013.

Galtung, J. and Ruge, M. (1965) 'The Structure of Foreign News: The Presentation of the Congo, Cuba and Cyprus Crises in Four Norwegian Newspapers', *Journal of International Peace Research*, 1, 64–91.

Gans, H. J. (1980) *Deciding What's News* (London: Constable).

Gelber, K. and McDonald, M. (2006) 'Ethics and Exclusion: Representations of Sovereignty in Australia's Approach to Asylum-Seekers', *Review of International Studies*, 32(2), 269–289.

Gerges, F. (1999) *America and Political Islam* (Cambridge: Cambridge University Press).

Ghannam, J. (2011) *Social Media in the Arab World: Leading up to the Uprisings of 2011*, http://cima.ned.org/sites/default/files/CIMA-Arab_Social_Media-Report_2.pdf, date accessed 28 May 2011.

Ghosh, P. (2012) *Hillary Clinton Condemns Anti-Islam Film*, http://www.ibtimes.com/hillary-clinton-condemns-anti-islam-film-full-text-788950, date accessed 10 November 2013.

Givens, T. and Luedtke, A. (2005) 'European Immigration Policies in Comparative Perspective: Issue Salience, Partisanship and Immigrant Rights', *Comparative European Politics*, 3(1), 1–22.

Glasser, B. and Strauss, A. (1967) *The Discovery of Grounded Theory: Strategies for Qualitative Research* (Chicago: Aldine).

Gottschalk, P. and Greenberg, G. (2007) *Islamophobia: Making the Muslim Enemy* (Lanham: Rowman & Littlefield Publishers).

Grabar, O. (2003) 'The Story of Portraits of the Prophet Muhammad', *Studia Islamica*, 96, 19–38.

Gurdilek, R. (1993) *35 Reported Killed, 60 Injured in Muslim Rampage*, http://www.apnewsarchive.com/1993/35-Reported-Killed-60-Injured-in-Muslim-Rampage/id-350c3270658f92691dd20e67da17a4fe, date accessed 10 November 2013.

Haber, M. and Koblin, J. (2008) *60 Months in the Red Zone*, http://observer.com/2008/06/60-months-in-the-red-zone/, date accessed 1 November 2013.

Han, E. and Rane, H. (2013) *Making Australian Foreign Policy on Israel-Palestine: Media Coverage, Public Opinion and Interest Groups* (Carlton: Melbourne University Press).

Hansen, R. (2006) 'The Danish Cartoon Controversy: A Defense of Liberal Freedom', *International Migration*, 44(5), 9.

Hanson, F. (2010) *Australia and the World: Public Opinion and Foreign Policy*, http://lowyinstitute.cachefly.net/files/pubfiles/LowyPoll_2010_LR_Final.pdf, date accessed 8 November 2013.

Haraszti, M. (2006) 'The "Cartoon" Controversy: The Need for Respect in Freedom', *Springer-Verlag*, 4(13), 13–16.

Harb, Z. (2011) 'Arab Revolutions and the Social Media Effect', *M/C Journal: A Journal of Media and Culture*, 14(2), http://journal.media-culture.org.au/index.php/mcjournal/article/viewArticle/364, date accessed 22 November 2013.

Harb, Z. and Bessaiso, E. (2006) 'British Arab Muslim Audiences and Television After September 11', *Journal of Ethnic and Migration Studies*, 32(6), 1063–1076.

Harcup, T. and O'Neill, D. (2001) 'What Is News? Galtung and Ruge Revisited', *Journalism Studies*, 2(2), 261–280.

Harkness, S. S. J., Magid, M., Roberts, J. and Richardson, M. (2007) 'Cross the Line? Freedom of Speech and Religious Responsibilities', *American Political Science Association*, 40(2), 275–278.

Helm, L. (1991) 'Translator of "Satanic Verses" Slain', *Los Angeles Times*, 13 July, 4.

Herald Sun (2004a) *How to Keep Ahead*, 20 October.

Herald Sun (2004b) *Siding with Savagery*, 22 October.

Herman, J. (2005) 'Freedom of the Press Under Threat?', *University of New South Wales Law Journal*, 57.

Hill, J. (2012) *Syria's Propaganda War*, http://www.theglobalmail.org/feature/syrias-propaganda-war/183/, date accessed 2 November 2013.

Hitchens, C. (2007) Published 2012, *Hitchens '07: Danish Muhammad Cartoons*, http://www.youtube.com/watch?v=LZZ96SArpuc, date accessed 10 November 2013.

Holsti, O. (2004) *Public Opinion and American Foreign Policy*, revised ed. (Ann Arbor: The University of Michigan Press).

Hughes, G. (2008) *Lies, Bombs and Jihad*, http://www.theaustralian.com.au/news/features/lies-bombs-and-jihad/story-e6frg6z6-1111117491538, date accessed 10 November 2013.

Huntington, S. P. (1993) 'The Clash of Civilizations?', *Foreign Affairs*, 72(3), 21–49.

Inglehart, R. and Norris, P. (2009) *Muslim Integration Into Western Cultures: Between Origins and Destinations*, http://dash.harvard.edu/bitstream/handle/1/4481625/Norris_MuslimIntegration.pdf?sequence=1, date accessed 20 August 2013.

Ismael, M. (2012) *Levant Scholars' Union: 'Innocence of Muslims' Film Is Anti-Islam Incitement*, http://sana.sy/eng/21/2012/09/12/441224.htm, date accessed 10 November 2013.

Jensen, H. R. (2008) 'The Muhammad Cartoons Controversy and the Boycott of Danish Products in the Middle East', *European Business Review*, 20(3), 275–289.

Joffe, G. (2007) 'Confrontational Mutual Perceptions and Images: Orientalism and Occidentalism in Europe and the Islamic World', *The International Spectator: Italian Journal of International Affairs*, 42(2), 161–177.

Kamali, M. H. (1999) *Freedom of Expression in Islam* (Kuala Lumpur: Ilmiah Publishers).

Kaplan, C. (2009) 'The Biopolitics of Technoculture in the Mumbai Attacks', *Theory, Culture & Society*, 26(7–8), 301–313.

Karim, K. (2006) 'American Media's Coverage of Muslims: The Historical Roots of Contemporary Portrayals', in Poole, E. and Richardson, J. (eds) *Muslims and the News Media* (London: I.B. Tauris).

Katz, E. and Lazarsfeld, P. (1955) *Personal Influence: The Part Played by People in the Flow of Mass Communication* (New York: Free Press).

Khalid, M. (2011) 'Gender, Orientalism and Representations of the "Other" in the War on Terror', *Global Change, Peace and Security*, 23(1), 15–29.

Khondker, H. (2011) 'The Role of New Media in the Arab Spring', *Globalisations*, 8(5), 675–679.

Kitch, C. (2002) 'Anniversary Journalism, Collective Memory, and the Cultural Authority to Tell the Story of the American Past', *Journal of Popular Culture*, 36(1), 44–67.

Kitzinger, J. and Barbour, R. (1999) 'Introduction: The Challenge and Promise of Focus Groups', in Barbour, R. and Kitzinger, J. (eds) *Developing Focus Group Research: Politics, Theory and Practice* (London: Sage).

Klocker, N. and Dunn, K. (2003) 'Who's Driving the Asylum Debate? Newspaper and Government Representations of Asylum Seekers', *Media International Australia: Incorporating Culture and Policy*, 109, 71–92.

Kontominas, B. (2009) *Journalists Guilty of Photographing Army Base*, http://www.smh.com.au/national/journalists-guilty-of-photographing-army-base-20090925-g5rv.html, date accessed 8 November 2013.

Kull, S. (2003) *Misperceptions, the Media and the Iraq War*, http://www.worldpublicopinion.org/pipa/pdf/oct03/IraqMedia_Oct03_rpt.pdf, date accessed 10 November 2013.

Kumar, D. (2010) 'Framing Islam: The Resurgence of Orientalism During the Bush II Era', *Journal of Communication Inquiry*, 34(3), 254–277.

Kumar, M. (2012) 'Introduction: Orientalism(s) After 9/11', *Journal of Postcolonial Writing*, 48(3), 233–240.

Kurzman, C. (2012) *Islamic Statements Against Terrorism*, http://kurzman.unc.edu/islamic-statements-against-terrorism/, date accessed 5 September 2013.

Larrson, G. (2005) 'The Impact of Global Conflict on Local Contexts: Muslims in Sweden After 9/11 – The Rise of Islamophobia or New Possibilities?', *Islam and Christian-Muslim Relations*, 16(1), 29–42.

Lentini, P., Halafoff, A. and Ogru, E. (2011) 'With Guarded Optimism? Evidence from Focus Groups of "Mainstream" Australians' Perceptions of Muslims', *Islam and Christian-Muslim Relations*, 22(4), 409–432.

Lewis, B. (1990) 'The Roots of Muslim Rage', *The Atlantic Monthly*, http://www.theatlantic.com/magazine/print/1990/09/the-roots-of-muslim-rage/304643/, date accessed 7 March 2014.

Lippmann, W. (1922) *Public Opinion* (New York: Macmillan).

Lopez, F. B. (2010) 'Towards a Definition of Islamophobia: Approximations of the Early Twentieth Century', *Ethnic and Racial Studies*, 34(4), 556–573.

Louw, P. E. (2003) 'The "War Against Terrorism": A Public Relations Challenge for the Pentagon', *Gazette*, 65(3), 211–230.

Love, E. (2013) *Boston Marathon Bombings: Breaking the Pattern*, http://www.aljazeera.com/indepth/opinion/2013/04/2013417638216948.html, date accessed 8 August 2013.

Lynn, N. and Lea, S. (2003) 'A Phantom Menace and a New Apartheid: The Social Construction of Asylum Seekers in the United Kingdom', *Discourse and Society*, 14(4), 425–452.

Maasho, A. (2011) *Ethiopia Jails Two Swedish Journalists for Aiding Rebels*, http://uk.reuters.com/article/2011/12/27/uk-ethiopia-sweden-journalists-idUK TRE7BQ08P20111227, date accessed 11 November 2013.

Macnaughten, P. and Myers, G. (2006) 'Focus Groups', in Seale, C., Gobo, G., Gubrium, J. and Silverman, D. (eds) *Qualitative Research Practice* (London: Sage Publications), 65–78.

Malloch, M. and Stanley, E. (2005) 'The Detention of Asylum Seekers in the UK; Representing Risk and Managing the Dangerous', *Punishment and Society*, 7(1), 53–71.

Manning, P. (2006) *Us and Them* (Sydney: Random House).

Marr, D. and Wilkinson, M. (2003) *Dark Victory* (Sydney: Allen & Unwin).

Marshall, S. (2011) *Reporting the Arab Spring: 'These Stories Will Go On and On'*, http://www.journalism.co.uk/news-features/reporting-the-arab-spring–these-stories-will-go-on-and-on-/s5/a546485/, date accessed 28 September 2013.

Martin, P. and Phelan, S. (2002) 'Representing Islam in the Wake of September 11: A Comparison of US Television and CNN Online Message-board Discourses', *Prometheus*, 20(3), 263–269.

Mazrui, A. A. (1990) 'The Satanic Verses or a Satanic Novel? Moral Dilemmas of the Rushdie Affair', *Alternatives: Global, Local, Political*, 15(1), 97–121.

McCleary, J. (2011) 'The Boat as a Prop in Election Theatrics Constructing Maritime Asylum Seekers as a "Problem"', Honors thesis, http://ses.library.usyd.edu.au/bitstream/2123/8275/1/Jessica%20McCleary.pdf, date accessed 8 November 2013.

McClelland, R. (2011) *Tackling Home-Grown Aussie Terrorism*, http://www.thepunch.com.au/articles/tackling-home-grown-aussie-terrorism/, date accessed 8 November 2013.

McCombs, M. and Shaw, D. (1972) 'The Agenda-Setting Function of Mass Media', *The Public Opinion Quarterly*, 36(2), 176–187.

McKay, F. H., Thomas, S. L. and Blood, R. W. (2011) ' "Any One of These Boat People Could Be a Terrorist for All We Know!" Media Representations and Public Perceptions of "Boat People" Arrivals in Australia', *Journalism*, 12(5), 607–626.

McKay, F. H., Thomas, S. L. and Kneebone, S. (2012) 'It Would Be Okay if They Came Through the Proper Channels': Community Perceptions and Attitudes Toward Asylum Seekers in Australia', *Journal of Refugee Studies*, 25(1), 113–133.

McLaren, L. and Johnson, M. (2007) 'Resources, Group Conflict and Symbols: Explaining Anti-Immigration Hostility in Britain', *Political Studies*, 55, 709–732.

McLoughlin, S. (2007) 'Islam(s) in Context: Orientalism and the Anthropology of Muslim Societies and Cultures', *Journal of Beliefs and Values*, 28(3), 273–296.

McNamara, L. (2009) 'Counter-Terrorism Laws: How They Affect Media Freedom and News Reporting', *Westminster Papers in Communication and Culture*, 6(1), 27–45.

McQuail, D. (2005) *McQuail's Mass Communication Theory*, 5th ed. (London: Sage).

The Media, Entertainment and Arts Alliance (2007) *Official Spin: Censorship and Control of the Australian Press 2007* (Queensland: The Media, Entertainment & Arts Alliance).

Mellor, N. (2012) 'The Culture of Witnessing: War Correspondents Rewriting the History of the Iraq War', *Language and Intercultural Communication*, 12(2), 103–117.

Miladi, N. (2006) 'Satellite TV News and the Arab Diaspora in Britain: Comparing Al-Jazeera, the BBC and CNN', *Journal of Ethnic and Migration Studies*, 32(6), 947–960.

Mill, J. S. (2011(1859)), *On Liberty* (Luton: Andrews UK).

Modood, T. (2006) 'The Liberal Dilemma: Integration or Vilification?', *International Migration*, 44(5), 4–7.

Morey, P. and Yaqin, A. (2011) *Framing Muslims: Stereotyping and Representation After 9/11* (Cambridge: Harvard University Press).

Morgan, M., Lewis, J. and Jhally, S. (1991) *The Gulf War: A Study of the Media, Public Opinion, and Public Knowledge* (Massachusetts: Center for the Study of Communication).

MSNBC (2011) *Ethiopia Jails Two Swedish Journalists for Aiding Rebels*, http://www.msnbc.msn.com/id/45794529/ns/world_news-africa/t/ethiopia-jails-two-swedish-journalists-aiding-rebels/, date accessed 8 November 2013.

Muedini, F. (2009) 'Muslim American College Youth: Attitudes and Responses Five Years After 9/11', *The Muslim World*, 99, 39–59.

Mummery, J. and Rodan, D. (2007) 'Discursive Australia: Refugees, Australianness, and the Australian Public Sphere', *Continuum: Journal of Media and Cultural Studies*, 21(3), 347-360.

Musaji, S. (2011) *Muslim Voices (Part 1) Fatwas and Statements by Muslim Scholars and Organisations*, http://theamericanmuslim.org/tam.php/features/articles/muslim_voices_against_extremism_and_terrorism_part_i_fatwas/, date accessed 5 September 2013.

Musleh, M. (2011) *The Arab Revolutions Will Not Be Tweeted*, http://972mag.com/the-arab-revolutions-did-not-happen-because-of-social-media/, date accessed 28 September 2013.

Nacos, B. (2009) 'Revisiting the Contagion Hypothesis: Terrorism, News Coverage, and Copycat Attacks', *Perspectives on Terrorism*, 3(3), 3–13.

Nacos, B. L. and Torres-Reyna, O. (2003) 'Framing Muslim-Americans Before and After 9/11', in Norris, P., Kern, M. and Just, M. (eds) *Framing Terrorism: The News Media, the Government and the Public* (New York: Routledge).

Nacos, B. and Torres-Reyna, O. (2007) *Fueling our Fears: Stereotyping, Media Coverage and Public Opinion of Muslim Americans* (Lanham: Rowman and Littlefield).

Nash, C. J. (2005) 'Freedom of Press in the New Australian Security State', *University of New South Wales Law Journal*, 28(3), 900–908.

The New York Times (1993) 'The Publisher of "The Satanic Verses" in Norway Is Shot', 12 October, 3.

The New York Times (2007) *The Iraq War as We See It*, http://www.nytimes.com/2007/08/19/opinion/19iht-ediraq.1.7168564.html?pagewanted=all&_r=0, date accessed 1 November 2013.

Nikels, H. C. (2007) 'Framing Asylum Discourse in Luxembourg', *Journal of Refugee Studies*, 7(4), 397–417.

Norris, P., Kern, M. and Just, M. (eds) (2003) *Framing Terrorism: The News Media, the Government and the Public* (New York: Routledge).

O'Doherty, K. and Augoustinos, M. (2007) 'Protecting the Nation: Nationalist Rhetoric on Asylum Seekers and the Tampa', *Journal of Community & Applied Social Psychology*, 18(6), 576–592.

Oates, S. (2006) 'Comparing the Politics of Fear: The Role of Terrorism News in Election Campaigns in Russia, the United States and Britain', *International Relations*, 20, 425–437.

Obama, B. (2012) *President Obama's Speech to the UN General Assembly – Full Transcript*, www.theguardian.com/world/2012/sep/25/obama-un-general-assembly-transcript, date accessed 10 November 2013.

Oh, O., Agrawal, M. and Rao, H. R. (2011) 'Information Control and Terrorism: Tracking the Mumbai Terrorist Attack Through Twitter', *Information Systems Front*, 13, 33–43.

Olding, R. (2012) *Muslims Inundated with Messages of Hate*, http://www.smh.com.au/nsw/muslims-inundated-with-messages-of-hate-20120918-263gj.html#ixzz26oqzFaUr, date accessed 23 September 2013.

Oliver, A. (2013) *Australia and the World: Public Opinion and Foreign Policy*, http://lowyinstitute.org/files/lowypoll2013_web_1.pdf, date accessed 8 November 2013.

Organization of Islamic Cooperation (2008) *1st OIC Observatory Report on Islamophobia*, http://www.oic-oci.org/uploads/file/Islamphobia/islamphobia_rep_may_07_08.pdf, date accessed 25 September 2013.

Organization of Islamic Cooperation (2012) *5th OIC Observatory Report on Islamophobia*, http://www.oic-oci.org/uploads/file/islamphobia/reports/english/islamphobia-report-2012.pdf, date accessed 25 September 2013.

Panagopoulos, C. (2006) 'Poll Trends: Arab and Muslim Americans and Islam in the Aftermath of 9/11', *Public Opinion Quarterly*, 70(4), 608–624.

Papacharissi, Z. and de Fatima Oliveira, M. (2008) 'News Frames Terrorism: A Comparative Analysis of Frames Employed in Terrorism Coverage in US and UK Newspapers', *The International Journal of Press/Politics*, 13(1), 52–74.

Parker, A. (2012) 'Brits Join Prophet Film Fury', *The Sun*, 22 September, 2.

Parks, L. (2007) 'Insecure Airwaves: US Bombings of Aljazeera', *Communication and Critical/Cultural Studies*, 4(2), 226–231.

Parliament of Australia (2011) *Seeking Asylum: Australia's Humanitarian Program*, http://www.aph.gov.au/binaries/library/pubs/bn/sp/seekingasylum.pdf, date accessed 7 March 2014.

Pearson, M. and Busst, N. (2006) 'Anti-terror Laws and the Media After 9/11: Three Models in Australia, NZ and the Pacific', *Pacific Journalism Review*, 12(2), 9–27.

Pedersen, A., Hansen, S. and Watt, S. (2006) 'The Role of False Beliefs in the Community's and the Federal Government's Attitudes Toward Australian Asylum Seekers', *Australian Journal of Social Issues*, 41(1), 105–124.

Peek, L. (2003) 'Reactions and Response: Muslim Students' Experiences on New York City Campuses Post 9/11', *Journal of Muslim Minority Affairs*, 23(2), 271–283.

Perry, B. and Poynting, S. (2006) 'Inspiring Islamophobia: Media and State Targeting of Muslims in Canada Since 9/11' *TASA Conference 2006, University of Western Australia and Murdoch University*, 4–6 December 2006, http://www.tasa.org.au/conferences/conferencepapers06/papers/Indigenous%20issues,race,%20 ethnicity%20and%20migration/Perry,Poynting.pdf, date accessed 7 March 2014.

Pew Research Center (2007) *Iraq War Coverage Drops Off in Second Quarter*, http://www.journalism.org/2007/08/20/iraq-war-coverage-drops-off-in-2nd-quarter/, date accessed 7 March 2014.

Pew Research Center (2008) *Unfavorable Views of Jews and Muslims on the Increase in Europe*, http://www.pewglobal.org/files/2008/09/Pew-2008-Pew-Global-Attitudes-Report-3-September-17-2pm.pdf, date accessed 29 August 2013.

Pew Research Center (2010) *Public Remains Conflicted Over Islam*, http://www.pewforum.org/files/2010/08/Islam-mosque-full-report.pdf, date accessed 5 September 2013.

Pew Research Center (2011) *The Future of the Global Muslim Population: Projection for 2010–2030*, http://www.pewforum.org/files/2011/01/FutureGlobalMuslimPopulation-WebPDF-Feb10.pdf, date accessed 20 August 2013.

Pew Research Center (2012a) *The World's Muslims: Unity and Diversity*, http://www.pewforum.org/files/2012/08/the-worlds-muslims-full-report.pdf, date accessed 20 August 2013.

Pew Research Center (2012b) *Faith on the Move: The Religious Affiliation of International Migrants*, http://www.pewforum.org/files/2012/03/Faithonthemove.pdf, date accessed 8 November 2013.

Pew Research Center (2013a) *The World's Muslims: Religion, Politics and Society*, http://www.pewforum.org/files/2013/04/worlds-muslims-religion-politics-society-full-report.pdf, date accessed 20 August 2013.

Pew Research Center (2013b) 'Most Expect "Occasional Acts of Terrorism" in the Future', http://www.people-press.org/2013/04/23/most-expect-occasional-acts-of-terrorism-in-the-future/, date accessed 1 August 2013.

Phillips, J. (2013) 'Asylum Seekers and Refugees: What Are the Facts?', http://parlinfo.aph.gov.au/parlInfo/download/library/prspub/HGNW6/upload_binary/HGNW6.pdf;fileType=application%2Fpdf#search=%22library/prspub/HGNW6%22, date accessed 8 November 2013.

Pierson, P. (1993) 'When Effects Become Cause: Policy Feedback and Political Change', *World Politics*, 45, 595–628.

Pintak, L. and Ginges, J. (2009) 'Inside the Arab Newsroom: Arab Journalists Evaluate Themselves and the Competition', *Journalism Studies*, 10(2), 157–177.

Poole, E. (2002) *Reporting Islam: Media Representations and British Muslims* (London: I.B. Tauris).

Poole, E. and Richardson, J. (eds) (2006) *Muslims and the News Media* (London: I.B. Tauris).

Powell, K. (2011) 'Framing Islam: An Analysis of U.S. Media Coverage of Terrorism Since 9/11', *Communication Studies*, 62(1), 90–112.

Poynting, S. and Mason, V. (2007) 'The Resistible Rise of Islamophobia: Anti-Muslim Racism in the UK and Australia Before 11 September 2001', *Journal of Sociology*, 43(1), 61–86.

Poynting, S. and Noble, G. (2004) 'Living with Racism: The Experience and Reporting by Arab and Muslim Australians of Discrimination, Abuse and Violence Since 11 September 2001', http://www.humanrights.gov.au/sites/default/files/content/racial_discrimination/isma/research/UWSReport.pdf, date accessed 7 March 2014.

Rahman, F. (2002) *Islam* (Chicago: Chicago University Press).

Rane, H. (2009) *Reconstructing Jihad Amid Competing International Norms* (New York: Palgrave McMillan).

Rane, H. (2010a) *Islam and Contemporary Civilization: Evolving Ideas, Transforming Relations* (Carlton: Melbourne University Press).

Rane, H. (2010b) 'Media Content and Inter-Community Relations', in Rane, H., Ewart, J. and Abdalla, M. (eds) *Islam and the Australian News Media* (Carlton: Melbourne University Press).

Rane, H. (2011) 'The Impact of Maqasid Al-Shariah on Islamist Political Thought: Implications for Islam-West Relations', *Islam and Civilisational Renewal*, 2(2), 337–357.

Rane, H. and Ewart, J. (2012) 'The Framing of Islam and Muslims in the Tenth Anniversary Coverage of 9/11: Implications for Reconciliation and Moving-On', *Journal of Muslim Minority Affairs*, 32(3), 310–322.

Rane, H., Ewart, J. and Abdalla, M. (2010) *Islam and the Australian News Media* (Carlton: Melbourne University Press).

Rane, H., Nathie, M., Isakhan, B. and Abdalla, M. (2011) 'Towards Understanding What Australia's Muslims Really Think', *Journal of Sociology*, 47(2), 123–143.

Rane, H. and Salem, S. (2012) 'Social Media, Social Movements and the Diffusion of Ideas in the Arab Uprisings', *Journal of International Communication*, 18(1), 97–111.

Reporters Without Borders (2010) *Journalists Under Threat from Anti-Terrorism Law*, http://en.rsf.org/turkey-journalists-under-threat-from-anti-30-03-2010, 36878, date accessed 8 November 2013.

Reporters Without Borders (2011) *Upheaval in the Arab World*, http://www.rsf.org/rapport/RSF_BILAN_MOYEN_ORIENT_2011_GB.pdf, date accessed 29 August 2013.

Ricchiardi, S. (2007) *Obstructed View*, http://www.ajr.org/Article.asp?id=4301, date accessed 1 November 2013.

Richardson, R. (2010) 'Sending a Message? Refugees and Australia's Deterrence Campaign', *Media International Australia*, 35, 7–18.

Romano, A. (2004) 'Journalism's Role in Mediating Public Conversation on Asylum Seekers and Refugees in Australia', *Australian Journalism Review*, 26(2), 43–62.

Rostboll, C. F. (2009) 'Autonomy, Respect, and Arrogance in the Danish Cartoon Controversy', *Political Theory*, 37(5), 623–648.

Rostboll, C. F. (2010) 'The Use and Abuse of "Universal Values" in the Danish Cartoon Controversy', *European Political Science Review*, 2(3), 401–422.

Roy, E. (2004) *Downer Accuses Journalist of Giving Comfort to Terrorists*, http://www.abc.net.au/pm/content/2004/s1225277.htm, date accessed 1 November 2013.

Rucht, D. (2004) 'The Quadruple "A": Media Strategies of Protest Movements Since the 1960s', in Van de Donk, W., Loader, B., Nixon, P. and Rucht, D. (eds) (2004) *Cyperprotest: New Media, Citizens and Social Movements* (London: Routledge), 25–48.

Ruigrok, N. and van Atteveldt, W. (2007) 'Global Angling with a Local Angle: How U.S., British, and Dutch Newspapers Frame Global and Local Terrorist Attacks', *The International Journal of Press/Politics*, 12(1), 68–90.

Rushdie, S. (2000) *The Satanic Verses* (New York: Picador).

Ryan, M. (2004) 'Framing the War Against Terrorism: US Newspaper Editorials and Military Action in Afghanistan', *Gazette: The International Journal for Communication Studies*, 66(5), 363–382.

Saeed, A. (2007a) 'Media Racism and Islamophobia: The Representation of Islam and Muslims in the Media', *Sociology Compass*, 1(2), 443–462.

Saeed, A. (2007b) 'Trends in Contemporary Islam: A Preliminary Attempt at a Classification', *The Muslim World*, 97, 395–404.

Said, E. (1978) *Orientalism* (London: Penguin).

Said, E. (1997) *Covering Islam* (New York: Vintage).

Said, H. (2012) *Hundreds of Syrians Protest Against the Offending 'Innocence of Muslims' Film*, http://sana.sy/eng/21/2012/09/14/441563.htm, date accessed 10 November 2013.

Salem, F. and Mourtada, R. (2011) 'Facebook Usage: Factors and Analysis', *Arab Social Media Report (ASMR)*, 1(1), 1–18.

Sardar, Z. and Davies, M. (2010) 'Freeze Framing Muslims', *Interventions: International Journal of Postcolonial Studies*, 12(2), 239–250.

SBS Dateline (2004) 'Mark Davis and John Martinkus Interview Transcript', *Broadcast* 20 October.

Sells, M. and Qureshi, E. (2003). *The New Crusades: Reconstructing the Muslim Enemy* (New York: Columbia University Press).

Senate Submission (2004) *Supporting Statement for John Martinkus Detailing the Circumstances of His 2004 Kidnapping in Baghdad and the Response of Foreign Affairs Minister Alexander Downer and the Department of Foreign Affairs*, file:///C:/Users/Halim/Downloads/Martinkus%20-%20supporting%20 statement%20to%20submission%204%20(1).pdf, date accessed 7 March 2014.

Shaheen, J. (2003) 'Reel Bad Arabs: How Hollywood Vilifies a People', *Annals of the American Academy of Political and Social Science*, 588, 171–193.

Simons, G. and Strovsky, D. (2006) 'Censorship in Contemporary Russian Journalism in the Age of the War Against Terrorism: A Historical Perspective', *European Journal of Communication*, 21, 189–211.

Simons, M. (2010) *Stewart Didn't Breach Ethics on Source: Journalists' Union*, http://www.crikey.com.au/2010/06/17/stewart-didnt-breach-ethics-on-source-journalists-union/, date accessed 8 November 2013.

Sivanandan, A. (2006) 'Freedom of Speech Is Not an Absolute', *Race and Class*, 48(75), 75–76.

Slone, M. (2000) 'Responses to Media Coverage of Terrorism', *Journal of Conflict Resolution*, 44(4), 508–522.

Stephens, A. (2006) *Publics in Western Countries Disapprove of Muhammad Cartoons: but Right to Publish Widely Defended*, http://www.worldpublicopinion. org/pipa/articles/breuropera/171.php?nid=&id=&pnt=171, date accessed 10 November 2013.

Steuter, E. and Wills, D. (2009) 'Discourses of Dehumanization: Enemy Construction and Canadian Media Complicity in the Framing of the War on Terror', *Global Media Journal*, 2(2), 7–24.

Stout, D. (2007) *2 G.I.'s, Skeptical but Loyal, Die in a Truck Crash in Iraq*, http://www.nytimes.com/2007/09/13/washington/13troops.html, date accessed 1 November 2013.

Strother, S. G. (1989) *The Dispute over 'Satanic Verses'*, http://articles.orland osentinel.com/1989-03-02/news/8903030222_1_satanic-verses-book-chains-booksellers, date accessed 10 November 2013.

Tayob, A. (2006) 'Muslim Responses to Integration Demands in the Netherlands Since 9/11', *Human Architecture: Journal of the Sociology of Self-Knowledge*, 5(1), 73–90.

Tazreiter, C. (2004) *Asylum Seekers and the State: The Politics of Protection in a Security-Conscious World* (Aldershot: Ashgate).

Thomas, H. (2007) 'Pawns in a Political Play', *The Walkley Magazine*, 46, 9.

Thurston, A. (2012) *Ethiopia, Anti-Terrorism and Human Rights*, http://sahelblog. wordpress.com/2012/02/06/ethiopia-anti-terrorism-and-human-rights/, date accessed 8 November 2013.

Tolan, J. (2002) *Saracens: Islam in Medieval European Imagination* (Cambridge: Cambridge University Press).

Tolan, J., Veinstein, G. and Laurens, H. (2013) *Europe and the Islamic World: A History* (Princeton: Princeton University Press).

United Nations High Commissioner for Refugees (UNHCR) (2013a) *Asylum Trends 2012: Levels and Trends in Industrialized Countries*, http://www.unhcr.org/ 5149b81e9.html, date accessed 8 November 2013.

United Nations High Commissioner for Refugees (UNHCR) (2013b) *Refugees: Flowing Across Borders*, http://www.unhcr.org/pages/49c3646c125.html, date accessed 9 November 2013.

Van Atteveldt, W., Ruigrok, N. and Kleinnijenhuis, J. (2006) 'Associative Framing: A Unified Method for Measuring Media Frames and the Media Agenda', *Paper presented at the annual meeting of the International Communications Association*, International Congress Centre, Dresden, Germany.

Van de Donk, W., Loader, B., Nixon, P. and Rucht, D. (eds) (2004) *Cyberprotest: New Media, Citizens and Social Movements* (London: Routledge).

Warren, S. (2009) 'You Wouldn't Read About It: Press Freedom Is Never a Given Gift from Government', *Walkley Magazine*, 56, 29–30.

Weakliem, D. (2005) 'Public Opinion, Political Attitudes, and Ideology', in Janoski, T., Alford, R., Hicks, A. and Schwartz, M. (eds) *The Handbook of Political Sociology: States, Civil Societies, and Globalization* (Cambridge: Cambridge University Press).

Welsch, M. and Schuster, L. (2005) 'Detention of Asylum Seekers in the UK and USA: Deciphering Noisy and Quiet Constructions', *Punishment and Society*, 7(4), 397–417.

Wicks, R. H. (2006) 'Emotional Response to Collective Action: Media Frames About Islam and Terrorism', *Journal of Media and Religion*, 5(4), 245–263.

World Public Opinion (2005) *The American Public on the Islamic World*, http:// www.worldpublicopinion.org/pipa/articles/views_on_countriesregions_bt/92. php?nid=&id=&pnt=92&lb=btvoc, date accessed 29 August 2013.

Yamaguchi, K. (2012) 'Rationalization and Concealment of Violence in American Responses to 9/11: Orientalism(s) in a State of Exception', *Journal of Postcolonial Writing*, 48(3), 241–251.

Yilmaz, F. (2011) 'The Politics of the Danish Cartoon Affair: Hegemonic Intervention by the Extreme Right', *Communication Studies*, 62(1), 5–22.

Yousif, A. (2005) 'The Impact of 9/11 on Muslim Identity in the Canadian National Capital Region: Institutional Response and Future Prospects', *Studies in Religion/Sciences Religieuses*, 34(1), 49–68.

Zaller, J. (1994) 'Strategic Politicians, Public Opinion, and the Gulf Crisis', in Bennett, W. and Paletz, D. (eds) *Taken by Storm: The Media, Public Opinion, and U.S. Foreign Policy in the Gulf War* (Chicago: The University of Chicago Press).

Zayani, M. (2008) 'Arab Media, Corporate Communications, and Public Relations: The Case of Al Jazeera', *Asian Journal of Communication*, 18(3), 207–222.

Zelizer, B. and Allen, S. (2002) *Journalism After September 11* (London: Routledge).

Zeng, L. and Tahat, K. (2011) 'Picturing Terrorism Through Arabic Lenses: A Comparative Analysis of Al Jazeera and Al Arabiya', *Asian Journal of Communication*, 22(5), 433–448.

Zogby, J. (2013) 'American Attitudes Toward Egypt and the Muslim Brotherhood', *Zogby Research Services*, http://b.3cdn.net/aai/bb8329d81f05caa4c6_07m6bn93w.pdf, date accessed 7 March 2014.

Zuckerman, E. (2011) *The First Twitter Revolution?*, http://www.foreignpolicy.com/articles/2011/01/14/the_first_twitter_revolution, date accessed 23 September 2013.

Index

CPSIA information can be obtained at www.ICGtesting.com
Printed in the USA
LVOW10s1130060816

499279LV00017B/422/P